Praise for
How to Think Like a Woman

"Invigorating . . . Darkly funny . . . Penaluna tacks between rage and humor, biography and theory. Her writing is sharp and rousing. Her message is consoling and motivating. If this is what it means to think like a woman, sign me up." —*Wall Street Journal*

"Penaluna confirms not only that women have always engaged in philosophy, but that they have made unique and substantial contributions to the field . . . Refreshingly, she doesn't cast these four women as flat feminist heroes; instead, she paints Astell, Cockburn, Masham, and Wollstonecraft as complicated, conflicted figures who often found themselves lonely, disappointed, and alienated by their own intellects . . . Later in the book, Penaluna writes her own capsule biographies of various women thinkers throughout time . . . By giving us their names, she not only counteracts their omission from the canon, but fashions the beginnings of a new one entirely." —*The Atlantic*

"Provocative . . . An indictment of sexism in the field." —*New York Times*

"A much-needed revelation." —*Literary Hub*

"Intimate . . . Penaluna beautifully uncovers the philosophical stories of four influential but scandalously overlooked feminist philosophers . . . and delicately intertwines her own journey towards selfhood." —*Los Angeles Review of Books*

"*How to Think Like a Woman* serves as an alternate philosophical canon, where women and their intellect are deeply and rigorously examined." —*The Millions*

"Penaluna deftly tells the stories of four 17th and 18th century female philosophers, skillfully weaving their narratives into a rich exploration of her own experiences of patriarchy and sexism in academia."
—*The Observer* (UK)

"A work of empathy and intelligence . . . Let there be more such books."
—*The Scotsman* (UK)

"Incisive . . . Penaluna skillfully captures the thinking of these four women in impassioned prose as she challenges sexism in the canon . . . Lucid and frank, this blend of memoir, biography, and criticism makes a solid case for why representation matters."
—*Publishers Weekly*

"Thought-provoking . . . Engaging . . . A considerable achievement."
—*Booklist* (starred review)

"[Penaluna's] story of rebuilding and reimagining personally and professionally demonstrates defiant independence from patriarchal prescriptions and their shame and an embrace of feminist anger, ambiguity, and diversity of thought . . . [A] redemptive reclamation of the female voice in the study of philosophy."   —*Kirkus Reviews*

"A feminist rallying cry informed by centuries of thought on the 'woman question,' this elegantly written and intellectually rigorous memoir is a gift to women in male-dominated fields—and to everyone living a life of the mind while also trying to be a decent human being."
—**Ada Calhoun, author of** *Why We Can't Sleep:*
Women's New Midlife Crisis

"A sharp-eyed reappraisal of four brilliant women in history—and a provocative challenge to the philosophy bros."
—**Helen Lewis, author of** *Difficult Women*

"*How to Think Like a Woman* is a fascinating and illuminating work of nonfiction by a writer of real style and critical intelligence. Regan Penaluna has created an elegant synthesis of intellectual history, memoir, and feminist polemic that deserves to be widely read as a corrective to centuries of misogyny and erasure in philosophy."

—**Mark O'Connell, author of *Notes from an Apocalypse***

"In a world in which philosophy is not only sexist in underestimating women's actual and potential contributions, but actively misogynistic in pushing women out of the field, we need this book. Regan Penaluna's *How to Think Like a Woman* is at once a deeply personal and philosophically riveting meditation on four brilliant and inspiring female philosophers—Mary Astell, Damaris Masham, Mary Wollstonecraft, and Catharine Cockburn—that I learned so much from. A must-read for anyone who cares about what happens to women, young and old, in this needlessly and harmfully male-dominated profession."

—**Kate Manne, author of *Entitled:***
How Male Privilege Hurts Women

"Regan Penaluna's courageous book is a walk along the bluffs, amid the drowned gardens, telling of the sun and flood of her life. Along those bluffs four women from the past keep her company, awaiting the words she will speak of them and herself."

—**Alexander Nemerov, author of *Fierce Poise:***
Helen Frankenthaler and 1950s New York

HOW TO THINK LIKE A WOMAN

HOW TO THINK LIKE A WOMAN

*Four Women
Philosophers Who
Taught Me How to Love
the Life of the Mind*

REGAN PENALUNA

Grove Press
New York

Published simultaneously in Canada
Printed in the United States of America

First Grove Atlantic hardcover edition: March 2023
First Grove Atlantic paperback edition: March 2024

This book was set in 11.5-pt. Scala Pro
by Alpha Design & Composition of Pittsfield, NH.

Library of Congress Cataloging-in-Publication data is available for this title.

ISBN 978-0-8021-6272-4
eISBN 978-0-8021-5881-9

Grove Press
an imprint of Grove Atlantic
154 West 14th Street
New York, NY 10011

Distributed by Publishers Group West

groveatlantic.com

24 25 26 27   10 9 8 7 6 5 4 3 2 1

For my parents, my sisters, and Iowa

We cannot live in a world that is interpreted for us by others. An interpreted world is not a hope. Part of the terror is to take back our own listening. To use our own voice. To see our own light.

—Hildegard of Bingen, 1098–1179

Contents

Author's Note

The seed for this book was planted when I was thirty-one years old and newly divorced. I had just resigned from a full-time job with benefits as a professor of philosophy and moved out of my home near the Upper Iowa River. I'd invested over a decade in a life of the mind only to trade it all in for a small, cockroach-ridden apartment in New York City and an adjunct teaching job with no security and a ninety-minute commute. All the same, I knew if I didn't make the move, I'd break.

Once, being an academic philosopher had held the promise of making me into the person I always imagined I'd become—someone authentic, driven by her own compass. It would, I believed, fulfill my childhood dream of jumping headfirst into a life devoted to questioning—a life that would lead me to places of exceptional intellectual endeavor and beauty. It promised a career that would give me independence.

The truth is, philosophy is a hard place to make a career, but it's especially hard for a woman. The odds are against her from the start. It is a subject dominated by white men, many of whom aren't much concerned about the field's long history of oppression and how that oppression is still alive today, pulsing through texts, customs, habits of thinking, and behavior. The result is a climate that is unfriendly, sometimes even hostile, to women.

Philosophy has been and is still very much a field where you're rewarded for thinking in a way that ignores or is detrimental to women.[1] Where raw intellectual talent is heralded as necessary for success, this regularly works against women, who are viewed in the very texts being studied to have less raw talent than men. One study revealed that fields of research that highly prized "natural brilliance" also had low numbers of women PhDs.[2] Of all the subject areas scrutinized, including STEM, philosophy valued raw intelligence the most of all.[3] There are also studies showing that when teachers don't expect much from certain students, those students adopt a similar self-perception.[4] I believe this is a problem in philosophy, where greatness is rarely, if ever, expected of women. Rather than taking responsibility for the hostile climate, some men in the field simply doubt women's intellects.

These men see women primarily as a sex rather than as individuals. These men also see women's underrepresentation in philosophy as a result of choices women have made to study other things in an otherwise fair world rather than as evidence of women making decisions in a world that is in many ways limited to them or working against them. But most of all, they don't acknowledge that their skepticism of woman's intellectual capacity—expressed casually and with an objective air—impacts the self-perception and lives of actual women.

The word "philosophy" is from the ancient Greek and means "the love of wisdom," a pursuit, in theory, available to any curious, determined human being. Ideally, philosophy reflects human thought at its greatest magnitude and embodies a culture's quest for truth and self-knowledge. It matters that this endeavor has fallen short not only of truth but also of justice on several counts, including the treatment and understanding of women. Philosophers have been some of the most consistent and fruitful contributors to theories of women's inferiority, treating topics traditionally studied by women, such as parenting, caregiving, and other aspects of domestic life, with little interest, while the white male point of view is dramatized in countless thought experiments.

Of course, not all philosophy is like this. Feminist philosophy, critical race theory, and Queer theory all challenge the dominance of this view. In my experience, the problem is that these schools of thought are neither mainstream nor regularly taught in introductory courses; if they are on offer at all, it is typically as elective courses. In college philosophy departments, the mark of a "serious" philosopher is whether he knows his epistemology, metaphysics, and ethics—not, for example, his feminist philosophy, which is still largely dismissed as a political rather than a philosophical endeavor. Yet any person who knows their Nietzsche or has carefully studied the history of philosophy recognizes the hubris behind the assumption that some areas of philosophy—including the most abstract—are necessarily free of bias.

In this light, perhaps it's no surprise that some women report feeling uncomfortable speaking up in philosophy classes. Perhaps it's also not surprising that there are fewer women in senior positions in philosophy than in any other field in the humanities and in many of the sciences as well.[5] And in the *Stanford Encyclopedia of Philosophy*, an important touchstone for scholars and students, women make up only 10 percent of the most cited philosophers,[6] and all in all, women make up only 13 percent of authors in top philosophy journals.[7]

The plight of women in philosophy is part of a much larger story of the suppression of individuals who are not white, male, heterosexual, cis, and able-bodied. For instance, works by Black, Indigenous, and other People of Color (BIPOC) make up only 3 percent of articles published in the *Stanford Encyclopedia of Philosophy*, and from 2003 to 2021, Black academics contributed only 0.32 percent of all papers published in the top fifteen philosophy journals.[8] These numbers are appallingly even lower than the already tiny fraction of ethnic minorities with PhDs in philosophy.[9] Some scholars pin the lack of diversity on boundary policing—the act of dismissing work as unphilosophical that takes into account feminist, Queer, disabled, Black, and other marginalized perspectives.[10] The philosopher Shelley Tremain says gatekeepers in the field "diminish the importance of philosophy of disability, disqualifying it from the realm of what counts as philosophy."[11] Gayle Salamon, a Queer theorist in the English department at Princeton University, says she left philosophy after growing tired of the constant need to counter the belief that "the philosophy that I do is not quite philosophy."[12] I suspect a major reason there aren't many women and minorities in philosophy is because the double standard of justification is simply too exhausting. On top of teaching, researching, and fulfilling departmental duties, these individuals are under constant pressure to prove that they belong there in the first place.

These issues of inclusion and fairness were not at the top of my mind when I began studying philosophy. But my perspective started to shift when I accidentally came across the work of a woman philosopher from over three hundred years ago. I realized I didn't know of any women philosophers who had lived prior to the twentieth century. I also realized, abashedly, that I didn't know anything about the women philosophers of the twentieth century except their names. No one in my department studied or taught them; we didn't even have a course on feminist philosophy. I had internalized the misogynist notion that because none of them were being taught, none of them were worth looking into.

I was wrong. Over the next few years, I read about the lives and work of four brilliant and inspiring female philosophers: Mary Astell, Damaris Masham, Mary Wollstonecraft, and Catharine Cockburn. I discovered that in a time when women were forbidden to study at universities and male philosophers wrote extensively about the intellectual shortcomings of the female mind, these women pushed back. They highlighted the double standards of philosophers who promoted Enlightenment ideals of freedom and equality but did not extend those ideals to women. In reading about their works and lives, I started to reconnect to something deep inside myself. Astell, Masham, Wollstonecraft, and Cockburn were heroic voices from across time cutting through my frustration.

This book tells the story of how I lost myself in philosophy and then, through my discovery of these early feminist philosophers, found a path back to myself. Despite the centuries that separated us, we were united by our love of philosophy and our sorrow and anger. What does a woman do when she's told that she doesn't belong or that she's not as smart as a man because of her sex? Some let it roll off their backs, knowing their worth regardless of what they're told. I admire these women, but I'm not like them. I can't maintain that level of equanimity. I struggle, I doubt, but above all, I need answers—or at least attempts to explain what is happening to me and why. In this, I feel a kinship with these four philosophers.

Though not all of them devoted their entire careers to defending women, each was highly attuned to how patriarchy oppressed women and how philosophy could be used to counteract women's marginalization and suppression. Their legacy helped carve out an alternative vision for women's lives, in which they were no longer men's inferiors or dependents but their equals, capable of intellectual greatness and of making significant contributions to society. Nevertheless, you won't find them in textbooks or introductory courses on the history of philosophy. Most of us have forgotten them.

Before I begin my story, I should say that I decided not to name the institutions or faculties where I studied or taught, and I used pseudonyms for the people I personally interacted with. I am not interested in identifying any school or person because I do not want to draw attention to them as individuals, but rather highlight the features of my experience that I believe may be shared by others, especially women.

It's also important for me to acknowledge that the concept of woman is complicated by intersections of social categories, such as race, class, and gender. It is also dynamic, extending beyond the traditional sex binary to include other identities and orientations, such as nonbinary and trans. That said, this book is not a feminist treatise offering cutting-edge insights into sex and gender, although

I am inspired by contemporary feminist and Queer literature, which continues to inform my thinking. This book is about the awakening of my feminist consciousness through the rediscovery of lost feminist philosophers. It's about the challenges I faced trying to know myself while immersed in academic philosophy and also about how my own foibles and blinkered views contributed to my hardships. More than anything, though, it's about how I came to feel trapped by the concept of woman and how I've been grappling ever since with whether it's possible to be a woman and be free.

The lives and works of Astell, Masham, Wollstonecraft, and Cockburn are central to my story. I was drawn to Astell's audacious move to leave home for London and make a living writing philosophy, Masham's lifelong love for philosopher John Locke and how it shaped her as a thinker, Wollstonecraft's tumultuous romances and her struggle to free herself and women from the marriage plot, and Cockburn's heartening response to the conflict between motherhood and her writing. But this book is not a series of exhaustive biographies. I write about these philosophers because they were with me in some of my hardest moments and also because their lives clarify my own. In telling their stories, I began to understand my own story as part of a larger narrative, spanning centuries, about those of us who are wronged by philosophy and who, in our eagerness to make ourselves whole again, toil to make philosophy just and true.

A Woman Thinker

In graduate school, one of my professors told our class to consider the possibility that women weren't as smart as men. His words were clear and delivered to a room packed with students from various universities in the Boston area who had come to learn from him, Professor Berg, a renowned philosophy professor. I was one of only two women in the room, and until that moment I, too, believed I was there to learn how to think like Berg. I'd heard words like these before, as does any woman in the course of her life, but I always seemed to get past them. Now though, at age twenty-five, I was suddenly caught in their net, while others seemed to move swiftly through the apertures.

That day Berg had arrived at class as usual, plunking a thick stack of lecture notes on the table in front of us and thumbing through them to find where we'd left off. He was short and round, his waistline, he'd told us, the result of an inordinate appetite for cashews. I had been drawn to Berg's seminars because of his irreverence. He encouraged us to disregard recent debates in the academic journals, which he characterized as mere quibbling, and focus instead on the timeless messages of the great philosophers. This course was devoted to Plato's *Republic*, and according to the syllabus, that day's lecture was titled "The Female Drama."

I want to start with a request, I remember him saying. His voice was loud, and he looked ahead at no one but spoke to everyone. Our job, he said, is to make sure we aren't letting custom get in the way of truth. Then he asked: Why is it women have not achieved the highest levels of thought? That there are not many women in philosophy departments and haven't been throughout time? It might be politically correct to assume our culture has prevented women from taking on these roles, he offered, but it might not be philosophically sound.

He dabbed the corner of his mouth with a finger and scanned the room. He wasn't ashamed but instead proud of what he'd said, as if his statements were not only controversial but courageous.

I was confused. Until that moment, I'd thought of Berg as an ally. Only a few weeks earlier, he had pulled me aside to praise a paper I'd written. For a brilliant female colleague of mine who could read ancient Greek, he agreed to write recommendation letters. The class sat in silence for what felt like ages, and then he dove into a lecture on Plato's ideas about whether women are fit to rule.

As he spoke, I withdrew into my thoughts, questioning Berg's earlier support for my friend and me: Did he think we did objectively good work or work that was good *for a woman*? And then, why was it easy for him to objectify women's intellects—and so by extension *my* intellect—and invite a roomful of male colleagues to join him? Had he done this before, and had he been met with a roomful of silent listeners?

I had an urge to interrupt his lecture and say something, but my throat was tight and I couldn't isolate a single idea or sentiment. To speak felt dangerous, as if hundreds of wasps would escape my mouth. I didn't want to give the men in the room any reason to label me hysterical. I wasn't sure what I wanted to say. I had never studied feminist philosophy. Up to that point in my program, I'd gathered it was considered a fringe field. It wasn't on offer in my department, and I'd had no inclination to study it on my own. If pressed, I would have agreed that the nature of woman was unknown, as was the nature of man. Like most questions in philosophy, questions about the nature of things rarely had answers and often led only to more questions. Now I was beginning to see that not all questions were equal, and some, like the "woman question," had disturbing effects. I said nothing.

My silence in class that day haunted me. I continued in my coursework, but I was not fully present. A part of me was stuck back in Berg's classroom and on what he'd said, and the more I fixated on it, the less familiar I became to myself. I felt I'd been violently forced to acknowledge that perhaps I wasn't a thinker after all but rather a woman thinker—whether I wanted to be or not. And I wasn't even sure what that meant or whether it was at all a desirable thing to be.

I was raised to believe the shape of my life would be different from the shape of my grandmothers' and my mother's lives: if anything held me back professionally, it wouldn't be my sex or gender.[1] I was the oldest of four daughters, and my parents told us that girls could grow up to become anything boys could become. My dad habitually prefaced the family dinner with: "You can do anything you want if you put your mind to it." Then, before we took a bite, he had us recite it back to him in unison, which we did while rolling our eyes. This well-intentioned motto, thick with privilege, contained a pressure of sorts: I must become *something*. And this something, I imagined, would be no different from what a boy—who would one day be a man in the world—could do.

As a child, I wanted to understand the unknown, to pierce it, to formulate it, to draw it close. Where I grew up, in a small city in Iowa surrounded by a sea of corn and soybean fields, metaphysics abounded in the form of philosophy's cousin: religion. I was drawn to the idea of God and the attending sensations that kicked up when I imagined myself and humankind connected to a mysterious, absolute being. My childhood was full of metaphysical longing, a sense of wonderment at God's greatness, triggered by the melancholic clang of church bells at twilight and expansive starry nights interrupted by the bright lights of football games.

Yet I was troubled by certain details. In one of my earliest memories, I am perched at the edge of my bed, demanding God prove his existence by making me fly. In another, I am eight, seated in a pew during church service, drawing a chorus of devils singing hymns. The nun sitting behind me isn't impressed and takes away my recesses for a week. Far from being curious about the universe, the nuns and priests I knew seemed irritated by it. (I was relieved when my parents pulled me from Catholic school in third grade and put me in the public system.)

I continued to attend church and followed my parents as they switched from Catholic to Lutheran services. During these years, my mom had an eclectic group of friends of different spiritual persuasions whom I'd visit with her. And my favorite person of all was Stella, a farmer with somewhat of a secret life. She lived outside the industrial city where I grew up, amid the tilled geometries that spread over the hills like a quilt. Years before I met her, Stella had enrolled in seminary with the hope of becoming a Catholic priest during a liberal moment in the church. But by the time she graduated, the church had taken a conservative turn, and so instead she became a farmer. Still, she didn't abandon her studies altogether. My mom and I went to her house for the weekly Bible study she led for pastors and churchgoers to sharpen their interpretations of Scripture. I was there because I, too, wanted to learn more about my purpose in this life.

Stella was one of the first adults I admired besides my parents. Although I couldn't put it into words at the time, I intuited that belief wasn't merely a subscription to a set of ideas and practices but involved an emotional orientation to the world. I saw how fear, joy, and awe acted as invisible forces harnessing facts and experiences into meaningful moments. I wanted to deliberate about beliefs, test them for their strength, and I was drawn to people who shared a similar sensibility: wonder coupled with questioning. Stella got this. She maintained that the Bible was intended to stand up to critical analysis, and that a person must challenge the text to bring it to life. She often did this by encouraging us to embody the people of Scripture—to step outside of ourselves and imagine a way of being that was different from our own and that would deliver us to a new perspective on reality.

I continued to visit Stella almost every week with my mom when I was thirteen, and, through her example, I began to see the outline of what a life shaped and guided by philosophical ideas and principles could look like. It was a power; it was liberating.

Little by little, some things started to bother me about Stella and her Bible study. Where once I saw only a stable character, noble and compassionate, I now detected stagnancy and intellectual resistance. Stella's mind was open to questions but only within the confines of her vocation. This shift in my perception was subtle, like the way a cloud passing overhead slightly alters the tonality of the visible world, except in my case the vibrant colors never returned. I couldn't see Stella uncritically anymore.

When I stepped back and observed the other members of Stella's circle from this angle, I saw a similar pattern. Most people here weren't questioning their faith—at least not in this space. Yet I wanted to feel that such a break with religion was possible, because that was true to the natural leanings of my angsty thoughts. I was yearning for more immersive experiences to challenge me.

Above all else, Stella seemed isolated in her encampment, despite the small community that formed around her on Wednesday nights. I couldn't imagine that as my future; I wished for a larger, more dynamic community. After a year, I stopped visiting her. Only well into my adulthood would I appreciate how Stella, because of her audacity for striving to become a Catholic priest and thinking women equal to men, had been driven to the margins of an intellectual world. And how, in the face of this defeat, she had created a community of sympathetic minds.

In the following years, I had other religious episodes, at Bible camp and weekly peer-group meetings with a local pastor. Each of these experiences, though unique, ended in a similar way to my experience with Stella: the ecstasy wore off when I apprehended the limits of how far people were willing to question their own lives, which often didn't seem far enough to me.

I longed to connect to something greater than myself, to ponder reality and my place in it. I wasn't looking for a personal god. I was after truth, which didn't promise to yield a universe that I would like but rather one that was real. By the time I was seventeen, nothing about religion delivered. It was like a collapsed vein. When an on-again, off-again boyfriend passed me a note signed "Your friend in Christ," I shuddered and knew my love affair with religion (and him) was over.

I soon found a replacement. At college, I took my first philosophy course and discovered it was the one area of study that spoke to my yearning to know the truth. From the introductory level on, it was devoted to theories of the self in the world. It spoke to the part of me that once, under different circumstances, I might have called the soul.

I fell in love with the field during a class on early modern philosophy I took the fall semester of my sophomore year. It was held in a room above a guitar shop, which the university rented because space was in short supply. Thick, short-pile carpet covered the floor, muffling the sounds of footsteps and shifting desks as the students settled in. The furnishings were similar to what you would find in a typical corporate office rather than a traditional university classroom. The one window looked out on the hallway. It was uninspiring but convenient.

Twenty or so students sat facing the professor at the front of the room. He was middle-aged, Polish, and habitually wore black skinny jeans and a dark gray T-shirt. He was only on campus for the fall semester; the rest of the year he ran a humanities institute in Europe, and it seemed the success of his academic life abroad made him feel less pressure to perform here, resulting in a casual, fluid lecturing style.

He slowly paced in front of class along an invisible path extending ten feet in front of him, then he would turn and do it again, for ninety minutes. He had a habit, when he was in the middle of a thought, of making a prelinguistic sound, a sort of oral bookmark, waiting for the idea to form. At first, the other students and I thought it distracting, but after a few classes we got used to it. It was like a hypnotic anchor, but instead of making us passive, his habit of mumbling *dich ahhh* or *zeeee* while looking us in the eye or posing questions kept us in a state of ready attention.

He opened the class with a quote by the seventeenth-century French philosopher Blaise Pascal, that "man is equally incapable of seeing the nothingness from which he emerges and the infinity in which he is engulfed." Then he interpreted: "You see, humans exist between two infinities . . . *ahhh, dich ahmm* . . . one of events stretching into the past . . . *ehhhh* . . . and one of events extending into the future. This is what our reason tells us. We have no insight into why things are this way. Or why we appeared when we did in this infinite chain." He paused, looking around the room, then continued: "What we do in the face of this knowledge . . . *dich ahhhhh* . . . is what defines us. Meaning starts there."

I suddenly had the image of an expansive black space with a string of spheres, representing humanity, extending into the vast emptiness. The classroom itself folded into the experience, and it now carried an electric charge running through matter itself: the desks, the walls, the chalkboard, and the floor. I was aware of my body, the fleshy, wet finite self suspended in the electrifying unknown. In that moment it struck me as undesirable—impossible, even—to proceed in life without acknowledging this live wire. It had driven Pascal to religion. Once it would have done the same for me. But instead, it drove me further into philosophy. I wanted to push off into this dark. As long as I was surrounded by texts and thinkers who were working on ways of making sense of who we are and where we find ourselves, I would be comfortable existing in metaphysical uncertainty. If the truth was painful, or if it mapped out for us the great unknowns of existence, I believed its pursuit was worth it. There was a sort of power and freedom in knowing the limits of our condition.

There was also great pleasure. Philosophers throughout history have written about the nature of intellectual pleasures, how they bring the most sustaining enjoyment to a person's life. I experienced it too. A painful truth was pleasurable because it was authentic. And to spend hours caught up in philosophical ideas brought a steady joy similar to what I'd once had contemplating God.

Although in many ways I felt at home at the university, another part of me felt like an oddball. My peers were mostly from the East Coast, and their high school education seemed rigorous in comparison to mine. Most of them had studied literature in some depth, had a grip on history, and had some idea how to write a persuasive essay. They spoke multiple languages fluently. I didn't know what an Advanced Placement class was until I arrived on campus my freshman year. I had a lot of catching up to do, and I worked hard to fill the gaps. I supplemented my studies with outside reading. I combed secondhand bookstores for classics and introductions to philosophy and literature. I got high marks in my coursework, and my professors knew my name. Still, I became increasingly preoccupied with my imperfections. I was frustrated by—sometimes ashamed of—my uneven knowledge and upper-midwestern accent. At home for vacation my sophomore year, I corrected my mother's English. My dad called me a snob.

Around this time, I started dating a philosopher. His name was Alex, and he was a graduate student in the philosophy department who had been my teaching fellow for an ethics class the year before. Alex told me I was smart and that I had the potential to be a good professional philosopher, if I wanted to be. I was flattered and relieved to hear it, thinking maybe I wasn't as rough as I'd thought. We continued dating, and during my junior and senior years I continued my philosophy coursework. I started to consider what I wanted to do after graduation. Dating Alex gave me insight into what life was like as a philosophy graduate student, and it seemed incredible: spending one's days studying and teaching. I loved seeing him combing the stacks looking for old books or walking across the quad, head bent over a text, questioning after the substance of reality. He cut a romantic figure, and I imagined myself one day doing the same.

That there were only a handful of women in my upper-level philosophy classes didn't bother me, just as it didn't bother me when I learned there were only two women in Alex's graduate program. I had good grades, good recommendations, and I was propelled by the belief I'd learned from my youth that if I had sufficient talent and worked hard, I had a chance. My aim was to earn my PhD and then get one of those rare jobs working as a college professor.

In the fall of 2000, I enrolled in a PhD program at the same university I'd attended as an undergraduate. The program was renowned for its coursework in the history of philosophy. It was a course of study I was especially drawn to, because it would allow me to focus on the greatest texts by some of the greatest thinkers of all time. I was offered a full scholarship. The university was also in the same city where Alex lived and taught. He was writing his dissertation and teaching philosophy at another college in Boston, and once I started graduate school, we became serious and talked of getting engaged. That fall, I began my coursework and started my teaching assistantship. I lived in a ground-floor apartment overlooking a small garden covered with dark green climbing vines, and every morning after I woke, I sat at my table eating bread from the local bakery, drinking tea with milk, and reading philosophy. I spent hours taking notes, writing in margins, interrogating the text, rebuilding systems in my mind. It was everything I'd wanted, and yet, as the year progressed, I couldn't shake the feeling that something was off. I was utterly lonely. I chalked my unhappiness up to personal neuroses and grad school life, because when I looked around, I could see that many of my fellow grad school students were miserable too.

The graduate students in my program were cordial, and some of them became friends, but there was an undercurrent of competitiveness. We faced an uncertain future in a terrible job market that we were told was only getting worse. A friend invited me over for coffee and quiche. Over our cups and empty plates, I cross-examined her on her thesis, drilling into what I thought wasn't clear. It made me feel better, as if I were behaving like a true philosopher, but it made her teary and defensive. She didn't want to talk about it anymore. Before that day, she'd confessed to me in despondent moments that she might leave the program to become a plumber or a yoga instructor. She was one of the brightest graduate students, but she suffered from an inferiority complex, and I took advantage of her vulnerability. I figured if I could discover a weakness in her thinking, then I would validate my presence in the program—something I felt I needed to do, since I often doubted my own abilities. We never talked about philosophy again.

Once, when a student received an A-plus on a paper in the hardest course in the program, we all envied her for it. My response was to never take that class so I could avoid any direct comparison. To avert potential failure, I took fewer risks. I didn't pursue what I was most interested in but rather what would help my GPA and help me stand out in the job market.

I started to think I wasn't good enough. Curiosity was no longer my prime motivation. The need to prove myself was. I didn't see I was suffering from anxiety and depression. I was high functioning and made it to class and got good grades. But I tormented myself to the point of anguish by overanalyzing conversations and the contributions I made in class. I believed intelligence was something you were born with—that though you could hone your skills, your core brilliance was something you simply had (or didn't have). In support of this notion, my professors and classmates spoke about so-and-so's smarts as if they developed in a vacuum. I came to see my academic classes as a special sort of test. A chance to prove—or disprove—my native wit. If I didn't grasp a concept immediately, I took it as evidence of my dimwittedness. It didn't occur to me until later in life that intelligence could also be accumulative, a function of effort and curiosity, a construct dependent upon a community and its norms.

Then, after my first year in grad school, Alex got a job at a small college in Iowa. It was a coincidence that it was located in my home state; it was the only department with an opening in his area of expertise that was hiring. We were excited by the idea that maybe when I was done with my coursework in Boston, I would join him in Iowa and angle for a full-time job there with him.

One day on my return to the library from lunch, a woman in the program caught up with me to ask a question. She wanted to know how I was coping in a long-distance relationship. Her partner lived in another country, and she said she was having a hard time. I didn't tell her how sad and isolated I was, how I hadn't connected with anyone since Alex had left, how I'd become terrified of sharing my philosophical ideas for fear of being judged, how I felt estranged not only from others but also from myself—or the part of myself I was proud of. Because I was too wrapped up in self-pity to be authentic and kind, I said something false. I told her that being away from Alex hadn't been ideal, but it had given me more time for my work. She scoffed, perhaps sensing I was holding back.

Then I took that class with Berg. The struggle that once had seemed entirely individual was now compounded by the slow, dawning awareness that things might also be harder because I was a woman. I'd heard rumors that a visiting professor had recently left because he had been accused of harassing some of the female graduate students. In the wake of this scandal, the male professors kept their distance or treated us with indifference. It was as if they equated the absence of physical or verbal harassment of women with the presence of departmental support. But fear and indifference are also corrosive.

I noticed some of the professors seemed on edge around the female graduate students. One told me that department faculty couldn't meet with graduate students outside of office hours, a rule that appeared to apply only to female students. I felt like an outcast when I heard stories of my male colleagues bonding with their mentors over beers, having dinner in each other's homes, and sharing stories and jazz CDs. Reaching out and forming basic connections with professors was fraught with anxiety, and my sense of isolation expanded. I was asked to write a recommendation for a professor who was up for tenure. When I described him as "a friend," I was encouraged by another professor to replace the word with something less personal so it wouldn't be misconstrued by the administration as sexual. My response was to scrutinize my own behavior for signs of inadvertent sexual signals, which increased my timidity. A professor confessed to me in an elevator that his recent book had gotten no reviews. I brought him a dozen ears of corn from Iowa to cheer him up and left them in the department refrigerator for him with a note. Afterward, I worried my gesture was too public and would be taken the wrong way. I tried to remove them, but he got to them before I could.

One afternoon in a coffee shop, a friend at another university confessed she had exchanged sexual favors for recommendation letters from her mentor. She was a talented philosopher and a feminist; he was known as an advocate for women and minorities in philosophy. When he learned she had Reiki training, he asked her to give him sessions while both were naked. She agreed—a decision that earned her glowing professional support but privately gave her great shame. I concentrated on her story, feeling a mix of sadness and anger about how women's bodies were sometimes treated as bargaining pieces in academia. I wondered whether I would ever be asked to do something similar, believing I would say no but unsure whether that was the truth.

I confessed to a professor that I didn't like how quiet I'd become in his seminar—especially compared to my male classmates, who remained talkative. He patiently listened, but he clearly didn't know what to say. I could tell no one had ever come to him with this kind of personal problem, and I was embarrassed for making him uncomfortable. After a long pause, he told me he could cold-call on me in class if it might help.

What's insidious about all this is that my department was otherwise a stimulating place to study. My professors were brilliant, and I came away with a rich understanding of major texts in the history of philosophy. What I experienced was mild in comparison to the stories I heard about other departments. But I did inhabit a male-oriented environment in which some professors didn't believe there was a problem or thought it was enough to present themselves as advocates of women's advancement in the field.

It would have helped to have known by my mid-twenties that my malaise wasn't all my fault and that external forces were at work making things harder for women, especially ambitious women in men's spheres. My experience has shown me that women are more likely than men, especially in their formative years, to feel like imposters. Our culture underestimates the difficulty a woman faces doing something her grandmothers and mother were not encouraged or allowed to do. It wasn't a fluke that after I left home and struck out on my own, I doubted myself and had trouble regaining my confidence. A critical perspective on the condition of women, something philosophy is exceptionally well suited to provide, would have been a great salve. But mainstream academic philosophy didn't take this sort of perspective seriously, and for this reason, it exacerbated my self-devaluation and despair.

After three years of graduate study, I finished my courses without ever studying a woman philosopher. I'd become more passive, less inspired, and less confident about my ideas and powers of thought. To my dismay, I had come to resemble the stereotypical woman described by the great philosophers.

On the Prejudices of Philosophers

About twenty-six hundred years ago, Western philosophy was born in Greece and along with it, the "woman question."[1] Some of the first philosophers of Western civilization described reality as generated by a cosmic strife between opposites: Hot and cold. Wet and dry. Male and female. "For there would be no harmony without sharps and flats, no living beings without male and female, which are contraries," said Heraclitus.[2] He also said you cannot step into the same river twice, which could be interpreted to mean that everything changes. I wonder: Did he ever consider whether the contraries themselves were in flux? Might male and female not be meaningful essences, let alone opposites? As far as we know, he didn't say.

What we do know is that the surviving fragments of his philosophy don't challenge ancient Greek gender norms. For the most part, men and women went about their daily lives quite differently. Girls were not educated as well as boys, learning only the rudiments of reading and writing. Their whole existence revolved around the home and the demands of men, whom they served.[3]

This arrangement benefited the philosophers immensely—and they knew it. They were well aware that philosophy was an expensive activity. To have the leisure to get lost in abstractions and ponder the nature of the universe, a philosopher could not spend his days worrying about dinner, laundry, or the incessant demands of a young child. Where did his freedom come from? You need good luck, said one ancient philosopher. And not to have been born a woman, said another.[4]

Or a slave.[5]

Although it was rare, some ancient philosophers took exception to the view that women were complete subordinates. Around 532 BCE in Croton, a beautiful and prosperous seaside city located in the toe of southern Italy, Pythagoras founded a school of philosophy devoted to mathematical and theological insights. Women were allowed to study and teach in the school. Pythagoras and his followers postulated that women were men's intellectual equals and that the two were capable of friendship.[6] Nevertheless, from what remains of their writings today, it seems they didn't want to shake things up too much. Men and women studied separately, and but for the few women in Pythagorean schools, the rest were to carry on with their traditional social roles. What's more, the friendship that brought the sexes together required women's obedience. A harmonious asymmetry is how the Pythagoreans liked to think of it, and in the case of marriage, as one ancient historian put it, Pythagoreans held that wives were "not to oppose their husbands at all," and that wives "would achieve a victory if they gave in to their husbands."[7]

A half century after Pythagoras opened his school, a smart young man with a sizable inheritance cruised the Mediterranean, hitting the intellectual hot spots with the aim of becoming a wise man.[8] His name was Democritus, and he earned the moniker "the laughing philosopher" because of his purported joviality and his insight that cheerfulness is largely a state of mind.[9] Even so, there were things that irritated him. "To be ruled by a woman is the ultimate outrage for a man," he wrote.[10] Men and women are not merely opposites but antagonists, he proclaimed, and men must dominate women.

He also held that reality was composed of minuscule particles called atoms, an idea modified by the poet and philosopher Lucretius three hundred years later and then incorporated into Lucretius's own model of the natural world, which some scholars today say was foundational to modern science.[11] Lucretius lived as an Epicurean, elevating the pleasures of the mind above those of the body, because they were more in a person's control and therefore more stable and lasting. He said a life without philosophy is "a struggle in the dark."[12] A struggle, apparently, that he believed women were fated to.

Lucretius wrote in his poem *On the Nature of Things*—a work that would go on to influence poets including Virgil, Milton, Wordsworth, and Whitman—that men should be kind to "the race of women" because "'tis right for all men to have pity on the weak." And "all the race of men far excels in skill and is much more cunning." Lucretius said men who defend womankind were "blinded by passion, and assign to women excellencies which are not truly theirs." These men and all women were outside the bounds of reason, fumbling around in the dim realm of nonphilosophy.[13] They literally couldn't argue with him.

An origin story: One night in 407 BCE, the philosopher Socrates dreamed of a baby swan that grew plumage and then flew away. The next day he was introduced to Plato, the swan of his dreams, who became his student. Another origin story: Plato was the child of rape, a product of his father having forced himself upon his mother, who was then forced to marry her rapist.[14]

Plato grew up in a rich and powerful family, and, like many young men in his circle, spent hours with Socrates in the agora discussing politics and philosophy. After Socrates died, Plato traveled the Mediterranean to learn about new ideas, and on his return he opened an academy for philosophy in Athens. He also came away from his journeying with a bold, new view of women. Plato was the first person in the ancient West to permit women to study the same subjects as men in the same space at the same time. In response to this encouragement, women enrolled and rose high in the academy's ranks. Some of them even dressed like men, though it's unclear whether this was because they wanted to or were required to—or because they hoped to discourage male colleagues from sexually harassing them. Plato and other academy directors were mocked for opening their doors to females, but they insisted that women could be anything men could be, including philosophers.[15]

There was of course a caveat. Plato thought that women could do anything men could do, but never as well. He wrote, "There is no special faculty of administration in a state which a woman has because she is a woman, or which a man has by virtue of his sex, but the gifts of nature are alike diffused in both; all the pursuits of men are the pursuits of women also, but in all of them a woman is inferior to a man."[16] However, women might act in supporting roles as men's "companions and colleagues."[17]

Twenty years after Plato opened his academy, a seventeen-year-old orphan boy with slender calves, small eyes, and a love of clothes and rings enrolled.[18] His name, Aristotle, means "best." His father, once a medical doctor to a powerful Macedonian king, had died when he was ten. Little is known about his mother, except that she died when he was young. His guardian helped him secure a spot in Plato's prestigious Athens school.[19] What was it like for a teenage boy to study with women at a time when this sort of thing didn't normally happen? He was known to keep a nice haircut.[20]

Aristotle left the academy twenty years later, after Plato's death. He traveled to Asia Minor, where he had the support of Hermias, a local ruler who was later tortured to death.[21] Aristotle was attracted to Pythias, a young female relative of Hermias, and the two married and traveled to Lesbos, a volcanic, forested island rich in marine creatures and plants. Here, Aristotle combed the beach, collecting specimens for his taxonomy. He believed that every living thing had a purpose, a way of being that best fulfilled its nature, and one way to study its purpose was to look at its biology.[22]

It's tempting to speculate on Pythias's life. In 1938, Kate Campbell Hurd-Mead, an obstetrician and feminist from Danville, Quebec, wrote that Pythias worked alongside Aristotle and was an embryologist fascinated by animal generation.[23] There are no ancient sources to back this up. I imagine Hurd-Mead, who over the course of her own career as a physician had become increasingly interested in women's role in the history of medicine, suspected Pythias did these things. Perhaps Hurd-Mead saw a pattern emerge in her personal and archival work, in which male researchers were reluctant to credit the women who collaborated with them. I can see Pythias myself working out the principles of generation while she picked the beach for creatures, belly taut with child, warm Mediterranean sun on her back, a bag of octopuses on her shoulder. But it's also a disturbing image, given what Aristotle concluded from these surveys.

The female is like a "disabled male," he wrote. A "natural mutilation."[24] Aristotle saw the unformed, bloody clots of menses as evidence of women's biological passivity. To him, a mother's eggs and uterus provided the material for generation, but it was the father's sperm that gave the fetus shape and the spark of life. One sex needed the other in a dynamic that existed not for convenience or harmony's sake but rather because it was, as he says, "natural."[25]

Some scholars insist that in these passages Aristotle was only *describing* women's biology and how it functioned—not suggesting anything about how women should act or be treated in society. To understand Aristotle's view of women's inferiority as he intended it

to be understood, you need to turn to his ethics and political philosophy.[26] In these works, he tells us that women were destined to
be ruled by men. Women's reason was weak, and they were unable
to control their passions, making them unfit both for public life and
philosophy. Capping off these dismissive pronouncements, he added
that men who were intellectually stunted were suited for slavery.
Aristotle himself had several slaves on his own estate.[27]

Some years into their marriage, Aristotle carried his ideas, along
with his wife and their only child, a daughter, also named Pythias,
from Lesbos to his homeland of Macedonia. Here Aristotle was tasked
with educating the young Alexander the Great, who came away from
his tutorials with an appreciation of many topics, including Homer's
works and natural slavery. The soon-to-be emperor would one day
sell tens of thousands of his captured enemies into slavery.

In 334 BCE, Aristotle picked up his family again and moved
to Athens, where he started his own school of philosophy called the
Lyceum. Sometime during this period his wife, Pythias, died, and Herpyllis, Aristotle's servant or lover (sources aren't clear which, though
most suspect she was both), stepped in to care for his daughter.[28]
They eventually had a son, to whom Aristotle dedicated a book of
ethical philosophy, a tremendous work on the good life. (By the final
chapter, it becomes clear that only free, wealthy men—"gentlemen"—
can lead such a life.)

More than two thousand students enrolled in the Lyceum over
the course of its 250-year history, but not one of them was a woman.[29]
"To a woman silence is a crowning glory—whereas this does not
apply to a man," Aristotle wrote in his *Politics*.[30] What did Pythias,
her daughter, or Herpyllis know of Aristotle's theories about women?
Did they care? Were they horrified? Could they even read his work?
There is no record.

Aristotle scholars like to point out what they see as displays of
Aristotle's generosity toward women. That in his will, he asked for his
bones to be buried next to Pythias's, at her request, and that he left

his estate to Herpyllis. One scholar suggests that perhaps Aristotle didn't sleep with Herpyllis when Pythias was alive.[31] Another scholar ignores Herpyllis's existence altogether.[32] It's as if these academics want Aristotle to be not just a philosopher but also a good husband—a good man. A gentleman like the one you find in his ethics.

I sometimes wonder what Aristotle was like in bed. Did gold chains hit his chest? Did he like to tongue ass? What do we ignore about Aristotle to take him seriously, for his legacy to endure? What must we ignore in ourselves?

"Aristotle was right to think the female less perfect than the male," wrote Galen of Pergamon, a philosopher and doctor to Roman gladiators who lived in the second century. "She is colder; for if among animals the warm one is the more active, a colder animal would be less perfect than the warmer."[33] Like Aristotle, Galen concluded that women contribute little to generation, as men have active seed, whereas female gametes are more like "wind eggs."[34] Galen also wrote about how his father was supportive, but his mother was irascible: she excoriated him, his father, and their slaves. Galen died around the year 200, but his ideas had a huge influence on philosophy and medicine in Europe and the Arab-Islamic world for the next fourteen hundred years. In the ninth century, Galen's ideas made their way into the Middle East, India, and Pakistan through the work of scholar Hunain ibn Ishaq of Baghdad, who translated over one hundred of Galen's texts into Syriac and Arabic. In the early sixteenth century in Europe, Galen's works were standard reading for medical students.[35]

In the late fourth century, Augustine of Hippo, a philosopher and recent convert to Christianity, did not accept Aristotle's idea that women were by nature inferior.[36] They were, he wrote, men's spiritual equals and capable of the highest order of thought. In his dialogues, his mother, Monica, appears as such a brilliant philosopher that the men in her midst report that they are "unmindful of her sex, [and] we might think that some great man was seated with us."[37] Augustine also held that women had free will, and he defended the integrity of a woman who'd been raped, arguing that the tragic event hadn't corrupted her because her will was oriented toward goodness. But his doctrine of the will also had a dark side. Where Aristotle located a woman's submission in her nature, Augustine attached it to her freedom.

Augustine was an influential interpreter of early church litera-ture, and he insisted that the biblical story of Adam and Eve was not a parable but rather a historical fact.[38] The original decision by Eve to eat the forbidden fruit was a free choice but a bad one that had consequences for womankind: "It is not the nature, but the fault of the woman which brought her to get a master in her husband."[39] To pay for Eve's mistake and earn a place in heaven, a woman must freely choose her submission.

To not do this was evil. Augustine wrote that a young, unmarried woman was a temptress even without trying, her body encouraging men to sin. (The sexual appetites of those who weren't heterosexual men didn't figure as much in his philosophy.) Augustine himself enjoyed sex with his concubine so much he struggled to quit: "Grant me chastity and continence but not yet."[40]

Augustine believed some women escaped the rule of men. They were either in convents or in heaven.

"A disinclination to talk is a glory for woman but not for man," said Ibn Rushd, a medieval philosopher from Cordova, Spain, whose body of work is written as a commentary on Aristotle's texts.[41] Not that he thought all women should be silent. "Since some women are formed with eminence and a praiseworthy disposition, it is not impossible that there be philosophers and rulers among them."[42]

Thomas Aquinas, another medieval philosopher inspired by Aristotle, wrote, "For what is appropriate for the ornament of a woman or her integrity, that she is silent, proceeds from the modesty which is owed to women; but this does not relate to the ornament of a man, instead, it is fitting that he speaks."[43]

In 1245, Aquinas began his studies at the University of Paris, where Aristotle was mandatory reading for all students and became the model for higher education across Europe, including at the University of Oxford (founded in 1096) and the University of Cambridge (founded in 1209). And until 1920 for Oxford and 1869 for Cambridge, women were barred from enrolling at these institutions. They were not allowed to study in the new preparatory schools, where young boys were familiarized with the protocols and language of academia. In the halls of the university, as opposed to the monastery, philosophy became a more formal discipline, requiring technical argumentation.[44] The language of the university was Latin, and the ancient Greek texts, recovered from the East, were translated. Meanwhile, nuns were learning less Latin, and it would soon disappear altogether from their education. And so, at the dawn of the university, during a moment of incredible intellectual flourishing that the West had not seen since ancient times, women were at multiple disadvantages: unable to read, write, or speak the discourse of higher learning.[45]

It would therefore have been exceptionally hard for a woman to mount a sustained and public defense of her gender in the face of statements such as this one by Aquinas about women: "She has the capacity for understanding but her capacity is weak. The reason for this is on account of the changeableness of nature, her reason weakly adheres to plans, but quickly is removed from them because of emotions."[46]

In the 1400s, the printing press was invented, turning out thousands of copies of Latin and Greek editions of Aristotle's texts, as well as scores of texts spuriously attributed to the philosopher.[47] One of the latter, *Aristotle's Masterpiece*, emphasized women's inferiority and passivity and was used by medical practitioners in America up through the mid-nineteenth century.[48]

In 1500, while on a trip to England, Desiderius Erasmus was impressed by the erudition of his good friend Thomas More's daughters, and concluded that females could handle the same classical education afforded males. In fact, Erasmus believed it was the only way to keep girls, whom he saw as far more curious—and more easily tempted to sin—than boys, distracted.[49] "Weaving, for example, is an occupation that leaves the mind free to listen to young men's chatter and to reply to their banter, but a girl intent on her books has no thought for anything else," he wrote.[50]

A boy's education makes him a Renaissance man, Erasmus thought, a virtuous character with intellectual depth fit for citizenship. Whereas a girl's education makes her a docile virgin, ready to serve a man as a wife and a mother.[51]

In the sixteenth century, many nunneries in the Protestant countries of northern Europe closed, which meant there were fewer places where women could get a formal education.[52] Meanwhile, examinations at Oxford included questions like these: "Whether nature intends a woman?" "Whether woman's nature is as intelligent as man's?" "Ought Aristotle to have included a wife among the goods of a philosopher?"[53]

In Europe over the next few hundred years, the few girls who were educated in challenging subjects such as philosophy, mathematics, and classical literature were mostly the daughters of the aristocracy and were taught by private tutors.[54] Even then, their studies rarely matched that of their male peers. And, if French moralist

Jean de La Bruyère is to be believed, there was not much incentive for these young women to strive. In 1688, La Bruyère described an educated woman as "a fine piece of armour, artistically chiselled, admirably polished, and of exquisite workmanship, which is only fit to be shown to connoisseurs, of no use whatever, and no more apt to be used for war or hunting than a horse out of a riding-school is, though it may be trained to perfection."[55]

In 1615, sixty-nine-year-old widow Katharina Kepler of Germany— the mother of Johannes Kepler, a philosopher and astronomer who formulated the laws of planetary motion—was accused of witchcraft. Some of the allegations: One girl's arm lit up in pain after Kepler lightly touched it. A woman fell ill after she drank an herbal remedy that Kepler made. Another neighbor saw Kepler levitate.[56]

At the time, a popular 130-year-old handbook, *Malleus Malefi-carum* or *The Hammer of Witches*, instructed civil officers on how to identify and interrogate witches. It also propagated a grim view of women: "What else is woman but a foe to friendship, an ines-capable punishment, a necessary evil, a natural temptation, a desir-able calamity, a domestic danger, a delectable detriment, an evil of nature, painted with fair colours!"[57] The book helped bring mostly women to trial, especially those interested in knowledge, science, and medicine.[58] Around twelve thousand people (some estimates report as many as sixty thousand) were executed for witchery in Europe between 1500 and 1700, and law faculty at universities were sometimes tasked with deciding whether a person was guilty.[59]

Members of the University of Tübingen questioned Katharina under the threat of torture.[60] Johannes, a faculty member at the time, decided to step in and defend his mother himself. He provided deft and detailed responses to each charge, revealing them to be mere products of paranoia and fear. After that his mother was freed.

Johannes never took another case, however. He still believed in witches.[61]

The English philosopher Thomas Hobbes never married and spent most of his adult life in the home of an aristocratic family with whom he traded counsel and tutoring for lodging, political access, and the leisure to do philosophy. He also received regular massages.[62]

In 1651, Hobbes wrote that in the state of nature, men and women are equal. By this he simply meant that outside civil society, a person is obligated to no one; a person is free to do as he chooses. He added that in the state of nature children were in their mothers' custody. These are impressive statements considering they were made at a time when most people believed women were men's natural subordinates and fathers the natural guardians of children. They also make Hobbes's descriptions of civil society all the more disturbing, because women don't seem to be there. The rulers are men. The heads of families are fathers. There is no mention of women. No mention of mothers. *Where did the women go?*[63]

Hobbes wrote during a period following a series of major civil wars in England, devising a political philosophy he hoped would keep the peace. Perhaps he concluded that for harmony's sake, he had to silence the women.

Baruch Spinoza wrote that the aim of civil society was to protect freedom of thought and expression. More specifically, the freedom to do philosophy. He did not think women capable of such profound thought and concluded they could not be citizens. In his 1677 work *Tractatus Politicus*, in the chapter titled "Of Democracy," he wrote, "One may assert with perfect propriety that women have not by nature equal right with men . . . thus it cannot happen, that both sexes should rule alike, much less that men should be ruled by women." And why? "Men and women cannot rule alike without great hurt to peace."[64] But why? "But of this enough."

These are the final words of his political treatise.

Gottfried Leibniz corresponded with women about philosophy, though he apparently had a hard time imagining their daily lives. In 1697, he wrote, "I have often thought that women of elevated mind advance knowledge more properly than do men. Men, taken up by their affairs, often care no more than necessary about knowledge; women, whose condition puts them above troublesome and laborious cares, are more detached and therefore more capable of contemplating the good and beautiful."[65]

David Hume is typically portrayed as a gentleman of the Enlightenment. He was generous with his friends, and after a day of philosophical breakthroughs, he would shelve his research and play backgammon. In 1739, he gave us the problem of induction: There is no necessary reason for B to follow A. We are misled to think our ideas of the sensible world are certain, let alone predictive of the future. He said we know extremely little about this place we find ourselves in: there is no reason to believe that because the sun rose today it will rise tomorrow.

Hume's robust skepticism of traditional modes of thought didn't apply to all his ideas. For example, to Hume it made good sense that people were more comfortable with men fooling around than with women. The double standard of chastity was a rational response to the fact that it was harder to be certain about the identity of a child's father than of its mother. And in the absence of such certainty, Hume continued, the father wouldn't want to care for the child.[66] He also argued that though slavery was immoral, men of Europe were superior to Blacks and Native Americans.[67] He wrote, "I am apt to suspect the Negroes, and in general all other species of men to be naturally inferior to the whites."[68]

Decades later, in 1784, Immanuel Kant proclaimed the Enlightenment injunction *Sapere aude!* "Dare to know!"[69] His ideas about the nature and limits of knowledge shifted the entire focus of philosophy for centuries to come, upending traditions and forcing a Copernican revolution in thought. He also said about an African man that "this scoundrel was completely black from head to foot, a distinct proof that what he said was stupid."[70]

In the eighteenth century, moral philosopher Lord Chesterfield wrote in a letter to his sixteen-year-old son: "Women, then, are only children of a larger growth." He also wrote, "A man of sense only trifles with them, plays with them, humors and flatters them, as he does with a sprightly forward child; but he neither consults them about nor trusts them with serious matters."[71] (The subtitle of a compilation of letters to his son is *On the Art of Becoming a Man of the World and a Gentleman*.)

Some context: by the time the Enlightenment was reaching its peak in the late eighteenth century, women's formal education in Europe was worse than it had been in decades. Even those who believed women were capable of abstract thought were convinced their station in society didn't necessitate rigorous textual studies. A woman's education was tailored specifically to her class and place in the world, which was almost always assumed to be in the home.[72]

In 1821, G. W. F. Hegel wrote that the law of the state was universal, but the law of woman was familial and subjective. The difference between the two was a tension, the supreme opposition in ethics. He put it another way: Men are more like animals and women are more like plants. A woman, like a plant, "is a more peaceful unfolding whose principle is the more indeterminate unity of feeling."[73]

In the early nineteenth century, when some universities were opening women's colleges, Auguste Comte, known as the "first philosopher of science," wrote that the "natural law" revealed significant gender differences and that women were intellectually inferior to men. Comte held this to be incontrovertible, satisfying his standard for philosophical truths: that they derive from facts verifiable by the senses and scientific investigation.[74]

Comte was married to Caroline Massin, a seamstress and independent-minded woman, who left him after seventeen years. He described her as recalcitrant, unwilling to perform her wifely duties, and her self-assertion struck him as abnormal, evidence of her "manhood."[75] She was smart, "a woman of rare moral and intellectual qualities," but that's not why he'd married her. He'd wanted her affection, which he said she'd refused to give him: "There have been none of the compensations of a loving disposition, the only special quality in which women are irreplaceable."[76]

In 1871, Charles Darwin attacked philosopher John Stuart Mill for proposing that women were men's intellectual and moral equals, deserving equal rights. Darwin argued that the "chief distinction in the intellectual powers of the two sexes is shewn by man attaining to a higher eminence, in whatever he takes up, than woman can attain—whether requiring deep thought, reason, imagination, or merely the use of the senses and hands."[77] Darwin had women assistants, including his daughter Henrietta, who helped edit his book *The Descent of Man*, in which he made these statements.[78]

In 1873, Edward Clarke, a professor of medicine at Harvard, wrote a book called *Sex in Education, or, A Fair Chance for the Girls.* In it, he wrote against girls' higher education in the United States, fearing it would quash their natural inclination to procreate and be good mothers.[79] Clarke relied on Darwin's arguments. His book was a national bestseller.

Friedrich Nietzsche makes for wonderful reading for a budding philosopher because he challenges the presuppositions of the greats who came before him with such brevity and eloquence. He could also be delightfully playful and rude, as when he called his fellow philosophers cowards for failing to acknowledge the subconscious, nontheoretical motives behind their work. In a chapter of *Beyond Good and Evil* titled "On the Prejudices of Philosophers," Nietzsche wrote, "Gradually it has become clear to me what every great philosophy so far has been: namely, the personal confession of its author and a kind of involuntary and unconscious memoir; also that the moral (or immoral) intentions in every philosophy constituted the real germ of life from which the whole plant had grown."[80] On the page, Nietzsche is temperamentally more like a poet than a philosopher, and he was suspicious of the systematic method of academic philosophers.

Women's rights and equality were vigorously debated at the time Nietzsche was writing, and his philosophy provided a frame for many of these discussions.[81] His argument that all values are grounded in psychology rather than objective truth inspired a reexamination of the philosophy of personhood. Nietzsche challenged his readers to accept that they were ultimately motivated by their unconscious drives and to embrace themselves as forces of self-assertion. This opened up new ways of thinking about the concept of woman: What was the thrust of woman's subconscious desire? Who was woman if she was no longer defined by convention?

Nietzsche's answer is notoriously slippery. On the one hand, his philosophy of self-expression would seem to validate calls for women's liberation, and he encouraged a view of women as sexual beings. He endorsed the education of women at the university level and encouraged his sister to get her doctorate in philosophy.[82] He also said things like this: "Women in general do not love any art, are not knowledgeable in any, and have no genius." As if to prove his claim that philosophy is a kind of unconscious memoir, he maintained that women were bad cooks who "delayed human development." He suggests that a cure for women's neuroses—which were brought on by the struggle for equality and rights, no less—is pregnancy. But the philosopher was provocative and loved irony, and it's possible these passages were intended to be interpreted with a wink.

In 1946, Ludwig Wittgenstein gave a series of lectures at the University of Cambridge. On one occasion, he broke from his oration and turned to one of his best and favorite students, G. E. M. (Elizabeth) Anscombe—the only woman in the room, whom he'd fondly nicknamed "old man"—and told her: "Thank God we've got rid of the women!"[83]

By the 1970s, women made up nearly half of students enrolled in universities and teachers' colleges in the US—more than ever before.[84] Around this time, John Lucas, a renowned British philosopher, published a paper in the journal *Philosophy* on the innate differences between men and women. "There are no conclusive arguments about feminine abilities and attitudes. But the discoveries of the scientists, so far as they go, lend some support to traditional views."[85] He went on to say that there was reason to view the sexes as intellectually distinct and therefore requiring different treatment.

In 1979, Richard Swinburne, an influential philosopher and professor emeritus at Oxford, wrote, "In the actual world, very often a man's withholding benefits from another is correlated with the latter's suffering some passive evil either physical or mental. Thus if I withhold from you certain vitamins, you will suffer disease. Or if I deprive you of *your wife* by persuading her to live with me instead, you will suffer grief at the loss."[86] When Swinburne considered the "actual world," did he also imagine the actual wives? I wonder how these women appeared to him. Perhaps he imagines them quietly at home, baking bread, wiping honey from children's mouths, sweeping dusty floors—or preparing themselves to be bedded by a man who may or may not be their husband. I can't help but wonder: Is the wife happy? Is she easily persuaded by this male philosopher? Does *she* suffer? Do I dare project moral agency on her? But I digress, because Swinburne envisioned these "actual" wives to be ready for the plucking. And when the cunning philosopher arrives, it's the wife who is snatched up, and the cuckold who suffers.

◆◆

Weak. Pitiable. Submissive. But a child. What a horrible list!

I learned what the great philosophers said about women on my own outside of class. Except for Berg, my other professors skipped over these statements, signaling something dark best left alone. However, I was drawn to their words—I couldn't ignore them—and so I made a record instead, collecting them in notebooks. Although the topic was depressing, paradoxically, my note taking was therapeutic. I discovered a power in witnessing a pattern—a gratifying transcendence, which offered me a reprieve, however brief, from the grinding down of sexism. Contemporary French philosopher Luce Irigaray says the act of women recovering their voices without letting themselves be reduced to patriarchal discourse involves, in its earliest phase, a "playful repetition."[87]

Or, as I thought of it, the protolanguage of feminism, the baby talk of consciousness raising: I see oppression here, and
    here
         and here
      and there.
As my notebooks filled, it was harder for me to suppress the uncomfortable feeling that the great philosophers whose ideas I planned to devote my life to saw me as a problem.

What made this more difficult was the expectation that I shouldn't let it bother me. "I don't care about that sort of thing" was what a professor told me about a prospective graduate student who'd told me she was unsure about the climate in our department and disappointed that there were no feminist philosophy courses on offer. I inferred it was a virtue for women in philosophy to be cool, unflappable.

Yet I felt constitutionally incapable of such indifference and frustrated that it was expected of me. The philosopher Elizabeth Anderson describes freedom as "the ability not to have an identity that one carries from sphere to sphere but, rather, to be able to slip in and adopt whatever values and norms are appropriate while retaining one's identities in other domains."[88] I couldn't shake my identity as a woman when I was doing philosophy. It trailed me like a stray dog.

Although I'd grown quieter and less expressive in graduate school, I knew this wasn't me actualizing my womanly essence or fulfilling my feminine destiny. Not that I had much else to show for myself. I was a pilot flame of potential that only I seemed to notice, and if I failed to ignite as a philosopher, I believed it was on account of my person and not my sex. Even though my self-esteem was fragile and I felt very alone, when I stared into the carnival mirror of the philosophers' words, I took them not as a sign of who I was but rather as a warning: because I was a woman, I would always struggle in this field. I was unnerved by the possibility that my unease would become a permanent feature of my thinking self.

That was when I decided a change in environment might help, and I left Boston as soon as I could. The day after I completed my coursework, I packed up my apartment, loaded up my Honda Civic with my books and clothes, and drove for two days across the country to the small Iowa town where Alex lived. I longed to put physical distance between myself and my department, believing it would give me perspective on the questions that swirled in my head, swooping at me like crows: Was philosophy for me? And, if so, what sort of thinker was I?

Discovery in the Margins

I moved into Alex's apartment, which sat above a cell phone shop in a row of brick buildings on the main street. The space was clean, cheap, and grandmotherly—nearly every surface had its own doily. My favorite feature was the view from our bedroom window perched a story above the town parking lot, where I could watch the sunset reflect off the limestone bluffs in the distance. The vista, although nothing compared to the grandeur of the cliffs along the Mississippi, still afforded a sense of boundlessness. To look out from even this modest height, because the view was true, was an inspiration of sorts, and conferred its own degree of freedom.

Alex and I were engaged and had set a date to be married in the spring. Although for most of my young adult life I'd dismissed marriage, I changed my mind after being with Alex and took comfort in knowing that at least something in my life was settled. The department that employed Alex offered me a job teaching a midlevel philosophy course after a department member had unexpectedly fallen ill. I had always loved teaching, having earned a stipend as a teaching fellow, and so I leapt at the opportunity. I took pride in the responsibility and enjoyed making abstruse topics meaningful to my students. I delighted in cultivating my students' confidence and sense of awe, probably because it was something I'd wanted for myself. Along with an income, I was provided with my own office and access to the college library, which included borrowing privileges at major research universities in the Midwest. A friend who taught at another university called this college backwater, a derogatory term he also used for the more prestigious university where he taught. I'd also heard the term "service" to describe the work of professors at more teaching-heavy institutions like the one where I was now working. But these elitist attitudes didn't change how—when I was able to step outside my disappointment in myself and frustrations with the academy—I relished the work. I was researching ideas, igniting the intellects of my students, and getting paid for it. The department also mentioned there would be more courses for me to teach in the future. Now I had what I needed to do philosophy for the next year or two and was in a good position to find a topic for my dissertation. The moment crystallized into a sensation of pleasure, as if the expectations I had for my life and the world around me were momentarily in agreement, a feeling intensified by the fact that it wouldn't last.

My adviser back in Boston was helping me navigate these early days of the dissertation. In many ways, he was the opposite of Berg. Professor Novak was critical of scholars like Berg who stripped philosophical questions of their historical context. Novak enjoyed digging into intellectual history, discovering patterns of thought that challenged traditional interpretations of the birth of modernity. This is how he'd made a name for himself. Yet few graduate students wanted to work with him. He was haughty and his writing was turgid—a poor match for his acuity—but I was eager to study with him because of the prospect of shaking up intellectual history. More importantly, Novak didn't ask his students to entertain ideas about women's purported cognitive deficiencies.

Novak emailed me a reading list. He suggested I focus on a group of little-known philosophers, the Cambridge Platonists, to see whether I could find something worthy of a dissertation that would sustain me over the next two years. He told me that as I progressed through the titles, I should send him my reflections, not worrying about whether he replied. It would be good practice for me, he said.

I was unsure of what he wanted in these notes and dreaded the act of writing into a void, but I started anyway.

It soon became clear to me that I was headed into a dull valley. My initial assessment was that these philosophers were resistant to ideas that ultimately propelled the scientific revolution, and though they complicated the canon, it wasn't something I wanted to devote many years to exploring. Just when I was beginning to regret my decision to focus on obscure thinkers, I came across something in the footnote of a rare monograph about the Cambridge Platonist philosopher Ralph Cudworth. Within these pages were brief mentions of a woman who shared his name, Damaris Cudworth (later, Lady Masham). On page 79, I learned that she was Ralph's daughter, and then in the annotation that she had written a philosophical treatise.

A treatise! I had no idea there were women philosophers in the age of John Locke. After some more searching through the digital catalog, I discovered that Masham had written two works of philosophy. Neither was in print, but both were available on microfilm from a library in Madison, Wisconsin. I quickly ordered them. Days later, my college's library notified me that they'd arrived. After I taught my class, I went to the bathroom to wash the chalk off my hands and looked up in the mirror, spotting a faint vertical wrinkle between my brows. Was this stress or wonderment carving my face? I grabbed my notebook and pen and headed to the library.

I loaded the microfilm into the scanner, turned on the light, and read as the works lit up the stacks around me in the dark back corner of the library. The author of the monograph had led me to expect that Masham's ideas weren't unique: "She was her father's daughter."[1] But much of what I read wasn't at all like her father's philosophy. In those facsimiles of 310-year-old pages were the words of a woman fluent in the language of the leading philosophers of her day, offering a defense of women's minds. Women were, she said, as capable of navigating philosophy and science as men. (Her father had written nothing about the condition of women.) I was hungry for more. Were there other women philosophers, and did they, too, believe women were wrongly suppressed and capable of great intellectual heights?

There were. Over the next few months, I came across a small but serious body of scholarship introducing me to many women philosophers of the seventeenth and eighteenth centuries. From the work of these incredible scholar-pioneers—and a close reading of primary texts—I tracked down an interesting story to tell about these women. The birth of Western feminism is taken to be—and sometimes criticized for being—rights based.[2] But for Damaris Cudworth Masham, Mary Astell, and Catharine Cockburn (Wollstonecraft would come later), I argued that rights were instrumental to responsibilities and that early women's liberation in the West took the form of duties to God. If men weren't going to willingly share power, then a woman could argue that God intended her to have it.

Novak was on board with this topic, too, and we set a date for the proposal defense (I would need to pass this stage to start writing the dissertation). It took place in Boston, in the fall of 2004, a year after I'd moved to Iowa and a few months after my wedding. On the day I laid out my case for the course of my research, Novak asked me what brought me there: "The ideas of these philosophers or the fact that they were women?" There was a right answer, of course. "Their ideas," I replied, explaining how my proposal was meaningful because it situated their arguments in a tradition.

But this wasn't true. Almost from the moment I discovered these women philosophers, I'd set out on a separate, more personal inquiry that had nothing to do with my dissertation. I thirsted to know how they became intellectuals and what obstacles they faced as women.

Initially, Mary Astell captivated me most.

One wou'd therefore almost think, that the wise disposer of all things, foreseeing how unjustly Women are denied opportunities of improvement from *without*, has therefore by way of compensation endow'd them with greater propensions to Vertue and a natural goodness of Temper *within*, which if duly manag'd, would raise them to the most eminent pitch of heroick Vertue.

—Mary Astell

A Room of Her Own

M ary Astell lived from 1666 to 1731 and published several works, including one with a title that instantly grabbed me: *A Serious Proposal to the Ladies.*

Within these pages, Astell offered complex arguments about the nature of mind and body and tackled some of the same issues of metaphysics and epistemology as René Descartes, who famously said, "I think therefore I am," and John Locke, who said, "No man's knowledge here can go beyond his experience." Yet her core message was rare: educate women so they can pursue personal happiness and contribute to society. I was amazed by Astell's boldness and unapologetic ambition, how she willed into existence a new, heartening vision for women's lives. And, as I discovered, she did this by casting a pitiless light on the sexist ideas of some of the most famous philosophers of her age.

The further I dug into her body of work, the more impressed and perplexed I became. She wrote four books of philosophy, political essays, and poetry—despite the considerable obstacles she faced as a woman in the seventeenth century. Astell was born during a time when about 25 percent of women in England could write, and the subjects that were socially acceptable for them to write about didn't include philosophy or literature.[1] Even girls of the upper classes received an education inferior to that of most boys, so that class was less determinative of the quality of one's education than gender.[2] Girls either attended finishing schools where they learned to knit, dance, and sing, or they did housework. The few girls who learned to read scholarly literature would discover a world of sexist theories awaiting them in print. They would also find it a challenge to discuss their ideas with anyone, because women were prohibited from most intellectual spheres. Coffeehouses, scientific societies, preparatory schools, and universities would not let the "fair sex" through their doors.[3] So how did Astell manage to write philosophical works and go on to become one of the most well-known intellectuals of her age?

There are not a lot of first- or secondhand accounts of Astell's personal life left to history. There are no journals and only a few letters, including some that were found years ago folded into an old pocketbook in a private home. As a never-married woman with no heirs, she had no one to care for her estate. Although no image of Astell has survived, a vivid picture of her personality emerges from her confessional poetry, a few private letters, and the meticulous work of historians, not to mention her philosophy, which has a personal tone.[4]

Astell grew up in Newcastle upon Tyne, in the far north of England, which today is about fifty miles south of Scotland. She was the youngest of two children, with an older brother, a mother, and a father who was employed in the local coal industry. Over the previous century, England had leveled nearly all its forests, and most homes were now heated with coal. Generations of Astell's family on both sides had been in the business of counting and weighing coal, and the revenue provided the Astells with a comfortable upper-class life. Her family gained status as "gentry" the year she was born.[5] This was a bright spot in an otherwise grim situation. By the time of Astell's birth, the local mines were running low, and soon larger, shallower reserves were unearthed near other cities. Astell's father, the last in her family to have a job in the coal industry, saw his profits shrink.

This did not bode well for Astell. Casting a long shadow over her childhood was the possibility that she might not have a dowry, which was essential to one day finding a husband of her station. The pressure to marry shaped the course of almost every girl's life, and as one contemporary put it, women "are understood either married or to be married."[6] Without a dowry, Astell would have to marry beneath her, and she would have to devote even more of her time to domestic drudgery. Like most girls, she spent much of her time in or around the home. She sat for hours in her family's parlor, clutching a sheet of linen and practicing her ornamental needlework, or she spent time in the kitchen baking bread.[7] But Astell was precocious and sensitive. She thought all of this domestic work tedious—bleak, even—as it was prologue to a life she was expected to lead but that she had a hard time imagining for herself.

She realized at a young age that she enjoyed learning. Many families of the gentry allowed their daughters to remain illiterate.[8] Not the Astells. For reasons that are now lost to history, they chose to educate their daughter. Formal schooling was not an option, because there were no girls' schools in Newcastle. When England was a Catholic nation, there were nunneries in most towns, and they sometimes educated girls.[9] By the time Astell was born, the former nunnery, St. Bartholomew's on Nun Street, had been a private residence for over a century. Fortunately, there was another option. Her uncle Ralph Astell, a local pastor at St. Nicholas Church and a bachelor, was tutoring her brother and agreed to tutor her too.[10] Starting at age eight, Astell stepped from the threshold of her home—freed from her domestic work, even if just for an hour or so—and walked a few blocks down the cobblestone road to St. Nicholas Church, with its spires rising so high into the sky that sailors at sea used them to navigate. Once there, she pushed open the heavy church door and went to a small room off the nave, where she met Ralph to study.

It's difficult to imagine Astell becoming the thinker she was without her uncle's early influence. He was in many ways an ideal mentor for a clever girl in an age otherwise hostile to women's intellects. He was sympathetic to the idea that women's minds

and experience were worthy of consideration and in a poem wrote
compassionately of a mother's pain in childbirth.[11] He also had a
diverse collection of books on history, religion, French, philosophy,
and logic, which he might have used during their lessons. Ralph's
one known shortcoming was that he was an alcoholic. When Astell
was eleven, he staggered drunk into the pulpit to deliver a sermon,
and for this he was replaced.[12] Now without an income, he moved
in with the Astells, whose home was already crowded with Astell's
mother, father, brother, aunt, and Mary herself. Nevertheless, the
tutorials continued, and it's possible this greater proximity brought
Astell and Ralph into more frequent conversation, accelerating her
lessons. What is clear is that Ralph observed his niece's irrepressible
brilliance and appetite for difficult concepts, and he decided she was
ready for philosophy.

Ralph had studied philosophy at the University of Cambridge
at St. John's College, and briefly at Emmanuel College, home to the
Cambridge Platonists.[13] (This was the same group of philosophers
that I first looked into for a potential dissertation topic.) It was the
dawn of the scientific revolution, a thrilling, if also anxiety-inducing
moment to be a philosopher. There was widespread concern in philosophical and theological circles that Thomas Hobbes's ideas, both
trenchant and persuasive, also promoted atheism. Hobbes held that
everything was made of matter and could be explained without invok-
ing immaterial substances like the soul, spirit, or God. The Cambridge
Platonists took Hobbes and any other atheistic-leaning thinkers to
be public threats, believing that the fabric of society—the codes of
ethics that bound people together and the institution of religion that
saved their souls—was at risk of deteriorating. They sought ways of
thinking about the material world that facilitated scientific progress
while also keeping God and religion central to their visions.[14]

All of this was instructive for Astell and set her on a course of
study that stretched into her teenage years. The Cambridge Platonists
impressed Astell with ideas she would one day integrate into her own

philosophy. Astell would reject materialism. She would see philosophy as the rational articulation of God's expectations for human life. Perhaps the Cambridge Platonists' most powerful gift to Astell was an ambitious model for what a philosopher could do: tell the world how best to usher in the new age of Enlightenment.

But it was still early days. Astell did not yet see herself as a philosopher. She first had to suffer a crisis of identity. When she was twelve, her father died, leaving the family with such limited money that they hardly qualified as gentry. It was now official that there was no dowry for Astell.[15] It didn't help that she was not particularly beautiful, as she herself reported, and had absolutely no means of attracting a desirable mate—that is, one that allowed her time to study.[16] Astell could no longer deny that her days spent in books would soon be over.

She also reached the conclusion that courting rituals were soul sucking.[17] She hated getting dressed up in fancy clothes and makeup and going to parties. "No satisfaction can I find / In balls and revelling," she wrote.[18] She wouldn't do "as other women do, / To dress and talk and make a shew."[19] It's not surprising that she had no social life. "I am Friendless."[20]

Compounding her difficult situation was the death of her uncle a year later. Ralph passed on his entire library to her in the hope that she would continue her studies. By her late teens, Astell was wringing her hands, confessing her frustrations in poetry. "I have wearied Heav'n with Prayers / And fill'd it's bottles with my tears," she wrote.[21] "What shall I do? not to be Rich or Great, / Not to be courted and admir'd, / With Beauty blest, or Wit inspir'd."[22] Astell fell into a depression, writing that no disappointments could "make me less who am already low."[23]

She was stubborn, willing to suffer loneliness. "I have higher aims," she wrote in a poem titled "Ambition."[24] "O happy Solitude, may I / My time with thee, & some good books employ!"[25] As a loner and a serious, brooding teenager, she filled the friendless void by studying more philosophy and contemplating God. "Heav'n alone must exercise my mind and quill."[26]

When she could, Astell read between her chores, sometimes inscribing notes in the margins of her texts with a graphite pencil. One book contained a discussion of women leaders in the early church who had no families and devoted their lives to study. Next to this section, she put an asterisk.[27] She bristled at the restrictions on the lives of women, and she was drawn to the freedom and power that intellectual activity gave her.[28] It delighted her to know that her ideas were guided by her own reason and not a man's. This freedom of conscience that men of her time theorized about, praised, and personally enjoyed—though rarely attributed to women—was something Astell unabashedly took ownership of. And she sought the pleasure it gave her. "And when I wou'd pleasant and merry be, / It is but thinking what my GOD has done for me."[29]

She was indignant that people would dismiss her as irrational because she was female. Society *must* be wrong. Her confidence stemmed from her firm conviction that she was smart. She also believed that God was on her side. She reasoned, along with the Cambridge Platonists, that God did nothing in vain. But she added her own twist: this implied that since women had reason—a fact undeniable to her—God intended for them to use it. "For since GOD has given Women as well as Men intelligent Souls, why should they be forbidden to improve them?"[30] In an age when reason was considered essential to the soul and salvation, Astell asserted the right of women to think.[31]

By her late teenage years, philosophy had become integrated into Astell's identity and sense of well-being. Philosophy was her path to salvation. Philosophy was her tool to navigate the challenges that came with being a woman. Philosophy helped her cope in a world all too ready to disregard her. And when she looked to her future, she saw herself as a philosopher. Even if it meant she would face hardship: "Let me obscured be, & never known / Or pointed at about the Town."[32]

Astell entertained no illusions that there was an obvious or easy path for her to live a life of the mind. "In a poor simple Girl 'tis a bold flight, / To aim at such a glorious height," she wrote.[33] Most philosophers of the seventeenth century attended university, including those from humble backgrounds, such as Hobbes and Locke, who had the support of mentors. The few English women philosophers who came before Astell were not helpful models either. Both Margaret Cavendish and Anne Conway were from wealthy, well-connected families. If their books didn't sell, they did not have to worry about how they would pay the rent or eat.

Some of the most successful male intellectuals of the age were bachelors. Robert Boyle, Descartes, Hobbes, Locke, and Isaac Newton viewed singlehood as symbolic of a commitment to truth and as a defining feature of the new, modern intellectual who was shepherding in the scientific revolution.[34] It was a life unimaginable for most women. To be unmarried was disadvantageous for a woman, putting her in a more precarious financial position than that of a widow.[35] Yet it had become clear to Astell that she didn't want to marry, and she expressed admiration for women who were single "out of choice and not necessitie."[36]

Some women of the gentry managed to live on their own in certain neighborhoods of London without too much stigma, working as governesses and schoolteachers.[37] These jobs were of no interest to Astell, who aspired to make a living as a writer. The courage to even imagine this for herself seems spun out of thin air. Even though London had more than 150 bookshops to feed the voracious appetite of its literate class, women were not living as professional writers.[38] The exception was Aphra Behn, who had had a successful career publishing poetry, fiction, and plays.[39] No woman had supported herself writing works of philosophy.

Astell decided to give it a try. In 1688, at age twenty-two, she scraped together all the money she had, just enough to live modestly for one year, sewed it inside of her clothing, and boarded a stagecoach for a two-week journey south to London. The roads were in terrible condition and coaches trundled along at walking pace, easy targets for robbers on horseback.[40] Most passengers made their trips unharmed, but there were cases of thieves who beat, raped, and killed passengers. Once, when a woman's ring was too difficult to pull off, a robber severed her finger. Not surprisingly, passengers prepared themselves for the worst. They wrote wills. They sewed hidden pockets into their hats, jackets, and bodices to conceal their money and gems. They carried faux wallets. Some brought pistols.[41] Before she left, Astell wrote in a poem that she welcomed death, even if it was horrifying and painful. If it was her time, then she would accept her fate.[42]

Out the window of her coach she might have seen vivid proof of crime. Along the road, there may have been bodies hanging from tall gallows carved hastily from tree trunks. This is what happened to robbers if they were caught. Designated citizens tracked them down, killed them, and strung them up in the same spot in which the crime had been carried out. Conditions inside the coach were not pleasant either. The ride itself was uncomfortable. Astell experienced frequent jabs to the ribs by her whalebone corset as the coach rocked and jerked. She shared the carriage with various other passengers, coming and going at the stops along the way. Full-body bathing was rare, even for members of the upper class. To counteract body odor, people applied scented pomade to their skin, which gave them a slick appearance. The fleas and lice that lived in wigs washed only once every six weeks made the rounds, biting those on board. The only opportunity to freshen up was at inns they passed along the way, where passengers paid for a moment of privacy to wipe off excess sweat with napkins and comb out vermin with pig-hair brushes.[43]

After two weeks, Astell arrived in London. She moved to Chelsea, a neighborhood that was home to a disproportionate number of single women working as teachers and governesses. She had distant relatives in the city she could call on if in trouble. Although her finances were meager and her future uncertain, Astell found much to love in her new life.

> *I find I can both eat and drink,*
> *And sleep and breathe, and move, and read, and think*
> *The Sun shines on me, flow'ers their odor yeild,*
> *If not in mine yet in my neighbours feild.*[44]

A year later, however, her circumstances had become dire. Not much is known about this period of her life, except that she was out of money and her London relatives were of no help. "I have pawned all my cloaths & now am brought to my Last Shift," she wrote on tattered and dirty paper in a letter to William Sancroft, archbishop of Canterbury.[45] "I desire ye charity of y^r grace," she continued. "I am a gentlewoman & not able to get a liflyhood."[46] She did not know him personally, but he had a reputation for supporting writers and had recently proposed a school of higher learning for women. It's possible that because of this, Astell suspected he would be sympathetic to her cause. She desperately needed a patron. Fortunately, Sancroft agreed to help, and he gave her multiple gifts of money and connected her to a publisher.[47] Soon after, she started working on her first book. In 1694, she published *A Serious Proposal to the Ladies, for the Advancement of Their True and Greatest Interest* and remained anonymous, referring to her authorship only as "a Lover of Her Sex." Anonymity wasn't unique to women authors. Sometimes male authors chose to remain anonymous, especially if their ideas were radical. Locke had left his name off his trailblazing political book *Two Treatises of Government*. But anonymity was expected of women, especially members of the gentry, for whom humility was a virtue and evidence of their moral worth.

Just as her poetry was rooted in personal experience, so too was *A Serious Proposal*. But now philosophy played a more robust role. It was an ambitious work, an ethics of the good life—a philosophical line of inquiry stretching back to Aristotle—but written specifically for women. And inside those pages, Astell described how a woman could live a happy life, one intimately tied to a life of the mind.[48]

One of the central aims of the book was to make the case for an all-women's college. Nothing like that existed at the time, and Astell hoped her readers would help her fund it. Without a college, she argued, women would have a hard time—in most cases an impossible time—learning to think for themselves. Her institution would be the place where women could do just that.

Although it was a radical idea, it wasn't entirely new. Just a few decades earlier, English philosopher Margaret Cavendish had written a satirical play called *The Female Academy*, and the philosophers Anna Maria van Schurman of Holland and Bathsua Makin of England had each proposed an all-women's academy.[49] But Astell was the first Englishwoman to offer a detailed argument grounded in philosophical principles and to propose that women study philosophy. And she did it all with such zesty language.

Her initial task was to persuade women that they needed a college. "LADIES," she wrote. "Since you cannot be so unkind to your selves, as to refuse your *real* Interest, I only entreat you to be so wise as to examine wherein it consists; for nothing is of worser consequence than to be deceiv'd in a matter of so great concern."[50] She wanted to acquaint women with their true selves. Women were as rational as men, she argued, and their business was to use their reason to lead a good and Christian life. Study was essential to religion, because religion was nothing "without a good Understanding."[51]

Part of the problem, as Astell saw it, was women didn't view themselves as reasonable creatures or in need of rigorous training. Instead, they preferred to spend their time doing frivolous things, like reading romances and plays. This bothered her. "How can she be furnished with any solid Principles whose very Instructors are Froth and emptiness?"[52] And as for the women who cared too much about

French fashion, she recommended they learn to appreciate French philosophy as well.[53] Critical judgments like these were common for Astell, but she was not a snob. She was hard on women because she believed them worth more than a life devoted to beauty practices. "To imagine that our Souls were given us only for the service of our Bodies, and that the best improvement we can make of these, is to attract the eyes of men. We value *them* too much, and our *selves* too little, if we place any part of our worth in their Opinion."[54]

To help her readers see women anew, she borrowed language from the latest science. She wrote that women were unaccustomed to thinking for themselves and were in an important sense indistinguishable from automatons. They move and speak, but they are mostly following orders from without and have an "unthinking mechanical way of living."[55] Here she invoked Descartes's division of reality into two substances: the mind, which is immaterial and thinking, and matter, which is its opposite—material and unthinking. These substances were governed by different laws, and the motion of material things was due to physical forces, whereas the activity of mind was rational. For Astell and many other early modern philosophers, reason was essential to freedom. To follow the commands of someone else was to be not truly free. A person must earn her own path to salvation. But Astell argued that women lived as if they were only matter in motion, as if they were just "Machins" devoid of mind.[56]

This metaphor was of critical importance, signifying for her a horror in plain sight: the indifference with which people normalized women's thoughtlessness and promoted it through unequal standards and conditions. She wanted her readers to be horrified too. Astell's writing is an unsettlingly powerful early critique of the invisible forces of patriarchy that encourage women to confuse their "real" interest with that of men and to do so with near mechanical regularity. Marxists would write about the concept of false consciousness more than two hundred years later, and although Astell and Marx differ in fundamental ways, Astell would agree that a part of our being is profoundly shaped by our social world, and to know and free ourselves, we must understand the external forces at work.

Astell didn't accept that women are naturally inferior to men and in need of direction. Instead, she stated, they are made that way through insidious social conditioning that begins when they are young and "spreads its ill Influence through all our Lives."[57] She argued that negative social belief systems disempower women by warping their self-perceptions, restricting their behavior, and thereby limiting their potential.[58] And it's men, through the freedom and power they wield at the helm of society, who encourage women to think against their self-interest.

This is why her college was necessary. It would provide a supportive environment where women could escape the intellectually hobbling world of men. In a stunning reversal of the norm that prohibited women from universities, she proposed a ban on men from her campus: "No impertinent Visits, no foolish Amours, no idle Amusements to distract our Thoughts," she wrote.[59] At her college, women would unlearn the dictates of men and heed the "Dictates of our Reason" and "regain our Freedom."[60] There, a woman would learn how to think for herself.

Astell insisted that her college would be outside of town, serving as a "blissful recess from the noise and hurry of the World."[61] Here a comparison with Socrates is interesting. He was skeptical of doing philosophy in the countryside, and said, "I'm a lover of learning, and trees and open country won't teach me anything, whereas men in the town do."[62] But as a male philosopher, Socrates could more easily withstand the pressures of city life. For example, a number of influential men of Athens didn't trust Socrates. They questioned whether he was a true philosopher and even sentenced him to death. Yet this didn't drive him into an existential tailspin. Here's another example: When Socrates learned from the Oracle of Delphi that he was the wisest person, which flummoxed him because he knew that he knew nothing, his response was cocksure: he sought powerful men who claimed to be smart and then tested whether he was wiser than they were. His confidence in his pursuit didn't waver much, because he was accepted and encouraged by a community of smart and powerful men who believed in his mind. Astell, on the other hand, knew that women lacked such reinforcement. Towns were engines of patriarchal thinking that served to grind women down. A woman's ability to think for herself was something Astell insisted would be best cultivated in a mutually supportive community that would foster the self-esteem and ambitions of its members.[63] Men had benefited from this kind of setup for ages but rarely acknowledged it as a condition of their genius. And now Astell wanted her college to do this for women.

Her college would be for women with an edge, who weren't satisfied with tradition, who were "sick of the vanity of the world."[64] It would be for those who were curious and humble in the face of their ignorance, those who were "desirous to know and fortify their weak side."[65] It would be for women to prepare for all stages of their life: singlehood, motherhood, and beyond.[66] It would be an insurance policy for married women. If a woman's relationship with her husband soured, she could take pleasure in books. And once her children were gone, she could educate others.[67] Women would be free to lodge and study for an indefinite amount of time. Her college would be home to an "Amicable Society" where members would cultivate "hearty well-wishers" and make "affectionate Friends."[68]

Women would study philosophy, including the works of Descartes and Nicolas Malebranche. They would read the works of Anne Le Fèvre Dacier, a French writer and scholar who supported women's education and translated the poetry of Sappho.[69] Most importantly, members of her college would learn to cultivate their souls to lead a good life.[70] Astell wrote that God gave humans reason and bodies to serve a purpose, which included regulating the passions. Once a person is in control of her desires, she must look to her nature to discover her talents, which were an indication of God's expectations

for her life. She would then be on a path to happiness and a contributor to social well-being.[71]

Astell feared that she would scare away potential members of
her college if she made the curriculum appear too demanding. So
she promised they would read only a few books of philosophy. She
also worried that it might sound boring. For this reason, she embel-
lished her descriptions:

> *Happy Retreat! which will be the introducing you into*
> *such a Paradise as your Mother Eve forfeited . . . Here*
> *are no Serpents to deceive you, whilst you entertain your*
> *selves in these delicious Gardens.*[72]

This wasn't pure manipulation. Astell believed that intellectual pleasures could be, if not as powerful, then nearly as powerful as physical
pleasures. These were also subversive statements at a time when
women were taught that indulging in sexual pleasure was sinful
and that lust for learning was shameful. Lady Mary Wortley Montagu, a contemporary who would eventually become a close friend
of Astell's, wrote, "Whatever learning a girl acquired . . . should be
concealed as though it were a physical blemish lest it arouse envy
and hatred."[73] But Astell insisted women had a right to experience
pleasures of the mind and described them in near-orgasmic terms:
"A Joy whose perpetual Current always affords a fresh Delight."[74]

When she wasn't writing, Astell devoted herself to cultivating a community of her own. Two people now central to her life were Archbishop Sancroft and Rich Wilkin, her publisher. She corresponded
with the philosopher John Norris, who studied at Oxford and was
an expert on continental philosophers such as Descartes and Malebranche. It was she who reached out to Norris. She may have heard
that he respected women's intelligence, and that he had previously

changed philosophical letters with a few women. Norris responded, kicking off a heady exchange about the love of God, in which Astell displayed her philosophical prowess. In 1695, the year following the publication of her first book, they published their letters. This bolstered Astell's philosophical credibility, which *A Serious Proposal* had helped establish. Astell had also hoped for a mentor in Norris. In one of her letters, she wrote, "I desire the Favour of you to furnish me with . . . Rules as you judge most convenient to initiate a raw Disciple in the Study of Philosophy."[75] For whatever reason, Norris wasn't tempted. He recommended some philosophers for her to read and left it at that.

A few years after she arrived in Chelsea, Astell formed friendships with some women in the neighborhood who became her closest and most loyal supporters: Lady Catherine Jones, Lady Anne Coventry, Elizabeth Hutcheson, and Lady Elizabeth Hastings. All four were unmarried aristocrats who devoted themselves to charitable causes and study. In this they were different from other women of their rank, who participated in court life, were married, and indulged in the foods and fashions of the day. Astell's friends were keenly interested in her work and were moved by her wish to advance women's place in the world. They saw Astell as their intellectual guide, asking her to recommend books and share her thoughts on multiple subjects. In return, these women became Astell's lifelong patrons, providing her with stipends to support her work.[76]

A Serious Proposal sold well and went through multiple editions. Astell imagined herself as head of the first all-women's college, but a few years after the book's publication, donations for the college were still not rolling in. There was a rumor that Princess Anne, next in line to be queen of England, considered donating £10,000, but the grant never materialized.[77] Supposedly the Scottish philosopher Gilbert Burnet, bishop of Salisbury, advised the princess against it because the college sounded to him like a nunnery in disguise. Astell had, after all, likened her institution to a "monastery"—not the best choice of words during a period when England was in the throes of fervent anti-Catholicism.[78]

In 1697, Astell published *A Serious Proposal to the Ladies, Part II*, which detailed a philosophical method, similar to the one Descartes describes in *Discourse on Method*, that women could employ from home to sharpen their minds. She would never receive the money necessary to open a college. But over the next few years, through the continued support of her friends, she published more treatises and political essays. With a stable community to back her up, she was able to maintain her focus on philosophy.

To the world outside her circle, Astell was known to be an earnest intellectual, protective of her time. One story tells of how an acquaintance stopped by her house only to be turned away by Astell herself, who yelled from her window that she was not home. She was prone to introversion and uninterested in small talk. She would stop conversations short if she was bored. Astell lacked the social graces of upper-class women: the desire to please others. One acquaintance described her as "strange" and another as "ill-favored and forbidding."[79] She wore black when most women of her class wore colorful silk garments imported from the East.

Yet with her friends she was warm and responsive. In letters, she shared gossip, asked about their health, and mused about picking orange blossoms on her next visit.[80] She was known to go out of her way to be kind and attentive to the wives of the well-known men with whom she discoursed. She wanted them to know that their minds mattered too. She used her leverage in the publishing world to help along the literary careers of other women. Her friend Lady Montagu went on to compose some of the best travel writing of the era.[81] Astell also encouraged the poet and philosopher Lady Mary Chudleigh to publish works in defense of women.[82]

Friendship's pull on her was gravitational, and she confessed to Norris her "strong Propensity to friendly Love" for women.[83] She imagined the bonds between women at her ideal college to resemble chaste marriages. For these reasons, some scholars suspect Astell was a lesbian. Other scholars contend that her relationships were platonic and that expressions of female associations were typically stronger at that time than they are today.[84]

I think Astell could have been attracted to women. I also think that Astell hoped women in her college would commit to each other like husband and wife, because such loyalty would inspire them to be less concerned with the pursuit of a husband, to look beyond the restraints of heteronormativity, to begin to see the world and their place in it anew. She wanted to prepare women to understand themselves and participate in the world not necessarily in the traditional roles of wives and mothers but rather as rational beings with individual talents. This vision called on women to adopt a new frame of mind.

But women's minds were not the only thing Astell wanted to change.

She was aiming to free women with philosophy, but also to free philosophy itself.

Unschooled women didn't often tell male philosophers how to think. This is partly why Astell's next book, *Some Reflections Upon Marriage*, in which she takes on prominent male philosophers, opens with criticism of a woman in the first few paragraphs. She wanted to bring the men in closer so she could draw her sword. It's also because Astell was a complicated figure, aligned with many of the conservative political positions of her day. Yet underneath some of her traditional views lay radical motivations.

One morning in 1699, Astell left her home to learn the news that Hortense Mancini, the Duchess of Mazarin, who lived only a few blocks away, had died. The duchess was born in Rome and grew up in Paris. She was one of the richest women in Europe, host to many parties—and the source of gossip about a widely discussed marital separation.[85] Upon her death, rumors about the duchess's exploits reanimated the city, and people debated whether she was right to have left her husband years before.[86] Astell was one of the philosophers to weigh in on the question. She published her thoughts after the duchess's death in her second book, whose full title was *Some Reflections Upon Marriage, Occasion'd by the Duke and Duchess of Mazarine's Case; Which Is Also Considered.* Despite the overwhelming evidence that the duchess's husband was cruel, Astell argued that she was wrong to have left him, since she had agreed to marry him in the first place.

The duke was a selfish, intractable man, who would wake his wife from sleep to tell her his dreams. A religious zealot, he insisted that their newborn baby abstain from food on days of fast, forbidding the duchess from nursing. He was embarrassed by female sexuality, and the sight of cow udders offended him so much that he considered asking his farmers to cease milking the animals. He thought about sawing off his daughter's teeth to scare away potential suitors. His wife's beauty provoked great anxiety in him, and he was jealous of anyone who spoke to her. He fired maids and turned away friends who enjoyed her company. He also blew through his wife's inheritance.

The duchess was only fifteen when she married the duke, who was twenty years her senior. She soon discovered the duke's brutality, and after enduring six years of marriage, she ran away from her husband. She sought refuge with a group of compassionate nuns, but it quickly became clear that her spirit had not been crushed by her oppressive marriage. As a prank, the duchess mixed ink in the holy water, which stained the nuns' fingers and faces when they used it to anoint themselves. She left Paris for England, where some members of the English royalty welcomed her. She settled into a home in Chelsea and began throwing her famous parties. She introduced the English to new dishes and flavors from France and Asia. Her revelries lasted well into the next day, when guests would stumble from her doorstep into the slanting morning light. She was unapologetic in her indulgences, and she enjoyed upsetting the expectation that women were meant to be quiet and submissive.

Although Astell led a tranquil, studious life compared to her neighbor, she sympathized with the duchess, agreeing that the marriage had been horrendous, a "misery none can have a just Idea of, but those who have felt it."[87] Yet Astell argued that a wife should conform to her husband's wishes.[88] Astell was a devotee of the Church of England during a period when dissenters were gaining ground. She was politically a Tory and defended the divine right of kings at a time when philosophers were proposing the natural equality of humankind. She also believed in a great chain of being and that social classes reflected not only economic hierarchies but also intellectual and moral ones, and that members of the upper class had the greatest capacity for knowledge and virtue.

At the same time, she argued that just because the wife was subordinate to her husband, this did not mean that women were subordinate to men. To drive the point home, she likened the job of being a wife to the job of being a pig farmer:

> Because GOD made all Things for Himself, and a Rational Mind is too noble a Being to be Made for the Sake and Service of any Creature. The Service she at any time becomes oblig'd to pay to a Man, is only a Business by the Bye. Just as it may be any Man's Business and Duty to keep Hogs; he was not Made for this, but if he hires himself out to such an Employment, he ought conscientiously to perform it.[89]

In other words, if you are going to marry, don't take your role as a wife personally. It's just a job. But more importantly, since you will be shackled to a man for life, you ought to choose your husband wisely. Don't marry "a Blockhead."[90] That had been the duchess's mistake.

The duchess's other mistake, according to Astell, was to take inspiration from the philosophies of the time that advanced ideas of freedom on the basis of individual rights. The idea of a social contract, that legitimate rule required citizens' consent, entered the political lexicon. Some thinkers went as far as to consider that if the political relationship was based on consent, then the marriage bond should be, too, and that if one party violated the inalienable rights of the other, then it was moral to dissolve the marriage. These kernels of liberal democracy that today we take to be cornerstones of freedom and modernity were the very things that Astell deemed harmful to women.

Astell was suspicious of the assertion that individual rights were the foundation of a fair and just society, because it focused on what individuals deserved and not on what they owed their community. It was a mistake, she argued, to insist on individual rights, because this concept encouraged people to insist on their prerogatives and to think little if at all about what they ought to do.[91]

She took on Thomas Hobbes for making this very mistake. To prove her point, she went right to the heart of his political thought: the state of nature. Hobbes described the condition of life in the state of nature as humans living outside of the laws and government of civil society in order to be completely free. It was undesirable because it was "solitary, poor, nasty, brutish, and short." Hobbes used the concept of the state of nature as a theoretical tool to justify why an individual would not want to live in such a state but would instead prefer to join civil society—even a society that was repressive. Astell disagreed. She pointed out that life independent of the laws of civil society wasn't awful, because most people weren't driven by selfish motives, but by love and devotion. In fact, if it weren't for the love of parents, there would be no human life at all. She mocked the notion of the solitary individual in the state of nature: "How I lament my Stars that it was not my good Fortune to Live in those Happy Days when Men sprung up like so many Mushrooms or *Terrae Filii*, without Father or Mother or any sort of dependency!"[92]

Astell also took aim at Locke, who argued for the equality of humankind on the basis of natural rights.[93] In his *Second Treatise of Government*, Locke wrote that rightful rule was based on consent between equals. He seemed to extend this line of thinking to the private sphere when he said that parental power was shared between two individuals who were natural equals. But in another passage, when he addressed what to do in moments of disagreement between parents, he defaulted to a notion of natural male superiority. "Every Husband hath to order the things of private concernment in his family . . . and to have his will take place in all things of their common concernment before that of his wife," he wrote.[94] His reasoning was based on his belief that a man was "the abler and the stronger."[95] Astell saw this contradiction and asked, "If *all Men are born free*, how is it that all Women are born slaves?"[96] And in another passage, "if Absolute Sovereignty be not necessary in a State, how comes it to be so in a Family?"[97]

Then she went after John Milton, the political theorist and author of *Paradise Lost*, who stated that no one "can be so stupid to deny that all men naturally were borne free, being the image and resemblance of God himself."[98] Milton denied that women were men's equals and expanded the power of men in the public realm, while retaining patriarchy in the private sphere.[99] Astell called him out: "How much soever Arbitrary Power may be dislik'd on a Throne, not *Milton* himself wou'd cry up Liberty to poor *Female Slaves*, or plead for the Lawfulness of Resisting a Private Tyranny."[100]

The shortcomings Astell saw in the philosophies of Hobbes, Locke, and Milton laid the foundation for her claim that there was something amiss in the male intellectual attitude. "There is a certain Pride in the Mind of Man, which flatters him that he can See farther and Judge better than his Neighbour."[101] She observed that the philosophical spirit guiding her age was suffused with egoism and smallness and led men to falsehoods.

This was a daring position to take at a moment when philosophers were painstakingly working out methodologies to lead them to objective truth. These same philosophers were aware of how a poor education, unfounded opinions, and custom inhibited this pursuit. Many of them were even critical of the universities, which they dismissed as bastions of Aristotelianism, an antiquated way of thinking. Yet almost none of them acknowledged how gender stereotypes biased their own thought.

Astell was writing at a critical moment in European intellectual history, when curiosity itself was no longer considered a threat to religion. Since Augustine in the fourth century curiosity for its own sake was considered an evil. But this distrust of curiosity started to let up in the sixteenth and seventeenth centuries, when philosophers began to view scientific discovery as a divinely sanctioned insight into God's creation.[102] Francis Bacon and other men of the scientific revolution were careful to refer to their pursuit of knowledge as "useful," by which they meant compatible with Christianity or even helpful for salvation. The influential political philosopher Jürgen Habermas describes this period as critical to modern democracy, the birth of the public sphere and open discourse.[103] Astell would have taken issue with this characterization.

She saw how this shift in attitude didn't apply to women, whose curiosity remained unrehabilitated and who were thought to be incapable of useful knowledge. Women continued to be criticized for wondering about the wrong sorts of things, and were still considered unfit for the new method of inquiry. And the curious women whose smarts men couldn't deny faced the disturbing likelihood that they would become scientific curiosities themselves.[104] Medical doctors at the time were persuaded by Galen's theory that women were colder than men and had slower thoughts. Women who had quick thoughts must not be female but rather hybrids they termed freaks of nature.[105] When Astell wrote that learned women were "star'd upon as Monsters, Censur'd, Envy'd, and every way Discourag'd," she was being literal.[106]

In spite of this pervasive sexism, or perhaps because of it, Astell insisted women's minds were better suited to grasp the truth than men's.[107] She wrote that women have an intellectual sensibility informed by both reason and love.[108] Love plays a critical role in knowledge, because it draws us toward objects. She argued that when our passion is fixed on God, then our intellects are curious to know God and his creation. Only in this way does the natural world unfold before the human mind, revealing its secrets. By contrast, the intellectual temperament of men falls short of this ideal. Whether by nature or nurture (Astell isn't decided), men are far more prone to selfishness and, so, capable of producing only distorted truths.[109] A case in point: men insist upon women's inferiority not because they have true insight into women's nature but rather because they selfishly want women to serve them.

Astell also argued that an expansion of women's social roles was key to improving society at large. Unlike men, women had a great capacity for benevolence, a species of love that causes us to care for others in our community.[110] She didn't accept the commonplace belief that women would best serve society as mothers and wives. Those roles were necessary, but they were not the only ones available to women. To extend their influence beyond the domestic realm, women would have to love themselves enough to foster their individual talents. It was through introspection, not the guidance of men, that women would find their direction in life. For women who might not enjoy submissive roles, Astell recommended looking for a life outside of marriage, encouraging them to seek roles traditionally denied to them, such as governors, rulers, poets, philosophers, and scientists.[111]

Here, Astell is at her most audacious. In place of the model of the bachelor intellectual, Astell posited the single woman. This intellectual has sharp reason and a strong sense of compassion, giving her insight into God's will and making her best suited to manifest it in the world. She wrote:

> Nor will Knowledge lie dead upon their hands who have
> no Children to Instruct; the whole World is a single Lady's
> Family, her opportunities of doing good are not lessen'd

but encreas'd by her being unconfin'd. Particular Obliga-
tions do not contract her Mind, but her Beneficence moves
in the largest Sphere. And perhaps the Glory of Reform-
ing this Prophane and Profligate Age is reserv'd for you
Ladies, and that the natural and unprejudic'd Sentiments
of your Minds being handsomly express'd, may carry a
more strong conviction than the Elaborate Arguments of
the Learned.[112]

Once women unhitched their minds from the system of beliefs that
told them they were irrational, worthy only to be followers, destined
to be men's subordinates, Astell argued, they would be the ones to
access a truly "useful" knowledge.

This reminds me of something the philosopher Irigaray once
said. She asks what a philosophy of woman's nature would look like
that didn't derive from the belief that women are inferior and destined for motherhood: "But to what reality would woman correspond,
independently of her reproductive function?"[113] It's an open question and one that Astell was also motivated by centuries ago. Astell's
answer was that a woman's sex should not be her defining feature
if she does not want it to be, because humans are foremost rational
persons. Even if a woman were to participate in a traditional female
role, it should not be because of necessity but rather because she
freely chose to do so. A sentiment that—despite her conservatism
in other areas—is strikingly modern.

After 1710, Astell stopped publishing and took up another project.
With funding from a few of her friends, she opened a charity school
in Chelsea for poor girls. Charity schools taught young, destitute children skills to help them take care of themselves and find jobs. Acting
as the school's director, Astell developed a curriculum that taught
students how to read, write, and knit.[114] Astell's students studied more

than students in other charity schools, though there is no evidence they read philosophy, history, or literature.

Still, she believed in the dignity of all humans, that each person, no matter her rank, had a degree of reason and autonomy she needed to cultivate to live well. And by teaching the girls of her charity school basic knowledge and skills, Astell saw herself setting them on a path to freedom. She loved the work and did it for fifteen years. Over the course of the school's history, more than 120 girls were educated to read and write, and most of them found a job after graduation. Once she stepped down as director, she remained involved with the school, working with members of the board to secure land for a new building.

In her later years, Astell also harbored a dream to write a textbook on philosophy for women that would inform them about epistemology and the natural world. She assigned friends chapters to write, but she had trouble getting anyone to follow through with the project.[115]

She spent her final two decades with friends, in conversation about religion and philosophy. Her devotion to God remained constant. Every Sunday she walked to church and back, ninety minutes each way, in heels, a hoop skirt, and a whalebone corset. In 1731, at the age of sixty-four, she was diagnosed with breast cancer. Her doctor recommended surgery, though at the time there was no anesthesia. Astell managed to survive the mastectomy but died a few months later from infection. A friend wrote that in Astell's final moments of life, she asked to have her coffin placed next to her bed and to be alone, contemplating the afterlife.

A short biography written about Astell two decades after her death brought her to the attention of some prominent writers. Samuel Richardson's novel *Clarissa* was inspired by Astell's life.[116] Then in 1916, Florence Smith, an English PhD candidate at Columbia University, came across Astell's work and decided to write her dissertation on Astell. That's when Astell came to the attention of Virginia Woolf.

Woolf read Smith's dissertation while researching long-forgotten women writers and intellectuals and was astonished by Astell's life. "Queen Anne died and Bishop Burnet died and Mary Astell died; but the desire to found a college for her own sex did not die. Indeed, it became stronger and stronger," Woolf wrote. Woolf also proposed a college for women, an idea she says originated with Astell.[117] Woolf was shocked that none of her contemporaries knew about Astell. "But what I find deplorable . . . is that nothing is known about women before the Eighteenth Century," Woolf wrote in "A Room of One's Own."[118] Astell's life as a single woman and her insistence that women needed a refuge to think for themselves were motivating forces behind Woolf's proclamation that a woman needs a room of her own to write.

But for the most part, Astell remained forgotten by history. For her forcefulness, Astell knew there would be some sort of fallout. In her case, as in the case of most women, it took the form of erasure.[119] That's the risk a woman takes when she steps into a space believed to be the natural territory of men, something Astell was well aware of. "I know not how the Men will resent it, to have their enclosure broke down, and Women invited to tast of that Tree of Knowledge they have so long unjustly *monopoliz'd*."[120]

But Astell didn't allow this to stop her, because her message wasn't for them; it was for women. "An Ingenious Woman is no Prodigy to be star'd on, for you have it in your power to inform the World, that you can every one of you be so, if you please your selves."[121]

In the early years of my marriage to Alex, when I was teaching and writing my dissertation, I could not stop thinking about Astell's ideas. I read her works over and over. And every time I did, I discovered a new meaning, another pithy line. I wasn't personally stirred by the religious dimension of Astell's theories. Anytime I read an early modern thinker, I expected to encounter some reference to the divine: a proof of God or a method for how to access His will. Those days

I treated the religious dimensions of early modern theories like the paintings in a gallery of Counter-Reformation art. These centuries-old religious arguments were like centuries-old artworks inspired by a sensibility that didn't fully resonate with modern secular life, yet at the very least I could appreciate their formal aspects and take pleasure in works well done.

Astell moved me in more personal and practical ways, for instance, making me aware of my own prejudices. Almost a year before, I'd given my first conference paper on an early modern woman philosopher at a university in the Midwest. A graduate student asked the first question: "What does she mean by 'woman'?" she said. "Does she mean all women or just upper-class white women?" I hadn't prepared for this question, and I paused, unsure how to continue. Then a professor jumped in, telling the questioner to let it go, to focus on what is liberating and good about this early feminist thinker. But the questioner didn't. She asked whether we could even call Astell a feminist, and found me afterward to tell me more about this moral blind spot in my scholarship—in myself. This was not how I wanted my first conference presentation to go, and I was annoyed. Because the graduate student was right. There was a monstrousness in Astell's ideas—and in me for ignoring it.

Social theorist Patricia Hill Collins writes about how power works in privileged intellectual spaces, such as colleges and universities. She says that "despite ideological commitments to equality, inclusivity, and belonging, interpretive communities have hardwired practices that, whether intentional or not, replicate existing social hierarchies."[122] I had been tempted to look beyond the fact that I'd drawn inspiration from a thinker who rejected and repelled other people based on class and what was implied: race. Astell was eager to point out gender bias in the work of male philosophers, but she had her own biases. *A Serious Proposal* was a proposal to the "Ladies," a term that connotes upper-class women, who at the time were almost exclusively white, wealthy women. In another passage, she says her college would provide scholarships for the "less fortunate," though it's not clear whom she means. She could have meant poor women, though it's more likely she had in mind the less fortunate women of the upper classes, such as she herself once was.[123] And, though she argued that all humans had souls and were capable of salvation, she believed God distributed talents unevenly (for the sake of social harmony), and some people were equipped with less intellectual hardware than others, differences that cut not along gender but rather class lines.[124] Her ideas weren't intended to cultivate the minds of women of the lower classes or women of color. For the purposes of her project, these women were inessential.[125] It's a disturbing moral shortcoming in a thinker who in other ways was an inspiration.

I sometimes thought of Astell as a "protofeminist," a female defender who would have thought differently had she been born later. But was that fair or true? Astell and I shared a lot, but it's actually quite odd to expect she would share my moral sensibilities. It's a sort of relativization that doesn't stand up to scrutiny. I suspect the impulse to relativize what is immoral in ourselves is the same impulse that keeps us from dealing with our shame.

Philosopher Julia Kristeva describes disgust as protective. When we see a pile of shit on the sidewalk, smell rotten food, see a dead body where we don't expect it, we retch, cover our faces, turn away. "Not me. Not that," she writes. Our disgust cushions us from a far more challenging confrontation with "a reality that, if I acknowledge it, annihilates me."[126] This includes ideas that offend us and challenge who we are and the choices we've made. When I first realized how I'd initially been indifferent toward Astell's dismissal of most women, I faced the ugliness of my own prejudices and privilege, and, as Kristeva predicted, my response was: *No, not this, not now.* I felt the urge to sweep it all under the rug and forget, to ignore, to move on to a different project. How easy to feel shame, outrage, and to shut down. How patriarchal of me.

There were other things Astell helped me see. Her chant that women belonged in intellectual spheres was invigorating. There was a sense of freedom in Astell's work that I was especially drawn to. Her concern that men have the liberty of entering a space designed for their intellectual flourishing, whereas women must either elbow their way in or make their own separate space from the ground up, exhorted me to take seriously the ways I didn't have the same access to knowledge or encouragement as my male peers. She nudged me to reflect on what I did in the face of this. When Astell observed that men were unappreciative of her intelligence, she built for herself a community of supportive women. This hadn't been my initial response.

Reading Astell made me feel raw. She cracked open my past, forcing me to revisit some of the false starts I'd made when I set out to live a life of the mind.

Enlightenment

I was a college sophomore when I called Alex for a first date. Before I searched his name in the university directory to call and ask him out for coffee, I had already imagined what it would be like to kiss him. He was five years my senior, and his preference for blazers and his status as a graduate student made him seem older still. He combed his brown hair straight, but it was on the brink of a curly rebellion, and when a stray lock fell over his blue eyes he pulled it behind his ear. As a teaching fellow, he always had a response to the most difficult questions his students asked him, and the theoretical ideas I'd barely understood in lecture became, by the end of his discussion section, objects I could grasp and turn around in my mind. When he answered the phone, he sounded surprised but happy to hear from me.

"You sound like Casey Kasem," I blurted. The disc jockey's Top 40 countdown voice had lulled me to sleep in elementary school. It seemed soothing to me, confident.

"Well, I'm only mildly offended," he answered. I inhaled sharply. Still, he agreed to go out with me.

We met at my favorite bookstore coffee shop on Newbury Street, and I ordered a raspberry chai latte and he a coffee with cream. We sat across from each other at a small table, and each time I shifted in my seat, I accidentally brushed his leg and was reminded of how tall he was. He was calm and smiled a lot. I told him I'd been reading Milan Kundera. I got the impression he didn't think Kundera was serious. Still, I shared my ideas with him. I was eager to impress.

The couple seated next to us stretched their arms across the table holding hands. Between them was a stack of books they'd picked out to browse. At one point the woman burst out: "I just love to learn with you!" I covered my mouth with my hand to keep from laughing out loud. They were too saccharine and self-serious. Alex and I stared at each other with wide eyes, bonding over what we wouldn't be like if we were ever a couple.

Soon, I was spending most of my free time with him, learning about Aristotle, the ingredients in a gimlet, and how to force narcissi to grow indoors in winter. He had been raised in Massachusetts by a single mother who worked at a school and performed in the local theater. His mother's father was wealthy, and Alex, his mother, and his younger brother spent weekends at his grandfather's home on the coast of Maine. We were charmed by each other's differences in background and taste. I shared my fascination with Nietzsche, the periods in history when writing and reading were dormant, and the disorienting qualities of the Mannerists. I had permanent bedhead and wore black. He studied the ancient philosophers in Greek and was captivated by the Renaissance and Enlightenment. We'd become that insufferable couple in the coffee shop, but I was beyond caring. I was falling in love.

One day at the Museum of Fine Arts, he took my hand and brought me to an ancient marble statue of a reclining woman, barely clothed. The diaphanous material of her gown caught on her shoulders and rippled down her side. It was a miraculous sensory illusion, how a carved rock could be made to appear light and unburdened. My mind switched between seeing frozen stone and seeing the lissome body of a young woman free to please. I felt the mystery of titillation give way to a sensation of compression inside me when I thought about the millions of eyes that had wandered this body for millennia.

As a child, I preferred to dress like a tomboy. I was friends with many boys and was sometimes even mistaken for one. I loved how boys were so physical when they played, but I also didn't want to

draw unwanted male attention to myself. My mother shared stories
about growing up in the projects of St. Paul, Minnesota—stories
of abuse and of greedy men chasing girls through deep snow. She
meant to warn and protect us. By my teenage years, I believed that
objectification was something that I could mostly avoid if I had luck
and was careful. I constantly readjusted my interpretation of reality
to perpetuate this belief, a task that became harder the more I moved
through the world. In college I discovered the male gaze in literature
and the halls of museums, which affirmed its dominance throughout
history. Still, this insight didn't completely encumber me. I believed
my professional future held opportunity for me and decided until
that future arrived, I could simply put my attention elsewhere, such
as in early modern ethics and epistemology.

That day in Boston, I took Alex farther into the museum, stopping before a two-thousand-year-old Aegean pot with hieroglyphic
figures of indeterminate gender. Standing before this piece, I felt
relief to be in the presence of something seemingly unrelated to
women's objectification. I thought of my hopes for myself—to be a
person who wasn't plagued by fear and anxiety. I concentrated on
the artist's intention, encouraging an entire constellation of questions to blossom.

A few months after we started dating, I invited Alex to a goth club.
When he strolled up to me on the sidewalk outside the venue, I suddenly had trouble concentrating on anything but him. He'd switched
out his blue jeans and button-down for a new pair of black Levi's
and a black T-shirt. I knew he'd done this for me, and the rest of the
evening I was drunk on the affirmation that he was falling for me as
much as I was falling for him. Plato says that beauty inspires its own
replication through looking, writing, and creating. Alex and I were
beautiful things talking about beautiful ideas, over and over again,
in a virtuous circle of reproduction. When we discussed philosophy,

it enriched my coursework, and as I fell for him, I fell more for philosophy.

We dated throughout my undergraduate years and spent weekends in Maine with his family, an erudite group who recited Shakespeare while rinsing lettuce and on special occasions listened to Handel's entire *Messiah* until well after midnight. Together we drank Manhattans on ice in the musty library, lounging on heirloom couches and dressed in formal wear—though we rarely went out. We were the occasion. Waves crashed on rocks behind us as we debated the Iraq War, whether to take out the sailboat the next day, and how to make Boston baked beans. Most topics were interesting: there was always someone to provide context or a contrary opinion. One warm August afternoon when the tide was coming in, Alex's aunt and I jumped into the channel in our clothes and found ourselves swimming in an Italian soup of large, translucent plankton. Salps, we discovered after post-swim research. Sailing occasioned talks on navigation; driving along the coast inspired a discussion of American architecture; hiking afforded lessons in botany. I could no longer walk through a forest without seeing *Liriodendron tulipifera*. I felt empowered by these moments with his family, as if they were smoothing the roughness of class that had been a source of anxiety in my early college years.

After a few years of dating, I shared a book with Alex's mother and aunt about the lost art of keeping house. It was thick, with double-columned pages in a tiny font, and filled with details such as how to fold a towel and how to make your own cleaning solution with sodium hydroxide. The author, a workingwoman of roughly my then age, laments that the secrets of her grandmothers had been practically snuffed out by feminism. The author herself identified as a feminist but posited that the movement went too far by treating domestic knowledge as inherently oppressive. Alex and I were less bothered by the feminist implications of the book. We found it to be an elegant example of human curiosity probing the mundane—in this case, housework—only to reveal surprising depths. I thought his mother and aunt would appreciate the author's meticulous research. Alex and I were getting more serious, and the book, which we'd purchased together at a Barnes & Noble just off the highway, was a hope for a home we might one day share.

I was slicing tomatoes in the kitchen while Alex's aunt and mother sat down on wooden chairs at the dining room table nearby. His aunt flipped through some pages and then handed it to his mother, who did the same before she closed it and deposited her ashtray on top.

After a bit, I asked, "So, what do you think?"

They gave each other a sideways look, and his mother turned to me.

"This is why we had women's liberation," she said. "So we wouldn't get saddled with something like this." She laughed, then lit a cigarette.

I nodded and thought about it while I continued slicing. Alex and I had already discussed domestic labor and agreed that we would share it. He cooked, folded fitted sheets, and loaded the dishwasher better than me. We were proud of these facts, viewing them as setting us on a course for an equal partnership. Just the same, I saw his mother's point. Although Alex and I had purchased it together, I had chosen to share the book with women. I hadn't passed it on to Alex's uncle, grandfather, or brother—a humorous thing to picture that was also instructive because it was humorous. How easily I'd fallen into stereotypical behavior when I wasn't thinking. There was a whole side of my being that was mechanical, reproducing actions that conformed to a larger interest that was in opposition to my deliberate and most cherished wishes for myself.

As Alex and I grew closer, something else was taking root. When we discussed philosophy, unsurprisingly, I typically went over terrain he had already plowed through as an undergrad. I fantasized about the day we would be intellectual equals, but like a cruel perversion of one of Zeno's paradoxes, with each step forward the goal seemed further away. One day, Alex and I were having a technical discussion of Spinoza, and I was eager to have him read a short essay I was working on. I felt sure he'd compliment my ideas, nudge me forward—maybe even push back on an idea or two. He read it in an hour, after which he suggested massive revisions. I was crestfallen. His comments were incisive and powerful, and I rewrote the essay. He read my next paper and suggested more revisions. Again, I rewrote.

This became a pattern between us—exceptionally painful, yet feeling, on my end, somehow necessary. I doubted my abilities enough to ask for his help, thinking his validation would dispel my insecurity and improve my confidence. Instead, the opposite happened: I started to question myself in ways I never had. I started to think it was too risky to invest wholeheartedly in developing my ideas without running them by him first. Similarly, it felt too risky to share them with anyone besides Alex, because clearly my ideas needed work. I told myself he was saving me from embarrassment. Yet, in choosing this way of being in philosophy, I was depriving myself of the benefit of sharing my ideas with others. These were my early formative years, when I should have been cultivating my intellect with different people, but my fear of making mistakes that other people might see drove me to intellectual isolation.

Over time, this dynamic came to feel strangling. It wasn't laying the groundwork for personal autonomy, let alone an equal partnership. All the same, I didn't stray from Alex, because I loved him and knew he loved me, and because I didn't expect philosophy to be such a boys' club. With him by my side, I was convinced it would be somehow easier. When he proposed, I accepted.

Later, when we'd been married two years and were living in Iowa, I would take walks on the bluffs overlooking the river. One time I noticed that some townspeople had planted community gardens just yards from the river's banks. Weeks later, the river flooded and overtook the land. I was saddened, remembering the gardeners' joyous industry during planting season, but I was not surprised. Floods weren't unheard of here. I walked the levee, looking down as the river lapped sprigs from a vegetable patch. Why hadn't anyone warned the gardeners, I wondered. Maybe they had, and the gardeners chose to believe that this season would be different.

I never wanted a subordinate role for myself in marriage and believed that this wish was sufficient to prevent it from happening. Looking back on this period, I've sometimes wondered why no one warned me about the asymmetry in my relationship. Why no one stopped me, looked me in the eye, and said, *What's happened to you?* It's possible they didn't see it. It's possible that for similar reasons I didn't stop it myself. The power imbalance wasn't unique to us. No one saw a problem because there was no problem to see. We were just a man and a woman participating in a love story common to partnerships across time.

It was around this time that I became curious about the women whose lives were tangled up with the lives of the great philosophers. I expected disparities in their relationships, too, and I longed to know how the women were treated and how they responded. In my free time, I did some research. What I discovered were many women—daughters, wives, lovers, students—who were stifled by philosophers or the culture of philosophy. In some cases (the historical record is woefully limited on women's subjectivity), I could even discern their reactions, some of silent acquiescence, some of anger and defiance. Whatever their reactions, these were the women behind the men.

The Women
behind the Men

Socrates was married, some say to two women at once.[1] His wife—or rather, one of his wives—was Xanthippe, forty years younger than he was and mother to his three sons. Socrates argued with her, and apparently she argued back. Once, in frustration, she poured piss over his head. For these reasons, she is remembered as a termagant. A fishwife. A shrew. (Her reputation inspired the Shakespeare play.) Socrates said, "I wish to deal with human beings, to associate with man in general; hence my choice of wife. I know full well, if I can tolerate her spirit, I can with ease attach myself to every human being else."[2]

As he strolled the Athenian marketplace, conversing with the sons of influential men, Socrates shared his belief that "the unexamined life is not worth living." He is also rumored to have said, "By all means marry, if you get a good wife, you will be happy. If you get a bad one, you will be a philosopher." Socrates likened himself to a gadfly, a pest waking men from their dogmatism with sometimes humiliating, unrelenting questions. Powerful men tried to swat him away, putting him on trial for impiety and for corrupting the youth of Athens. They sentenced him to die, and he drank the hemlock: a noble death for a noble calling.

An argumentative man is a gadfly, is a philosopher. An argumentative woman is a nettlesome tool for him to sharpen his wits upon.

* * *

In the year 1116, Peter Abelard, a famous Aristotle scholar at the cathedral school of Notre-Dame in Paris, fell in love with his student Heloise d'Argenteuil. He knew he would have no problem wooing her. "I was sure it would be easy: I was famous myself at the time, young, and exceptionally good-looking, and could not imagine that any woman I thought worthy of my love would turn me down."[3]

Heloise was educated in a convent, and by her late teens or twenties (her exact age is uncertain) she was renowned in Europe for being extraordinarily learned. Peter admitted, years later, that she knew more about classical literature than he did. And when you read her words, you cannot help but notice that her elegance outstrips his. They both excite your reason, but she guts you.

They first met when she was allowed to attend one of his philosophy classes. He was overcome by her presence. "In her looks she was not the least of women, but in her learning she was supreme," he recalled.[4] Peter got in touch with Heloise's uncle, at whose home she was staying, and convinced him to let him lodge there. The uncle, unaware of Peter's attraction, hired him to tutor his niece. Peter now had the chance to teach Heloise philosophy and to seduce her, and so he did. Many times, as she documented, in many places. Gardens, closets, and beds. In the relative privacy of a relative's home, they stole feverish moments, which Heloise lustily recalls as "abandoning ourselves to fornication." (Why am I surprised that in the twelfth century a woman unabashedly wrote how she loved to fuck?)

Then she got pregnant. She had the baby, and her family pressured the couple to marry. Peter agreed to do it on the condition they keep it secret—as master of his school he was expected to be chaste. But word got out, and he commanded Heloise to join a convent. This outraged some of her family members, who snuck up on him in the middle of the night and castrated him. He fled to a monastery.

Heloise named their son Astrolabe after an instrument perfected by the ancient woman philosopher and mathematician Hypatia to calculate the rising of stars on the horizon. When Heloise joined a convent, she couldn't bring her son with her, and so she gave him up to be raised by Peter's sister. A decade after they'd first met, Heloise was still mourning the loss of Peter's presence. She wrote, "My heart was never my own but was always / with you, / and now even more, if it is not with you / it is nowhere: / without you it cannot exist at all."[5]

Petrarch, the fourteenth-century poet, was overcome by Heloise's words and scribbled in the margin of his copy of their letters: "You are acting throughout with gentleness and perfect sweetness, Heloise."[6] Their letters inspired literary adaptations throughout history— Alexander Pope's, Jean-Jacques Rousseau's, and Michel Gondry's— which agree that Peter and Heloise's was a classic and tragic love story: two lovers forced by external pressures and greater goods to live apart.

And then there's the lesser-known story of how Peter confessed that he raped Heloise multiple times: "When you objected to it yourself and resisted with all your might, and tried to dissuade me from it, I frequently forced your consent (for after all you were the weaker) by threats and blows."[7] It's possible he was lying here to protect her virtue. Yet Heloise didn't care unconditionally about chastity. She'd written of the times they'd had intoxicating sex.

There's also Heloise's complaint that he decided things for her that she didn't want, but which she accepted as his subordinate. He demanded they marry when Heloise preferred being his mistress or "*whore*."[8] Marriage didn't ensure fidelity, she said. Heloise argued that philosophy and marriage were incompatible, citing Socrates and Theophrastus, a student of Aristotle, who argued that no wise man should have a wife.[9] Heloise respected these beliefs built into the practice of philosophy itself. And she believed that if she lived according to them, she would allow philosophy to thrive. She obeyed Peter's wish to spend the rest of her life in a nunnery, though she wrote him she would have "followed you / to Vulcan's flames if you commanded it."

She entered the pale future of religious life, a life without Peter's physical presence, a life that she observed was constructed by men and for men, in which abbots dictated the rules of convents. "The men who wrote the rules for monks were entirely silent about women, but they also laid down regulations which they knew did not suit women in the slightest," she wrote.[10] As Peter was the abbot in charge of her convent, she asked him to draw up a charter for it, but with her recommendations in mind. In a well-argued letter, she outlined justifications for comfortable clothing for menstruating women (rather than the traditional garb of tight, itchy wool), less manual labor, and moderate allowances of wine and food to make daily life bearable.[11] She said women were the weaker sex and couldn't meet the same challenges as men.

Peter responded that she needed to think more highly of her sex.

He must have thought highly of Heloise, because he incorporated some of her philosophical ideas from their correspondence into his works—without attribution.[12]

The philosopher and inventor of the modern scientific method, Francis Bacon, married a girl of fourteen when he was forty-five.[13] He started courting Alice Barnham when she was eleven. Years passed. Bacon was rumored to be gay and to spend most of his time away from home, busy with his work. The couple went into debt. When Bacon heard talk that Barnham was having an affair, he wrote her out of his will. He burned their letters. Even Barnham's early biographer sided with Bacon. He was nursing a "bruised pride and broken heart," and he "must have gone through many miserable hours."[14] Yet Bacon was known to value celibacy and singlehood as conducive to the pursuit of philosophy and science. He wrote, "Certainly, the best works, and of greatest merit for the public, have proceeded from the unmarried or childless men, which both in affection and means have married and endowed the public."[15] He directed that he be buried with his mother.

* * *

Descartes had an affair with a friend's domestic servant, which was so distracting to his work that he had to end the relationship. But before he did, it led to the conception of his daughter, Francine. When Francine was five, she contracted a fever and was covered in sores. Descartes visited her and spoke of her future. It was a rare, tender relationship for the otherwise reclusive philosopher.[16] Three days later, she died, and Descartes was overcome with grief, saying he'd never felt a greater sorrow.[17]

Even though Descartes corresponded with a few women about philosophy, holding their intellects in high esteem, when it came to theorizing about women's intellects in general, he was silent. This is disappointing because his philosophy contains the germ of what might have been a bold reconstitution of equality between the sexes. For whatever reason, he chose to stop short of the implications of his philosophy for women's minds. Philosopher Susan Bordo describes Descartes's reticence as a gender void.[18]

There is an apocryphal story that after Francine's death, Descartes constructed a life-size mechanical doll in her image that he carried with him everywhere he went. He purportedly used it as an emblem of his theory that animals have no souls. However, the story goes that he treated the doll as if it were alive. On sea voyages he would sleep with it near him, which motivated one captain, who was rattled by it, to cast it into the sea. This strange tale endured hundreds of years after Descartes's death. The story of the daughter he loved and, as Bordo put it, the "woman-machine," producing an unresolved, incompatible vision—a cipher of sorts, haunting the space of his gender void.

Jean-Jacques Rousseau's housekeeper, Thérèse Levasseur, was nine years younger than him and bore his five children. Rousseau didn't want them around and, after each of their births, dropped them off at the local orphanage.[19] The cruelty of this act made some biographers question whether the children were legitimately his. In any case, he eventually married Levasseur.

Radically new visions of women's roles in society had been emerging in prerevolutionary France, but Rousseau wasn't in support of them.[20] For Rousseau, sex differences bled into cognitive differences: he argued that women were not destined to think for themselves or to live on equal terms with men, let alone do philosophy. Men were capable of the reason conferred by autonomy and of being free citizens, but women were not; theirs was the "reason of obedience."[21] He wrote, "The whole education of women ought to be relative to men. To please them, to be useful to them, to make themselves loved and honored by them, to educate them when young, to care for them when grown, to counsel them, to console them, and to make life agreeable and sweet to them—these are the duties of women at all times, and they should be taught them from their infancy."[22]

Toward the end of his life, Rousseau suffered from paranoia, and scholars describe his existence as solitary. He even wrote a book about it, titled *Reveries of a Solitary Walker*. Yet Levasseur was there with him, folding his laundry, fluffing his pillow, and cooking his food. And she was with him at his bedside when he died.[23]

In the fall of 1791, Maria von Herbert, a young woman who'd studied the work of Kant, wrote him a letter. A man had broken her heart, she explained, and now the world was meaningless. She confessed to having suicidal thoughts and was struggling to accept Kant's moral philosophy, which deemed suicide immoral. "My reason abandons me just when I need it," she wrote, and his philosophy "doesn't help a bit."[24] Her dark mood persisted.

Kant responded, calling himself her "moral physician." He recommended she look not to the consequences but instead to the intention of her actions. He took her assumption that someone else could make her happy to be her mistake. He reminded her: "For the value of life, in so far as it consists of the enjoyment we get from people, is vastly overrated."[25]

In other writings, Kant says women are inferior to men in reason and virtue, and therefore destined to be ruled by them. Not that women are powerless. Kant reasons that in civilized society, a woman learns to be alluring to attract a husband who will support her and their children.[26] "Women will avoid evil not because it is unjust, but because it is ugly . . . Even many of her weaknesses are, so to speak, beautiful faults."[27] "As for scholarly women," he wrote, "they use their books somewhat like a watch, that is, they wear the watch so it can be noticed that they have it on, although it is usually broken or does not show the time."[28]

Kant's views were in stark contrast to those of his friend Theodor Gottlieb von Hippel, who argued in his treatise *On Improving the Civic Status of Women* for women's equal right to education, citizenship, and professional jobs, including university professorships.[29] Hippel joined Kant for meals in his home to discuss the philosophical debates of their time. As far as we know, Kant never wrote a response to Hippel's work.

Herbert didn't reply to Kant's letter. A year later, he asked a mutual friend about her. Learning this, she wrote to him a second time. She reported her mood hadn't lifted and that she'd given up the study of arts and sciences because "I don't feel that I'm genius enough."[30] In pursuing her studies, she'd lost her self-confidence and curiosity. "I only want one thing, namely to shorten this pointless life." She repeated her concern that her own experience proved that there was something wrong with Kant's philosophy. "Don't think me arrogant for saying this, but the demands of morality are too easy for me," she said.[31] There is nothing challenging about being good or doing what's right when you have no passion for life, let alone the wish to sin.

In his *Anthropology*, Kant wrote about midlife crises. How at a certain point, a man will either fall prey to his passions, living in debauchery and despair, or he will transform and lead a life directed by reason.[32] But according to this same text, women are incapable of following the law of reason. They will either yoke themselves to a man who follows the moral law or, as is implied here, succumb to passion and fall into hopelessness.

Kant didn't respond to Herbert's second letter. Perhaps his own philosophy led him to see her as a lost cause. His few efforts to appeal to her reason and save her from her crisis didn't work, affirming his philosophical view that as a female, she was incapable of being saved. She was not a man on the brink of a major moral transformation but rather an "ecstatical little lady" suffering from "a curious mental derangement."[33]

Herbert's letter was suggestive in some places. She wrote that if his philosophy couldn't give her a will to live, then Kant himself could "give me something that will get this intolerable emptiness out of my soul . . . I want to ask permission, in advance, to visit you."[34] And then she told him of the engraved portrait she had of him. A part of her seems to have hoped Kant would make love to her or be the husband who could give her life direction.

Her letter and the possible insinuations disturbed Kant. He collected their correspondence and sent it off to another young woman of his acquaintance with the title "Example of Warning."[35]

In 1830, Harriet Taylor was married, with two children and a third on the way, when she met the philosopher John Stuart Mill and fell in love. Taylor's husband, twenty years her senior, allowed her to live in a separate house where Mill visited her. The arrangement was scandalous, especially by Victorian standards. The social isolation that followed Taylor and Mill's experiment in living brought them closer together. They spent most of their time in one another's company, and when they were apart, they wrote each other frequently.

Taylor was interested in philosophy, economics, and politics—particularly women's rights, including the problem of domestic violence—and wrote articles and essays, some published, some unfinished. She also wrote the book *Enfranchisement of Women*. Mill wrote *On Liberty* and *Utilitarianism*, works that would transform philosophy for generations to come. Mill proclaimed that Taylor was significantly involved in many of his projects, including *On Liberty*: "It belongs as much to her as to me."[36] Mill even referred to her as his coauthor, insisting that they had worked together on every sentence. As for the rest of his opus, he said that she contributed aspects to it if not by writing then by dictating sections to him and helping him think through ideas. "In this wide sense," he said, "all my published writings were as much hers as mine."[37] Not everyone had such enthusiastic reviews of Taylor. They said she "bewitched" Mill, that he'd exaggerated her capacities and contributions, and—most importantly—that she had nothing to do with his best ideas.

Taylor's husband died in 1849, and she and Mill married soon afterward. Their marriage was short-lived. Taylor was sick and died a few years later. Except for the scholars who care to raise the specter of Taylor, she is unknown to most of us, and Mill is typically treated as the sole author of *On Liberty*. Book covers, encyclopedia entries, and so much scholarship assume this. Yes, it's difficult to know for certain who did what, but in the face of authorial uncertainty, our cultural default reveals itself: We know what Mill did, but what about Taylor? *Who was she, anyway?*

◆◆

The stories of these women and their relationship to philosophy made me think more carefully about my own attachments to the field and why, if it was so unpleasant, I stuck around.

I sometimes framed my own romantic and intellectual life as a ladder, believing I was improving myself and working toward a better understanding of the world. This image reflected Socrates's teaching as described in Plato's *Symposium*. In this dialogue, Socrates holds court at a dinner party, describing the relationship between erotic love and the truth. He says we desire individual lovers insofar as they embody beauty and truth, which he calls the good. And as with a ladder, we ascend rung by rung from one experience to another, as we realize that our lovers are imperfect instances of what we seek. Ideally, we reach the top of the ladder when we apprehend that the good can be grasped by reason alone—that is, by a means within ourselves. The result is edifying: happiness and self-sufficiency.

That's not how I felt, but I didn't understand why. Then I read Alcibiades's speech.

Alcibiades, who has been listening to Socrates, isn't convinced. And when it's his turn to talk, he shares a different notion of love and attachment: he's in love with Socrates—not insofar as Socrates embodies universals but rather for his unique traits. Alcibiades loves how Socrates talks, dresses, and behaves. He has no desire to leave Socrates and ascend a ladder; he wishes to continue lusting after this particular person. And he describes this love as a misery. Alcibiades is conscious that Socrates knows his vulnerabilities and his boorishness, and this awareness humiliates him. "There's something I feel with nobody else but Socrates—something you would not have thought was in me—and that is a sense of shame. He is the only person who makes me feel shame . . . There are times when I'd gladly see him dead. But if that happened, you understand, I'd be worse off than ever."[38]

Like Alcibiades, I wasn't as ennobled or happy as I'd expected. The philosophers Robert C. Solomon and Kathleen M. Higgins characterize a message of the *Symposium* to be "love misplaced can be degrading and humiliating."[39] I was in love with Alex. I was also in love with philosophy—not the generic, abstract love of wisdom. I was in love with a particular body of work, by Hobbes, Pufendorf, Aristotle, and others—the philosophy taught at my institution, the canon as it had been presented to me (despite the painfully brutal canon I discovered it was). I suspected these particular attachments might be holding me back. I felt both love and shame, but I didn't want to let go. I couldn't.

The thought of stepping away from either of my loves filled me with anxiety of an entropic nature, as if without them I would disarticulate into nothingness—or, what was maybe worse, into a lesser being, a half-ass. A wannabe. A shit-for-brains. My insecurities felt singular, unbearable—until I detected traces of similar feelings in the writings of Damaris Masham. A relationship with a more advanced philosopher had also given her a sense of self-worth and acceptance, and the loss of this relationship would destabilize her intellectual life in a way it wouldn't for him.

I see no Reason why it should not be thought that all Science lyes as open to a Lady as to a Man.

—Damaris Cudworth Masham

"Fitts" and Starts

Damaris Cudworth Masham was close to legendary philosopher John Locke. They were friends for more than twenty years. It was an intellectual, personal, and at times romantic exchange that began before her marriage and ended when Locke moved into her home with her husband and their children. No need to write letters when you can share ideas near the fire in the evenings. This was a period of great philosophical flourishing for Masham, during which she wrote her two and only works.

My understanding of Masham's inner life is taken from her letters to Locke, a few autobiographical sections of her books, and a poem. There are no full biographies of her. I spoke with one scholar who said that there is simply not enough material to write a monograph.[1] There are a few accounts by her friends that tell of her brilliance and beauty. There is—or was—a painting of her by the famous seventeenth-century artist Sir Godfrey Kneller, which Locke commissioned in addition to one of himself. Locke's portrait is still around, though Masham's is thought to be lost or to have burned in a fire at an estate along with other items of hers. Yet the remnants of her life captured in her letters and works tell the story of a stunning individual.

Masham was born in 1659 and grew up in one of the oldest and most important centers of research in Europe. Her parents were Damaris Cradock Andrews, daughter of the first governor of the Massachusetts Bay Company, and Ralph Cudworth, a philosopher and master of Christ's College at Cambridge. As a child, she lived on campus in the master's quarters and was exposed to more learning than most men—and almost all the women—of her time would ever see or know. At the same time, the restrictions on her life fragmented her participation in this world.

Cambridge didn't allow women to enroll until 1869. (The first degree awarded to a woman would come later still: 1948.) All university fellows were required to be single, and the few women on campus were family members of professors, visiting nobility, cooks, maids, or laundresses.[2] As a young girl, Masham would play in the master's private garden, where on the other side of its wall, university men, wearing regalia in different colors and styles to signal their level of academic achievement, would converse in Latin and Greek—languages Masham never learned growing up, despite having a father and two brothers who were fluent in both. Her father hosted guests in the college's dark, wood-paneled dining hall, where his portrait, along with those of previous masters, hung on the wall. One such guest (and a rare one at that, as she was a woman invited to campus because of her brilliant mind) was Anne Conway, a metaphysician and distant relative of Masham's on her mother's side.[3] Conway was close friends with Henry More, another Cambridge philosopher, making it likely she made multiple visits to campus, though there is no evidence that Masham met her. The women in Masham's early life show up in the historical materials only in shadow. Her relationship with her mother and her half sister from her mother's first marriage, for example, are unchronicled, and their roles in her life indeterminate.

The influence of her father is easier to trace. With his furrowed brow and auburn hair, Cudworth was a brilliant thinker and a popular professor who was unafraid of challenging prevailing views. As a central figure of the Cambridge Platonists, he defended a notion of God whose goodness prevailed over all his other attributes, and he criticized atheistic materialism, which he saw as defining of the new, empirical science.[4] In his masterpiece, *The True Intellectual System of the Universe*, he argued that contemporary materialists were not trailblazing but rather repeating the mistakes of ancient philosophers. Cudworth believed that all living things had a purpose, and the forces of nature were rational laws that accorded with God's goodness and wisdom. He was an early supporter of religious toleration, and in 1645 he urged the House of Commons to adopt more open-minded views.[5] He said, "All the several forms of religion are but so many dreams. And those many opinions about religion that are everywhere so eagerly contended for on all sides are but so many shadows fighting with one another."[6] Cudworth argued that central to the Christian religion was the cultivation of a good character, which required the exercise of reason. Humans could grasp the eternal and immutable laws of morality and pattern a life on their dictates. (This notion of Christianity as rational and character based was present in Astell's thought, too, and came from her own training in Cambridge Platonism, courtesy of her uncle.)

As a child, Masham was drawn to philosophy, but in a letter to Locke she wrote that she was "Diverted from it when I was Young . . . by the Commands of others."[7] She didn't identify who had held her back. What is certain is that this woman who was raised in a supreme intellectual environment, who was the daughter of a highly regarded philosopher, and who yearned to do philosophy was prevented from seriously pursuing it. At the same time, she managed to imbibe a great understanding of her father's philosophy, and when she was an adult, both Locke and Leibniz had her explain it to them.[8]

She saw the minimal investment in her intellect as symptomatic of a cultural force inhibiting the minds of women. In these early years she didn't set forth a path to freedom for women. Instead, she absorbed this oppression and then spun it out into a description of the world as suffocating and harmful to women's intellects; it was a place where women would live and die, vulnerable and without much control over their own thought. A poem she wrote in her twenties describes women's alleviation from subjugation as occurring after the biblical apocalypse. Only then, following the complete annihilation of the physical world, would men see that women were their intellectual equals and had been all along:

> *And our weak Sex I hope will then*
> *disdaine yt Stupid ignorance*
> *w:ᶜʰ was at first impos'd by men*
> *their owne high merits to inhance*
> *and now pleads custome for pretense*
> *to banish knowledg witt and sense*
> *Long have we here condemned been*
> *to Folly and impertinence*
> *but then it surely will be seene*
> *There's in our Souls no difference*
> *when we no longer Fetterd are*
> *but like to them o[ur] selves appeare.*[9]

She would develop a more optimistic view, but only years later, after she met Locke.

By age twenty-two, Masham was still living at home in Cambridge with her parents, but she was growing curious about life in London, then fizzing with new ideas and bold approaches. And so, around Christmas in 1681, when well-connected friends in London invited her to a party, she agreed to join them. She was beautiful, unmarried, and witty, and it was certain she would be noticed.[10]

A few weeks after the party, Masham received a letter from one of the guests. It was from the house doctor, who, as the letter suggests, had been taken with her. He was lanky, had a Roman nose, and according to fashion, wore a long brown wig tied in a loose ponytail. At forty-nine, he was more than twice her age. He was John Locke, already famous, though not yet the giant of philosophy we know today. Not yet the author of a landmark treatise on empiricism that would transform philosophy for centuries to come or of works on religious toleration and natural rights and equality that would inspire writers of the United States Constitution. He was a former diplomat, rising star, and medical practitioner who held a permanent post at Oxford. He was an entertaining guest at parties, but as his closest friends knew, he preferred intimate, intellectual conversation—just like Masham.

He asked Masham if he was being too forward by contacting her. Still, he couldn't resist referring to her as "Philoclea," the name of a ravishing character in a sixteenth-century romance who obsessed the protagonist, "Philander," the name Locke used to sign his letter.

Unlike the scholars Masham knew growing up, Locke was ambivalent about academic life, and despite his permanent post at Oxford, he spent most of his time in London, the seat of the latest experimental methods of inquiry. Oxford philosophers were in the grip of Aristotle's theories, which Locke considered outdated. He was of the view that philosophical insight came from varied experience and that the senses were the origin of all human ideas, which contradicted the rationalist theories of Masham's father and most other Cambridge Platonists. She must have found Locke's confidence and ideas refreshing. But if so, she kept it to herself. She penned a response to Locke saying that she wasn't interested in romance, but that might change.[11] Until then, she wanted to stay friends. She signed her letter "Philoclea."

Over the next few months, many letters passed between them. Their correspondence was playful, humorous, and cerebral. Locke was eager to learn more about Cambridge Platonism and he trusted Masham as a teacher. He called her his governess and praised her as an exceptionally brilliant woman. "It's not so," she coyly replied.

After so much discouragement from other people, it must have been flattering and seductive to have a renowned philosopher validate her intelligence. It was also overwhelming. When she received his letters filled with philosophical questions, she would sometimes become dark and moody. "I am extremly Angry with my self," she wrote Locke, and "with all the World." Her anxiety was profuse, and she referred to these moments under its influence as "Fitts," which she linked to the pressure to perform brought on by Locke's inquiries:[12]

> *You will see by this that I am the worst in the World at Answeareing Questions. The truth is, I have of late so Mortall an Aversion for it that . . . I almost wish sometimes that I were Dumb . . . I thought the other Day that if I lock'd my self up in my chamber I should certainly be free from this trouble, when before I had beene at rest an Houre in comes [your] Letter and another of three sides of a sheet of Paper all questions from one end to t'other, I have not answear'd it yet, nor beleeve I shall not these three months. Pray have a care that you provoke me not so much, and write any thing to me rather then ask me one question more, since I am so far out of Patience that I prefer'd being sick last Night before it.*[13]

In late spring that same year, Masham returned to Cambridge, and the distance helped her realize she was in love with Locke. "I onely write you now to let you know that you have a Governess who cannot forget you," she wrote.[14] Cambridge was a weak distraction. After a few months in Locke's company, Masham was no longer charmed by the intellectual milieu of her upbringing. "It is intollerable to live in a Place where it is not possible to spend one Houre in an agreable Conversation without being beholden to the Dead or the Absent Liveing for it, and that too in one of the most Famous Universities in the World."[15] She felt a "Profound Indifference for all things in the World," she said, and then, with her characteristic dark humor, added: "I have beene thinking therefore that the best improvement I can make by my Misfortunes will be to take advantage of my Temper and turne a Stoick."[16]

Now twenty-three, Masham was reaching the age when women were expected to be married, and it's likely that she hoped Locke would propose to her.[17] She may have imagined that her erudition would make her an especially attractive wife to Locke. Even better, it was something he would appreciate. What an exceptional, serendipitous pair they would make: two thinkers spending the rest of their days together theorizing and, perhaps, even raising a family.

It's less clear what Locke wanted from their alliance. Just before he met Masham, he was seeing a woman he referred to in letters to friends as "Valentine"—an affair that faded soon after he met Masham. He owned some property, and it's possible he could have financially supported a family.[18] He had a comfortable existence as a successful intellectual under the patronage of Anthony Ashley Cooper, the First Earl of Shaftesbury, a prominent and controversial politician. Locke is said to have once described a previous affair as something that "robbed me of the use of my reason." (It was commonly believed and endorsed by medical practitioners that too many ejaculations could diminish a man's intellectual prowess.)[19] With a financially stable, intellectually stimulating lifestyle, Locke may not have felt the urgency—or even the need—to marry.

Things were obviously different for Masham. Her romantic tie to Locke kept him within her orbit, and a marriage to him would cement philosophy into her future. This is likely why, of the two, Masham was more desperate in their letters, as she scanned their exchanges for signs of his interest in her. When Masham told Locke that she missed London, implying she missed him, his response was to send a work on navigation. She replied that it wasn't to her taste. "The first look into it Discourag'd me from proceeding farther," she wrote.[20]

In December, they decided to meet in London, almost one year after Locke first wrote to her. It must have gone well, because their next exchange is a poem they composed about two lovers, Clora and Damon, thinly veiled stand-ins for themselves.[21] Masham wrote first. She describes Clora and Damon's relationship as doomed, because

Clora's charms are too weak to attract Damon, who is more eager to do philosophy than fall in love and commit to marriage: "Resolve he would no Captive bee, / But set Himself by Reason free." After some time, Damon realizes he loves Clora, but he is slow to tell her. "Thy passion comes too late," Clora tells him.

In his contribution to the poem, Locke describes a warmer, more optimistic connection between Clora and Damon. Damon confesses his willingness to give up his singlehood to be with her: "My freedome I to you resigne / The freedome which you know was mine." He assures Clora that she is not "a toy / To please some idle wanton boy / I thought by this 'twould well be known / I now noe longer was my own." He is captivated by her: "Was I not always in your power?" Locke nears the close of the poem by acknowledging that the lovers have a strong friendship with a romantic future: "Who begins there must he there end?"

Weeks after this promising exchange, there was still no marriage proposal or even an intimation of one. Masham decided to ignore Locke and his many letters. Finally in April, she told him that her silence was his fault: "the Consequence of giveing me no Direction."[22]

Locke had a host of other problems. England was in the throes of anti-government plots, and Lord Shaftesbury, his friend and patron, had been accused of treason. Shaftesbury had fled to Holland, and since Locke was closely associated with him, the philosopher started to plan his own departure. Holland offered refuge as an enclave for religious and political toleration. Now facing an indefinite future, Locke may have decided to put a betrothal to Masham on hold. It was also possible he regretted being serious with her, and this political upheaval gave him an excuse to put distance between them.

When Locke moved to Holland in September, Masham refused to write him and slipped into a depression. The following June she reached out. She wrote that she was no longer angry with him. She had grown accustomed to the state of "Solitude" he'd left her in.[23] Locke, perhaps relieved to hear from her and feeling responsible for her unhappiness, invited her to visit him in Holland. Masham could not suppress her excitement and wrote to him about the many things they could do and see together. Toward the end of her letter, she allowed suspicion to seep in. It had, after all, been some time since they'd seen one another, and she wondered whether his invitation was sincere, whether he had invited her merely out of pity, and whether he expected they would actually spend time together. She told him that she did not want to make the long journey across the sea only to be left alone in his home as his "Housekeeper."[24]

His response was to not mention the trip again. Her spirits fell: "I find you are not in such hast to see your Governess."[25] He had turned her off marriage, which she wanted him to know but also wanted to make light of, because she wished to keep him in her life. She said she might join a new religious sect near him in Holland, but this teasing masked a personal struggle.[26] Masham was in the midst of an identity crisis: a woman whose first two decades had given her a deep appreciation of a contemplative life and who now faced a future in which the continuation of this existence was in jeopardy. Like most women at the time, the course of her life depended upon marriage. She may not have considered living on her own, a life that promised its own set of hardships. Masham wanted something for herself that didn't exist in her society except by happenstance: a marriage that ensured the persistence of her dignity and intellectual sophistication. But by formulating her freedom in terms of something the right man could provide, she was keeping with tradition. This was why she couldn't let go of Locke even when it was clear he was not going to propose.

In January 1685, two years after they exchanged their first letters, Masham told Locke that the overwhelming sadness she had written off as a character flaw in herself was in fact lovesickness. She expressed again that she missed him more than he missed her: "I think of my Pupil much oftener then he dos of his Governess."[27]

Months later, she knew she couldn't continue waiting around for him. She began to see the figure she would cut in history, and she did not like it: "Since of all the things in the World I should the most Hate to be thought a Neglected Mistress, and to Heare my Misadventure Sett to the Tune of the *Forsaken Maid*," she wrote.[28] And so Masham did what most single twenty-six-year-old women at the time did: she got engaged. In June, she wrote to Locke that she planned to marry soon, "that Puzling Difficultie about Matrimonie might Perhaps be soone Resolv'd."[29] She said nothing about her suitor and described her upcoming nuptials as something that, if they bothered him, would give her an "Uneasiness of Mind."[30]

Locke wrote her a response, which she received the day of her wedding and opened in the church. Whatever he said wasn't enough to change her mind. She married Sir Francis Masham, a widower with nine children who lived on a large estate in Essex, in the country, and she was legally no longer Damaris Cudworth but Lady Damaris Masham. In marrying, she became nobility.

A few weeks later, in what she felt was a chilly congratulatory letter from Locke, he apparently asked her why she did it. Was it the trappings of nobility? The gold or fancy embroidery? Or was it the prospect of having a family and children? For all of Locke's intellectual prowess, for all his insight into the ways in which tyranny restrained the natural freedoms of men, the great philosopher was unable or unwilling to conceive of, let alone sympathize with, how Masham's freedom was constrained in a way that his wasn't.

Masham never told Locke why she'd married Francis. It's possible she saw her marriage as a partial solution to the social problem she faced. Her new husband, thirteen years her senior, wasn't an intellectual by any stretch, but he had a large house, financial means, and the promise of affording her some leisure to live as she once had. Her first letter to Locke after her marriage suggests as much.

"There is no longer Madamoiselle C," she wrote to Locke, referring to her maiden name. She wished to continue their correspondence, and she promised that, despite her name change, she would remain the same person:

> *Do not then think that the Spirrit of Care, and Familie*
> *Affairs shall Intirely Possess me How deepe soever I may*
> *seeme to Have ingag'd my self in them I am at this time*
> *Willing to Beleeve what Has beene sometimes told me,*
> *That in some sort I am Capable of any Thing that I Have*
> *either a mind to Or that it otherwise Befits me to do.*[31]

The second half of this sentence speaks to the sort of psychological contortions Masham performed during this massive life change—a forced optimism packaged as hope. For the first time ever, she was in charge of supervising servants, managing household supplies, and raising stepchildren, but she imagined there must be a space somewhere in this new life for the cultivation of her mind.

Six months later, she wrote to Locke: "Household Affaires are the Opium of the Soul."[32] Her philosophy books, including titles by Marcus Aurelius, Descartes, and Henry More, shared shelf space with "My Receits and Account Books" and "my Spining Wheel."[33] She discovered there was no time for philosophy, trigonometry, or poetry now that her days were filled with learning how to run a home as well as take her place as a member of the nobility.

She was also pregnant and scared of dying in childbirth, a fear many women at the time shared. There was no anesthesia, and women relied on simple aids such as mulled wine and wooden birthing stools. Forceps were a recent invention, though not widely used, and if a baby was stuck in the birth canal, the midwife would pull it out with her bare hands. Otherwise, the mother was left to labor by herself. Francis was frequently away in London, and when he wasn't, Masham said, "the Business of this World Almost wholly imploys him when he is at Home, so that I have very little of His Company."[34] She felt abandoned, lonely. There was no one in the house she could converse with, and the dreary weather and remote country setting only increased her anguish.

With the time she had to herself, she wrote letters to Locke, who was still abroad. "For All my quarrel with you I cannot help telling you that there is scarse any thing I would not give to see you Here in my Closet where I am now writeing to You," she wrote.[35] "I Dreamt of Heareing from you last Night and I wish'd for it All This Day." She asked him to write her but not talk about her marriage, "for I am quite sick of that subject."[36]

Locke told her about his beautiful Dutch mistress. She replied, "A mistress is the most dangerous thing in the world to a friend" and wondered "whether I ever was more to you then an agreeable acquaintance."[37] She was left pondering what Locke could mean to her. Now that marriage and romance between the pair were no longer in the offing, she could build upon a friendship with a man who treated her as a dignified, rational person.[38]

Over the next few years, Locke encouraged Masham to find time to engage her mind. He asked her to write poetry, which she sent to him. She signed one letter to Locke as if she were an author: "I will Conclude like other Authors, Finis." In another she wrote, "You may see me in Print in a little While."[39] He also urged her to work on philosophy. He asked her to give him comments on his work, hoping she would identify problems. Unlike her younger self, she now expressed feeling intellectually up to the task, despite her weak eyesight.[40]

She had other concerns. She wasn't sure it was her place to get involved in current philosophical debates. Who was she to tell people how they ought to live? Her life would be much better spent focusing on her religious obligations.[41] Philosophy required time away from godly responsibilities, she argued, which are necessary to earning salvation. She would have to have a good reason to step away from her domestic work, to risk her own religious path, to do philosophy:

Religion is the Concernment of All Mankind; Philosophy as distinguish'd from It, onely of Those that have a freedome from the Affaires of the World; Which as They would Hinder the latter; May well Manag'd be Great Inforcements of the Former.[42]

Another reason she was resistant to practicing philosophy was because it would be taxing. "The Pleasures of This life are so Trifling and Transitorie, And Its Cares so many and Bitter, That I think one must be very Miserable and Stupid, not to seeke Ones sattisfaction in some thing else."[43] She knew this harsh, critical statement would throw Locke: "I Know not what Thoughts this will make you Have of me."

Masham's circumstance made it difficult for her to experience those pleasures of the intellect that philosophers throughout history extolled. She remained at the Essex estate, raising her stepchildren and her own son, all the time never quite fitting in. She was having a much harder time living in rural England than she let on in her letters to Locke. When she did write about it, years later in 1705, filling pages at the end of her second and final treatise, her descriptions were more like an existential nightmare. She described in the third person the struggles of being a smart woman in the world—especially in the country—yet some sections read as autobiographical.[44] She reported that a smart woman is intimidating and for this she is mocked and gossiped about all over town. Her local parson is too shy to speak with her. Her doctor worries that she is concerningly peculiar. Because she is intelligent enough to manage her own home, she makes her neighbors uncomfortable, and they rarely visit. Masham says the smart woman is at odds with society whether she wants to be or not; her very being is a threat to the world as such.

If a woman has the leisure to practice philosophy, Masham complains, she still faces additional criticism that a male philosopher would not experience—even the most persecuted among them, such as Socrates. She is "a Subject of Ridicule to one part of them, and of Aversion to the other; with but a few exceptions of some vertuous and rational Persons. And is not the incuring of general dislike, one of the strongest discouragements that we can have to any thing?"[45]

What might redeem the practice of philosophy for a woman, then, would be an idea that compensated for the social battering and self-doubt she would inevitably have to endure on account of her sex. But at the time, no idea moved Masham in this way. "The Spirrit of Government dos not yet so Possess me but that I am as readie to give an Account of my self as receive one of my Charge."[46]

When Masham was thirty-one years old, her life changed dramatically: Locke moved into her home.

William of Orange had become king, and with a new government in power, it was now safe for Locke to return to England. He visited Masham and Francis at their estate, Oates, a large brick manor on an acreage with gardens, which stood nearly thirty miles outside of London.[47] Locke had a chronic cough that was exacerbated by London air. He had many friends in the countryside, but Oates quickly became his favored escape from the city. Masham said it took some convincing to bring her husband around to the idea, but eventually he and Locke struck a deal. The philosopher would pay one pound a week in return for lodging for himself and his butler and one shilling for his horse. Locke took over two large rooms on the first floor of the house. He brought his telescope, chairs, and over four thousand books, his belongings spilling into adjacent rooms. He enjoyed his new lodging, and his friends referred to him as "the gentleman now within the moated castle."[48]

Locke became close to Masham's only biological son, Francis, who was taught according to Locke's philosophy of education.[49] When Locke took brief trips to London, Francis wrote to him. "Dear Mr. Locke," he said in one letter, "I long till you come down. I should be

very glad to see you for I love you mightily." Locke was attached to
the boy and wrote Francis into his will. In a striking sign that Locke
wasn't on good terms with Masham's husband and didn't trust him,
he insisted to his lawyer that Francis's father have no power over the
gifts Locke left him.[50]

Masham and Locke spent a great deal of time together. As their
friendship developed, they were unsure how to describe it. Masham
said to a friend that he was like a brother or father, and Locke said
it was something closer. Not surprisingly, their relationship sparked
rumors. Locke was accused of being a pimp. Although that must
have caused them all discomfort, it was likely worse for Masham's
husband. There is no trace left of what Francis thought about Masham
and Locke, but being a cuckold had negative social consequences:
he could lose his standing in social circles, including being denied
bows by subordinates and his seating in church. Wealthy cuckolds
often simply ignored the situation in the hopes that doing so would
quell gossip. This may have been what Francis did. The income from
Locke may have lessened the sting, along with Locke's willingness
to connect Francis to a powerful friend who helped solicit votes for
him in the 1701 election.[51]

There is evidence Masham tried to theorize about her relationship to Locke. In a mysterious passage in one of her works, she
discusses love and adultery. She writes that a wife's love of another
man competes with the love she owes her husband, but it does not
take away from the love she feels for her child. Masham could love
another man who was not her husband and still be a good mother.[52]

Locke introduced good conversation and a steady flow of
intellectuals—including Isaac Newton, who met with them both to
discuss religion and theology—into Masham's life. He connected her
to Awnsham Churchill of the Black Swan, a highly respected book
publisher who issued Locke's *A Letter Concerning Toleration* and *Two
Treatises of Government*. Churchill commissioned works that were
politically and socially reformist.[53]

Although Locke was essential to securing Masham's sense of self-worth as a philosopher, she wasn't Locke's "disciple," as one scholar put it.[54] It's women and their experiences that motivate and shape her books. In fact, her philosophy doesn't focus primarily on metaphysics or epistemology—though these ideas are there—but rather on the forces that inhibit women and keep them from participating in the life of the mind.

On December 22, 1694, Locke shared with Masham the philosophical exchange between John Norris and Mary Astell. Masham was then thirty-five and had been married and a mother for nine years. As she turned the pages of the correspondence, she realized another woman existed who was conversant in philosophy. Masham was frustrated that Astell and Norris endorsed Nicolas Malebranche, a French philosopher who proclaimed that mothers inflict irreversible cognitive damage on their babies while in the womb. She was troubled by their seeming acceptance of Malebranche's claim that God should be the only object of our love. And so in 1696, Masham emerged from relative obscurity, risking the censure she knew intelligent women faced, and wrote her first book, entitled *A Discourse Concerning the Love of God*.

Masham said her arguments flowed from her quill, taking only "a few hours" to complete. The result was a short treatise taking aim at Astell and Norris for defending Malebranche. Masham didn't disguise her displeasure. She accused the pair of publishing "unpremeditated Raptures of Devout Minds, not the Productions of Philosophical Disquisition."[55] Masham used the slight age difference between herself and Astell—she was eight years older—against her opponent, arguing that Astell wasn't sufficiently critical, but "a young Writer, whose Judgment may, perhaps, be thought Byassed by the Affectation of Novelty."[56] Astell had recommended in her *Serious Proposal* that women study Malebranche. Masham had a copy of her text and was perplexed by how a defender of women's liberty could condone such a twisted portrayal of mothers.

Years before, in 1672, Father Nicolas Malebranche had traveled to see what all of Paris had come to see: a peculiarity in a glass jar.[57] Malebranche was a well-known philosopher and a follower of Descartes. He was writing a book about error, and what he observed was a very interesting mistake.

The philosopher peered inside the jar, which held a human fetus suspended in alcohol. The specimen had skin as wrinkled as an old man's and an abnormally small forehead. Its thin arms were folded over its chest as if it were a corpse in repose, and between its tiny shoulders were markings in the shape of a miter. The fetus reminded Malebranche of a painting of Pope Pius V, which (he was informed) the mother of the fetus had stared at while pregnant.

Malebranche's philosophical imagination was titillated, and so he grabbed a quill and wrote. The mother, he explained, must have stared "intently" at the painting and given birth "to a child who looked exactly like the representation of the saint."[58] He labeled the fetus a "monster" and blamed the mother.[59] Malebranche insisted that women were far more reactive to sensations and images than men and were more easily engrossed by superficial matters. "A trifle is enough to distract them, the slightest cry frightens them, and least motion fascinates them," he wrote. This was because a woman's imagination, which Malebranche conceived to be a faculty that entertained images either made up by the mind or perceived through the senses, overpowered her reason. The effects of her imagination coursed through her body like blood but with far more strength and destructive force. A pregnant woman looking at a picture could activate the flow of her fascination's "spirits," which then would course through her body and rearrange the fetus's "delicate fibers."

That a mother's imagination could have such a distorting and permanent effect on her unborn children, said Malebranche, was due to a curse that hung over the entire human race. The temptation of Adam and Eve resulted in an intellectual handicap for all mankind, because it made humans reliant on their senses. Malebranche said that our senses did not reveal truth—only illusions—and it was necessary to escape the grip of sensation to see the magnificence of God and the true order of the universe.

He blamed mothers for this. The stain of original sin is transferred from a mother to her baby in the womb when her imagination shapes the infant's brain fibers and encourages the development of a temperament that prefers the physical to the ideal. A mother cannot stop it from happening, he said; she is "not a criminal." She is simply the conduit through which humanity is made rotten.

Malebranche published his first work in 1674, and over the course of two decades, his ideas rippled through Europe, eventually making their way to England, where, in 1694, they were translated into English.[60] The *Athenian Mercury*, a popular London biweekly magazine, published his theories, and one of its editors wrote a poem in his honor. A reading group in London formed to study *The Search after Truth*. The published correspondence between Norris and Astell was for Masham an irritating reminder of the influence of Malebranche's thought in England.

Masham argued that Malebranche's description of Eve was false:

> Children, [Malebranche] expressly tells us, become (through their Union with their Mothers) Sinners; and are in a state of Damnation before they are born into the World. But both the Apostle and Reason assure us, that where there is no law, there is no Transgression.[61]

She wrote that Adam's sin—not Eve's—was the reason that humanity was imperfect and needed Christ. She quoted Scripture, which she knew well: "*As in Adam all died, so in Christ shall all be made alive*, I Cor. XV. 22."[62]

Masham also took aim at the crux of Malebranche's philosophy: that God alone is the total and only cause of every action in the universe and that created things are causally inert, something Astell and Norris took seriously as a possible foundation for Christianity. It's an odd principle on the face of it but one that follows from the belief that God's power is his supreme attribute. Masham, on the other hand, believed that God's goodness and wisdom restrained his will. She deduced that his insight guaranteed that he did nothing in vain, like create sense organs that are the immediate cause of us seeing and hearing earthly things—not God. "For if . . . I do not truly see with my Eyes, and hear with my Ears; then all that wonderful Exactness and curious Workmanship in framing the Organs of Sense, seems superfluous and vain; Which is no small Reflection upon infinite Wisdom."[63]

I may seem to be heading down the path of an obscure seventeenth-century debate, but it's important to know that Masham was creating the logical conditions to persuade us that God gave things in creation causal powers. When a person or thing pleases us, we are not wrong in desiring it or loving it, which to her were the same things. By contrast, Malebranche, along with Astell and Norris, held that God alone should be the object of our desire; it would be idolatry to love anything else in this way. We can, however, feel benevolence toward the rest of creation.

Masham thought that this expectation was not only philosophically flawed but also humanly impossible to fulfill. She inserted parenting and mothering into her discussion to help make her point. "We love our Children, or Friends; It is evident also from the Nature of the Object, that we not only wish to them as to our selves, whatever we conceive may tend to continue, or improve their Being; but also, that Desire of them is a necessary Concomitant of our Love."[64] It would be impossible to go through life without loving people.[65]

She added sarcastically: "Only Heads cast in *Metaphysical Moulds* are capable of it."[66]

Masham identified another disturbing feature of Malebranche's philosophy that she thought Norris and Astell were oblivious to. Since Malebranche argued that we cannot love other things without sinning, then it follows that we must retreat from the world to be morally good. By this logic, she explained, it would then be "absolutely necessary to renounce the World, and betake our selves to Woods and Desarts: For it is impossible to live in the daily Commerce and Conversation of the World, and love God as we ought to do."[67] Masham was not surprised that Malebranche advocated a principle too abstract and removed from everyday life. He was a priest, leading a celibate life of contemplation. Under such conditions, people are "likelier to grow Wild, than . . . being Useful to others."[68]

Masham saw Astell's college for women as another instance of this antisocial trend, arguing that retreating wouldn't lead women to true insights about themselves and their place in the world. Rather, Masham believed that it encouraged selfishness by putting more emphasis on individuals and their needs than on their accountability to other people. It would lead to "dissolving Societies."[69] Masham criticized Astell's philosophy for partaking of the same sort of narrow, patriarchal thinking that Astell had criticized male philosophers for.

Masham held that knowledge of oneself and the world is the consequence of being social and forming loving attachments: "If we lov'd not the Creatures, it is not conceiveable how we should love God."[70] She argued that human cognitive development begins with seeking pleasure, the strongest principle in human nature, which God implanted in us to direct us to the good.[71] And she drew on careful observations she must have made as a parent who spent time in a nursery: from our first pleasurable perceptions, we desire to be in the presence of those things that bring us joy, for example, "when first we cry for the Fire, or the Sucking-Bottle."[72] Our pursuit of pleasure propels us to attach to other people and things of creation, knitting together an understanding of our universe with love and curiosity. Masham wrote that this process eventually leads us to wonder about the originating cause of our universe and then to "the Discovery of the Author of that Being, that produces what is lovely."[73] For Masham, it is absolutely necessary to first love creation in order to love and obey the creator.

A few years after her *Discourse* was published in English, it was translated into French, and it's possible that Malebranche read it before he died. I find it amusing that Malebranche was taken to task by a woman with "feeble brain fibers," and I imagine Masham did too. But what impresses me more is how the Masham of *Discourse* had transformed from the Masham who fifteen years before had written that it would take an apocalypse to make men and women equal. Once filled with gloom about the fate of women in the world, she came to see how the power of reason could release women from the tired conceptions of men. And mothers emerge from her philosophical vision in a vital role: the transmitters of love who set us on the path of inquisitive engagement with the world. Mothers help make philosophy possible.

There was only one review of Masham's *Discourse*, and it was published in French nine years later and written by a friend who owed her a favor.[74] It seems Astell read *Discourse* and was critical of it, though she believed Locke wrote it.[75] Almost no personal letters were exchanged between Locke and Masham after this period, making it impossible to know for certain what she was thinking at the time: whether she figured *Discourse* was a success or failure. Its publication did raise her profile, and afterward she corresponded with other leading philosophers of her day, including Gottfried Leibniz and Pierre Bayle. In these letters she also discusses the substance of her father's philosophy, revealing a tenderness for her father and his legacy. Her efforts were motivated by an eagerness for his work to be "more knowne in the World than it has hitherto been."[76]

For all of her insight into the philosophical debates of her day, none of these topics feature in Masham's second and final philosophical book, *Occasional Thoughts in Reference to a Vertuous or Christian Life*, published in 1705. As we learn in the first few pages, the book takes inspiration from a conversation Masham had about education with a group of mostly women who "expres'd much displeasure at the too general neglect of the Instruction of their Sex."[77] Masham said that they didn't reach a solution but that her book, written a few years later, was her answer.

She wrote that the fundamental problem wasn't that women were prevented from studying the same subjects as men and with the same rigor, though that certainly was a problem. Rather, it was that women's minds weren't free. Masham believed that humans were created to think for themselves, and their salvation depended upon it. "But God having made Men so as that they find in themselves, very often, a liberty of acting according to the preference of their own Minds, it is incumbent upon them to study the Will of their Maker."[78]

Women were actively discouraged from pursuing such freedom. "It is sufficient for this that no body assists them in it; and that they are made to see betimes that it would be disadvantageous to them to have it," she wrote.[79] She says that rational women were made to feel unattractive and "contemptible."[80] She blamed this on the selfishness and hypocrisy of men, who "are ever desirous to find out such Rules for other People, as will not reach themselves, and as they can extend and contract as they please."[81] Though men might "pretend to be their Masters," women are not made to serve them: "The Knowledge hitherto spoken of has a nobler Aim than the pleasing of Men."[82]

She reaffirmed the view expressed in her first book that self-mastery begins with curiosity and love but added an interesting new component: the questioning of the authority of one's teachers. Children, girls especially, were "brought to say, that they *do Believe* whatever their Teachers tell them they must Believe; whilst in Truth they remain in an ignorant unbelief."[83]

We should be guided only by those ideas whose truth is affirmed by the operations of our own mind, Masham asserted. She was an empiricist like Locke and rejected the concept of innate ideas. She wrote that all knowledge derives from the information we receive from our sense perceptions and our reflections on them.[84] She distinguished between simple ideas, which we receive passively, and complex ideas, which result from the mind combining simple ideas. We arrive at truth after discerning a connection between propositions that we form from our ideas: "Whether *certain*; *probable*; or *none at all*; according whereunto, we ought to regulate our Assent," she wrote.[85] Even though her epistemology was directly inspired by Locke, she disagreed with him on some topics, including the status of moral truths.

Locke believed that reflection on our experience reveals to us that moral truths are "immutable" but that if God were to change human nature, then morality would also change to accommodate the features of our new being.[86] Masham rejected Locke's idea that God's will could change the nature of the things themselves. As in her argument against Malebranche, Masham asserted the priority of God's wisdom and goodness, claiming that moral truths are "as unchangeable as the things themselves," and that the things themselves "cannot but be what they are."[87] In this, she sided with her father, who wrote that "there is an eternal and immutable wisdom in the mind of God" and that "it is the perfection of will, as such, to be guided and determined by wisdom and truth."[88] When a woman uses her reason, according to Masham, what she will discover is the will of God, which she can choose to follow or not. Additionally, she will perceive the far reaches of the injustices that shape her world. And here, the pleasure of contemplation will be mixed with notes of sadness.

The thinking woman will see that the freedom to reason belongs to everyone, though it was wrongly kept from her. "Religion is necessarily included, as being the Duty of all Persons to understand, of whatever Sex, Condition, or Calling they are of."[89] She will see men's double standards. She might notice, for instance, that Scripture describes chastity as a "duty to both Sexes," unlike the common practice of treating its infraction as "but a Peccadillo in a Young Man, altho' a far less Criminal Offence against this Duty in a Maid shall in the Opinion of the same Persons brand her with perpetual Infamy."[90] She will see how women have been wrongly prevented from studying all sorts of subjects—not just the ones that pertain directly to religion.

> *Now in the pursuit of that Pleasure which the exercise and improvement of the understanding gives, I see no Reason why it should not be thought that all Science lyes as open to a Lady as to a Man: And that there is none which she may not properly make her Study, according as she shall find her self best fitted to succeed therein; or as is most agreeable to her Inclination: provided ever, that all such Knowledge as relates to her Duty, or is, any way, peculiarly proper to her Sex, and Condition, be principally, and in the first place her Care.*[91]

Of course, there is the problem of how a woman would have the confidence to pursue rational thought when she'd received the message since she was a child that she was not destined for it or even capable of it. In what is perhaps an acknowledgment of this challenge, Masham recommended a two-tiered reformation. The first involves the individual: a woman cultivating her own autonomy of thought. The second involves society: providing girls with a rigorous education.

Masham knew that to advance her vision of reform, she would need to persuade men of the value of educating women. She settled on a focus that was both integral to her worldview and also wonderfully strategic: the importance of mothers and their role in maintaining social and political harmony. Mothers who had a rigorous education that instructed them how to think for themselves and follow God's law would raise smart sons who would one day be responsible for successful governance. She thought the current social and political situation wasn't ideal and the general lack of education for women would continue to "disorder Common-wealths and Kingdoms; disturb the Peace of Families."[92]

She believed that women were as smart as men but had a greater capacity for empathy, making them better suited to raise children: "For that softness, gentleness and tenderness, natural to the Female Sex, renders them much more capable than Men are of such an insinuating Condescension to the Capacities of young Children, as is necessary in the Instruction and Government of them, insensibly to form their early Inclinations."[93] I don't see Masham calling all women to be mothers in these passages; rather, she appears to be asking current and potential mothers to take their post seriously, because, as she views it, it's not a job that men can do as well.

This insistence on women's superior capacity for care, which Astell also described, bothers me, as it further entrenches patriarchal views. But it also has a few radical implications. It's why Masham thought that women ought to be the arbiters of parental decisions in the domestic sphere. And here again she breaks from Locke, who insisted that fathers should be the ultimate judge in any domestic dispute. Her heightened respect for home life anticipated modern feminist laws that support the rights of mothers and attempt to curb domestic violence.

In April 1708, at age forty-nine, Masham took a trip to Bath. She had recently fallen ill and was suffering from painful gallstones. She viewed her trip as an opportunity for revival.[94]

Locke had died three and a half years before, and not long after, a prominent friend asked Masham to write a short eulogy. In her tribute, which became a significant biographical resource for Locke scholars, Masham recounted his final moments, when she sat with him by his bedside through the night, reading him the Book of Psalms. By her account, there was no one else in the room. Masham's much younger stepdaughter, Esther Masham, who was close to Locke when she was a teenager, later wrote that she too was present.[95] Whatever the case, Masham's insistence that it was her alone with Locke at his death indicates that she wanted history to remember her.

Masham didn't survive her stay in Bath. A biographer who visited her grave around 1800 reported she was buried under a black stone in the middle aisle of Bath Abbey.[96] The etching on the stone, reproduced in full by the biographer and purportedly written by her son Francis, extolls her virtue and good parenting. But I'm drawn to where the dedication mentions her "small Treatises," her "Learning, Judgement, Sagacity, and Penetration, together, with her Candor and love of Truth," and—especially this final part—her lack of "Opportunities to make those Talents shine in the World." The pathos of this final passage, its insinuation of a life inhibited, despite prevailing in many ways, is crushing. Masham's son was acutely aware of what she could have been, if only her freedoms had extended the length of men's. This passage stands in contrast to the moments when she acknowledged the relatively modest freedom allotted her, which she met with a similarly modest aim: if one woman's soul was saved by her ideas, she once wrote, then her work was of value.[97]

Masham's gravestone no longer exists in the abbey, having mysteriously disappeared years ago, just as her portrait by Kneller has vanished. Some nineteenth-century scholars came across her work, one writing that she was "a person remarkable for her mind" and another that she deserved "a niche in the history of English philosophy."[98] But there were no reprintings of her books until 2005, in the US and the UK, and even those are no longer in print.

Oblivion threatens to swallow her whole.

While I was married to Alex and working as a professor, I had a sense of encroaching darkness. Not the kind that arrives after you die, when collective memory dissipates and you fade away, but the kind that creeps up in life. The sort of oblivion that is silence and obedience except—and this was the confusing part—I had a hand in letting it happen to myself.

The Demons of Doubt

O n a wintry morning flight to Boston, Alex nudged my arm, drawing me out of the gossip magazine I was reading to distract myself from my dissertation defense the next morning. He pointed across the aisle and up a row to where a woman who looked to be in her fifties was digging into her second single-serving box of Frosted Flakes. She was wearing a fresh pair of Vans, a thick black hoodie, and a dark wool neck warmer for a hat, which she held in place with her hand. Alex tried to suppress his amusement by leaning far back into his chair while he watched her take bites. I was surprised he was captivated. But did he see what I saw: a woman whose allure was enhanced by her shameless appetite for sugary cereal and, I imagined, many other things in life?

Alex returned to his book. I set my magazine down on the plastic tray table in front of me and shifted in my seat. The woman across the aisle was now reading a newspaper, the sheets crackling in the thin air as she turned the page, and I wondered if she was as cool and nonchalant as she seemed to be, and if so, how she had become that way.

In the two years since Alex and I had married, we hadn't managed to correct the original asymmetry that marked our partnership. Yet there had been outward progress. We'd secured permanent jobs at the small Iowa college, sharing the equivalent of a teaching load and a half that afforded us ample time for research. The cost of living in our town was low enough that we could afford to dine once a week at our favorite local restaurant, a tiny bistro off Main Street known for its chill vibe, whose logo was two frogs toasting each other. Here we'd sit at the bar drinking house margaritas, laughing, me wiping salt from my mouth, him giving more details to a story. Our conversations supported the illusion of parity, disguising how, more often than not, we were not on an equal footing but rather stuck in a psychic landscape of invisible highways diverting us from who we thought we'd be together. And in the meantime, I hoped my achievements in academia would one day deliver us to a place of equal ground.

I suspected that some of the lopsidedness of our relationship still had to do with my uncertainty about whether I was right for philosophy. No matter what I accomplished, the sense that I didn't belong dogged me. Masham wrote about what prevents a woman from committing to an intellectual life: the unwritten, automatic, continual message that she isn't fit for it. Censure, ridicule, and isolation are strong enough forces to make her doubt herself.[1] They beat her back like waves against a dinghy.

And then what?

Does she accept what they say about her after all? Do they overpower her, changing not only her behavior but also her thoughts about herself? How does she distinguish between discouragement and oppression? How does she know whether the waves are not a form of subjugation but a kindness? All these questions suggest that the epistemic state of many a thinking woman is one of self-doubt.

Here's an old trick philosophers use when doubtful: invoke a demon. Descartes famously used this technique when he wasn't sure whether he could trust anything he'd learned in school or from books and wanted to find one certain thing. As he sat alone in a small room with a quill in his hand, warmed by a fire, he wrote in his *Meditations* that he was unresolved about his ideas—including the existence of God. He noted that it was possible an evil demon had tricked his mind into believing there was an all-good God. Yet even the existence of the demon couldn't make Descartes doubt that he himself was thinking, an insight that formed the cornerstone of his thought and earned him the title of father of modern philosophy.

What is little known today, and what Descartes himself did not acknowledge, is that he likely got this idea from a philosopher whose book *Interior Castle*—an early modern international bestseller—he'd read in school. It was written by Teresa of Ávila, a sixteenth-century Roman Catholic nun and philosopher.[2] To Teresa's horror, demons rather enjoyed visiting her. In her autobiography, she described a moment praying alone in an oratory when a small demon appeared on her left side. He had an ugly mouth and flames shooting from his body, which cast no shadow. Not to be daunted by this and the many other visitations she received, Teresa argued that despite the demon's ability to make her doubt the substance of her thoughts, he could not make her question the act of thinking itself.[3]

It's not surprising that the philosopher who introduced the idea of radical doubt was a woman, since women learn to question themselves from a young age. Contemporary philosopher and artist Adrian Piper noticed this too. She says that women are especially adept at philosophical doubt because "their judgment, credibility and authority start to come under attack during puberty, as part of the process of gender socialization. They are made to feel uncertain about themselves, their place in society and their right to their own opinions."[4] Descartes's demon was only a prop, and he could walk away from it when he grew tired of his meditations. Teresa, on the other hand, believed her demon was a representation of the devil and labored to find a way to escape the existential nightmare it introduced into her life.

I didn't believe in demons, although I was familiar with self-doubt. For years I'd operated as if a hot-mouthed shadowless beast were on my shoulder, whispering in my ear. I engaged with it—the power of its words difficult to dismiss—hoping to discover something that would ultimately liberate me from it.

Our interactions went something like this:

A few months before I married Alex, I was on a train to London hours after learning I'd failed one of the three days of the comprehensive exams, which graduate students must pass before they start their dissertation.

DEMON: *not off to a good start*

My best friend from college, who'd moved to England right after graduation, was with me, and we were on our way to see an indie rock band. We sat next to each other on seats facing the back of the train. I tried to downplay my disappointment so as not to ruin our night. I didn't tell her how I was ashamed of the results and now wondering whether I should leave the program. We were turned toward each other in near darkness, the flitter of occasional streetlights illuminating the side of her face in strobe. I told her that I would have to retake the third day in the spring, postponing the start of my dissertation research for another six months. I watched her dark eyes looking into mine. She was also in a relationship with a former college teacher and had fallen into a depressive slump in post-college life. We met when we were eighteen, two years before I started dating Alex. My trip to see her afforded me a chance to be a version of myself that had almost vanished. The night before, we'd hung out in her living room, a narrow space made smaller by the precarious towers of books that Mark, her boyfriend and an Oxford professor, had collected over the years. She played the Cure as I lit a cigarette, two beers in, and she took photos of me dancing in a light pink sweater, an item and color the pre-Alex me would have considered "too preppy," and which in that moment I hoped to sully with the smoke rising up from the cigarette. As the nicotine hit the back of my throat, I closed my eyes.

The professor who sent me the results of my exam told me I wasn't the only one to fail this round and that I shouldn't worry because it was common.

DEMON: *the job market is bleak and you can't afford to be common in an ever-expanding pool of brilliant candidates. this is a sign that you aren't cut out for this*

The day before, I'd walked the Oxford campus. A light mist fell and my flats scuffed along the damp stone path. As I passed under the arched entrance to Magdalen College, where Hobbes had studied four hundred years ago, I had a reckoning. This university was beautiful, but I felt I didn't belong here. I didn't aspire to philosophical genius. I didn't aspire to the talent of great scholars either. My good grades didn't set me apart. I hadn't discovered a grand philosophical idea and wasn't sure I ever would. Months before, I had submitted a paper to the annual graduate student competition at my university. I didn't win. I did win the award for best teaching fellow, which I took to be foreshadowing of my future in academia: I was destined for a teaching position, one in which I would be hired to teach many classes, and my research, though important to earn tenure, would be secondary. I would be a steward of novices. To my surprise, I didn't mind this prospect. I even liked it. And in this sense, I was fine being classed a commoner in academia. Still, I needed to impress my professors, whose support would be critical to establishing my early career. Failing the third day of the exam didn't strike me as a way to inspire their confidence.

After our train reached London, my friend and I walked to the concert hall. Our tickets were for the ground floor, which was standing room only. We grabbed beers and hung out around the perimeter as the band members took their places. The bassist had just begun playing the first rolling notes when the drums, guitar, and lead singer crashed in, shockingly loud. The crowd responded by moving closer to the stage. My friend finished her beer and walked forward, disappearing into the sea of people. I resisted. To go forward would require me to forget, even briefly, how disoriented the exam results had made me. I could let go. I could take myself less seriously. But if I did, I believed no one else would take me seriously. I feared disappearing. Where did this fear come from?

I stayed put, watching as the guitarist, whose sinister goatee reminded me of a bestial god, strolled to the edge of the stage and leaned back on his heels. His figure cast a long shadow on the opposite wall, so that as he played it looked as though he were masturbating a ten-foot phallus. His dark chin-length hair, stringy with sweat, fell across his face as his head bobbed with the beat. The crowd shook and screamed for him to continue. I remained on the edge, sipping my beer.

During my graduate coursework, I had found it increasingly difficult to speak confidently in class or with my professors. I would sweat, stutter, and speak softly.

> DEMON: *these are physiological indications that you*
> *are in an environment where you are not equipped*
> *to thrive. leave*

There was one graduate student I would seek out at parties because he would dance close and well with me. There was another I would track down when I wanted to laugh. Once, this same friend and I walked outside and stopped on the sidewalk, discussing Aristotle. It was the first spontaneous conversation I'd had about philosophy with another person besides Alex, and I blushed, trying to express my thoughts. It was awkward, and a stranger stopped to ask if it was our first date. This conversation was an outlier, because typically when I wanted to talk philosophy, I didn't look for anyone to engage with, and they didn't look for me. I would just call Alex.

A few years later, once my coursework was done and Alex and I were married and had secured our jobs in Iowa, our colleagues would go to him for advice, stopping by his office to work out their ideas. I finally got it. I was the quiet one.

DEMON: *you're an imposter*

When had I become this timid?

DEMON: *maybe it's some sort of genetic, late-onset anxiety*

I had memories of being a freshman in a Great Books class where I learned about Plato and I was one of the two most outspoken students. That forthrightness hadn't changed until graduate school.

DEMON: *it's called weeding out. accept it. you're a prickly thistle, a problematic pigweed*

The late philosopher Sandra Bartky writes that emotions are important features of knowledge, and that how a person feels informs how she interprets the world. Bartky argues that in society men and women learn different emotional responses to stimuli, which develop into different ways of knowing. She was particularly interested in shame, the feeling that others judge you to be fundamentally defective or wrong. The typical response to shame is self-censorship and social isolation: to hide and conceal from others what you think is shameful about yourself. Shame makes a person speak tentatively, blush, apologize, and cringe.[5] Bartky observed that women experience shame far more frequently than men, because society constantly sends the signal that they are inadequate. This is especially the case in academic environments in which women intuit they are inferior and don't belong. Bartky describes the effects of shame's inner monologue: "Better people are not made in this way, only people who are weaker, more timid, less confident, less demanding, and hence more easily dominated."[6] The takeaway: to think like a woman is to be regularly ashamed of oneself.[7]

* * *

After my flight landed in the Boston snowscape on the day before my dissertation defense, Alex went to see his mother in a nearby town, and I went to my hotel. I logged on to my email. Professor Schmidt, my new adviser, had written, asking me to call him immediately. When I did, he told me that the defense couldn't go on.

DEMON: *uh-oh. why are you surprised?*

Apparently, Novak had called him the evening before from Europe to say that the dissertation wasn't ready to be defended and that I hadn't addressed significant areas of scholarship. Novak was also dismayed to discover many instances where it wasn't grammatical.

Novak was more senior and renowned than Schmidt and had been my lead adviser until he'd gotten a job in Europe. Before he left, he described my work to my current employer as "unusual, original, and important." He never shared this with me, and when he was lead adviser for my dissertation, he was hardly ever in contact, offering few substantive comments on my work. He'd agreed to stay on as the second reader and told me that another professor in the department would take his place and that he was entirely confident in Schmidt's ability to help me take my dissertation over the finish line. I was somewhat relieved. I'd hoped for more interaction and feedback. In the end, my experience with Schmidt was pretty much the same as my experience with Novak had been. Schmidt didn't comment much either.

Now, as I listened to Schmidt, I grew infuriated. Novak had received the dissertation weeks ago. Why was he only expressing these concerns now, the day before the defense? I hung up and walked to the department.

When I arrived, I found that Schmidt was not in his office. I continued down the hall to find Professor St. George, the chair of my committee. He waved and asked me to return in ten minutes when he was done meeting with a student. I stopped by the office of Professor Franklin, my third reader. She was the most junior member of the faculty. Her area of research was entirely different from my own, yet I was inspired by the fact that she was a smart, successful woman. She smiled and asked whether I was excited about tomorrow. She hadn't heard the news, so I filled her in. She listened and told me she was sorry but that she needed to defer to Schmidt. Before I left, she said to let her know what Professor St. George thought about the situation. As the chair of my dissertation committee, it was his job to ensure the defense was fair and conformed to university protocols.

It was dusk by the time I sat in St. George's office, across from him at his large wooden desk, upon which sat a single lamp illuminating the floor-to-ceiling bookshelves on either side of us.

"This is nonsense," he told me. "Schmidt cannot set a date and then call it off the evening before the defense. Go back to your hotel and get some rest," he said. "The defense will go on as scheduled."

DEMON: *but the role of the chair is not to read the dissertation but to ensure the process is fair. two of your readers do not believe it is good enough. bail out. save your pride or whatever is left of it*

I hardly slept that night.

DEMON: *why didn't you listen to me?*

The next morning I sat in a small conference room at the vertex of an oval table, and my readers were seated together at the opposite end. St. George called the defense to order. Professor Z, my fourth reader, opened with the comment that my work was an achievement, the first dissertation in the history of the department devoted to women philosophers. It was an encouraging preface, but the rest of the defense went by in a blur. When it was over, I was relieved. I stepped outside the door for fifteen minutes while the committee deliberated. When they let me in, they shook my hand. I'd passed with revisions. Congratulations, Dr. Penaluna, they told me.

I wanted those words to deliver me to the place I'd imagined a decade ago as an undergrad, to feel as if I'd crossed a threshold, invisible but potent, into the fellowship of the life of the mind. One reader expressed that I'd "responded with deftness and thoughtfulness that is rare in junior scholars." I certainly didn't feel scholarly. I was all nerves, a raging sea.

>   DEMON: *how melodramatic. see how you turn yourself*
>   *into a victim? you're a human with agency and*
>   *they are humans capable of compassion*

In early 2007, I made the requested changes to my dissertation and sent them to Schmidt. He wrote that it was sufficient and that I should submit it for completion of my PhD. I was surprised by how quickly he greenlit my pages after the defense debacle. Novak said nothing and would never reach out to me again. In March, a cardboard tube arrived in the mail, and I was officially done with graduate school.

Later, I learned that Novak and Schmidt gave two of my male colleagues ample feedback and support on their dissertations. These professors connected them to leading scholars in the field. Multiple drafts of their dissertations were commented upon. Mine went through one drafting process that got negligible attention until the day before the defense. Why didn't my readers connect me to others in the field and encourage me to seek feedback from leading scholars? I didn't understand why they didn't give me more frequent input, more precise edits. Why wasn't I mentored?

>   DEMON: *there are many possibilities. let's see: they*
>   *decided you didn't have the chops and so didn't*
>   *invest in you; they were not lit up by the work you*
>   *were doing; you failed to spark their intellect and*
>   *mentoring sympathies*

Or they were incompetent.

>   DEMON: *sure, in which case you should have spoken*
>   *up. that you didn't is your fault. you know there are*
>   *confident women who do well in philosophy*

This story is not for women who escape the limits of normal destinies.

> DEMON: *if you are smart enough you will pursue*
> *something relentlessly. your obstacles boil down*
> *to obtuseness, personal neuroses, victimization*
> *complex, or some combination of those*

I'm not sure what the actual constraints on my freedom to self-actualize were.

> DEMON: *exactly. you have no right to tell this story. shut*
> *your piehole!*

Years later I came across an article by the critic Lili Loofbourow introducing an expression that I thought uncannily captured some of my graduate school experience: "the male glance." Not to be confused with the male gaze, which objectifies women's bodies, the male glance does the opposite to women's creative work: it barely gives it a second look.[8] Those under its spell decide after cursory examination that the work in question isn't of much value. The male glance "looks, assumes, and moves on. It is, above all else, quick. Under its influence, we rejoice in our distant diagnostic speed . . . it feeds an inchoate, almost erotic hunger to know without attending—to omnisciently not-attend, to reject without taking the trouble of analytical labor." It turns away without a care.

A year passed. I continued in my teaching and scholarship, and the next spring found Alex and me sitting in square fabric chairs at a small circular table. We were in a private office at a mental-health clinic in Iowa whose slogan was "Promoting Recovery and Quality of Life." We'd arrived from work wearing our office attire, looking like the couples on the brochures scattered across the table before us: white, middle-class, performing sideways hugs with wide smiles. An easel with an enormous writing pad stood behind us, and we were surrounded by more chairs than could possibly fit around the table, so that they were all at slightly odd angles to one another. This included the ones we were seated in. My therapist, Kathy, a tall woman with long, wiry hair, sat across from us. I'd come to trust her, initially telling her I was there because I was unsure about my marriage but spending most of my time with her—forty-five minutes every other week, which was all the insurance covered—working to reduce my anxiety and depression, as if they were a house fire I could put out with my bare hands. I had asked her to set up this meeting. After almost a year of cognitive behavioral therapy and not much progress, I wanted to try antidepressants. Alex was unenthusiastic.

"I'm afraid she will change who she is," Alex told Kathy.

"This is why I want to take them," I responded.

"I'm afraid you will become someone I don't know," Alex explained. Turning to me, he said, "I do want you to be happy."

Later that week I started on medications. Over the next few months I tried various combinations of psychiatric drugs. My anti-depressant-induced mania was followed by days of zombie-like noth-ingness. My psychiatrist added another medication to diminish the swings. The voice of doubt grew quieter, but it wasn't gone.

> DEMON: *all this focus on female suffering is tiring; it's cliché*

I need to fix myself quietly, out of sight, and then I will return to the world.

> DEMON: *focus on something productive, like expanding the repertoire of female expression*

In the thirteenth century, after hundreds of years that saw few women philosophers in the West, more women suddenly appeared on the scene. Their philosophical specialty was suffering.[9] In the late Middle Ages, when the suffering of Christ came to be seen as a valid expres-sion of religiosity, women, who had long been exiled from philosophy

because of the belief that they were overly emotional, were now recognized as capable of grasping ultimate truth.

> DEMON: *look what beautiful ideas came from these*
> *thinkers who had far greater obstacles than you*
> *faced. and anyway, who's to say any of your suffer-*
> *ing is due to oppression?*

I'm not certain it is. How could I be?

> DEMON: *you're white, middle-class, and educated. you*
> *have no right to complain*

A few months later, I got a book contract with a university press based
on my dissertation. I wrote the book. I did it on my own, sharing nothing with anyone, not a paragraph, not a chapter, almost just as I had
done with my dissertation. That was a mistake. When a letter from
the publisher arrived months later, informing me that they would
not go forward with the book, that two of the three peer reviewers
thought it didn't address the relevant scholarly debates, I was crushed.
I shared this news with a scholar in the field whom I admired and
whose conference I'd attended. She told me that I shouldn't give up
and that my project was a good one. These setbacks were normal in
academia, she said. I should just keep pushing ahead. But I wasn't
sure I'd have the heart to do it again.

> DEMON: *she's being kind. take a hint for once. you're*
> *not cut out for this sort of thing*

A colleague wrote a recommendation for my third-year review. He
said that since being hired to keep my spouse around, I'd proved
my worth. I know this because all third-year reviewees are invited
to read their colleagues' letters of recommendation. This colleague
was smart and humble and lived with his wife on a small farm atop
a hill a few miles outside of town. Their kitchen sink was almost

always filled with piles of dishes, left there after extraordinary meals composed of squash flowers, raspberries, spinach, and fennel we'd picked in their garden. His wife told him that she would only have children if they had her last name, which he supported. If someone had meat on their plate at the end of a department meal, he broke from vegetarianism on the grounds that wastefulness was worse than eating meat, then scraped the remainders onto his plate and ate them. I crushed crab apples in their old cider mill with him. My colleague tossed in one with a worm, which I paused to watch as it bobbed with the other apples until it disappeared into the froth.

DEMON: *that your relationship with Alex was his reason to hire you doesn't mean you need to be ashamed of yourself*

I was.

DEMON: *whose fault is that?*

Mine?

DEMON: *your belief in your own victimhood is blinding you to your own powers and the humanity of your mentors. what are you refusing to face?*

That I don't belong. Like, I really, really don't belong in philosophy. It was a super overstretch to try. I have an average intelligence. I'm too sensitive.

DEMON: *no. something more. autonomy was always within your reach, yet you chose dependency. you made the decision years ago with Alex that you would play the passive role, because it was easier—it is a role readily available to women. and you hoped you would have a career and achieve self-sovereignty without investing the effort and bravery necessary to earn these things. and that this original decision was made from a desire to protect yourself is the greatest irony yet: you willed your own impotence to avoid the*

white-hot gaze of judgment that some part of you
believed you were incapable of surviving. your
depression, anxiety, and warped character, the fact
that your professors find you forgettable, are con-
sequences of your fear of using your own voice

That's insanely depressing.

DEMON: *that's because you don't want to take responsi-*
bility for yourself

How do I do that?

DEMON: *through self-respect*

How do I learn that?

DEMON: *by taking risks*

The risks seem greater for me than for men. The world can be harsh
and uninviting. When I open the door alone, when I imagine opening
it a crack, I feel the cold. I'm aware that I have only a few resources
to count on. The world calls me to stay inside, to sit back and listen,
to find the warm lap of a man.

DEMON: *maybe*

I love philosophy.

DEMON: *there was no promise that it would love you*
back

◆◆

In these years of uncertainty, when I felt like a foolish lover for pursuing philosophy and being with Alex, I was reminded of Masham.

Any true love at one point or another will hurt. It may turn sour,
it may rot, it may dissolve into habitual gestures. It may annihilate.
These are the risks of love, and Masham's message was to dive in
anyway.[10]

Not all philosophers agree with this message, which to them
would seem careless, dangerous, and ill-reasoned. Thinkers such
as Kant and Thomas Aquinas saw no transcendent value in loving

other humans. You can get your heart broken, get sick, or die. Therefore it's best to desire something unchanging, like God or the Good,
even if it's something incapable of loving you in return. It's a lonely
experience, but you're free from being gutted by another person. You
yourself become impervious. Godlike.

Masham was an early adopter of a different take on love, one that
is messy and sticky, one that leans into our sociability, one that asks
us to fall for our lover, to stitch our heart to our baby's so much our
stomach does flips. Her message is that the only path to enlightenment is transcendence through interdependence. The love of others
is a treacherous but necessary path and the only one available to us,
because we are not gods.

It's often a tougher path for a woman, because society can be
a hostile place for her to cultivate her subjectivity. It was true in the
seventeenth century, and it was true for me. Maybe, then, the common experience of being a woman in philosophy is to be effaced:
your feelings, your opinions, your presence, your life, your works,
your impact are belittled, glanced at, or ignored. The psychological
hurdles are one reason why today there are fewer women than men
in graduate programs across many disciplines, and even fewer who
rise to the top of their class, and why some women seem to come into
their own at a slower rate than men. Only years later, when men have
outpaced most women in their careers, will women begin to discover
how they nearly snuffed themselves out. Just like I was doing. I took
Masham's recommendation to be: Do not retreat. A woman's path
to self-knowledge requires her to risk losing herself to find herself.

I will go further, and affirm, as an indisputable fact, that most of the women, in the circle of my observation, who have acted like rational creatures, or shewn any vigour of intellect, have accidentally been allowed to run wild.

—Mary Wollstonecraft

Love and Loathing

The problem was, I was quite good at losing myself. Masham indicated in the most abstract terms the direction I had to go, but I was still stumbling around. Because the world makes it easy for a woman to choose self-diminishment—and often rewards her for it—I had to remain extra vigilant but not so aloof that I was risking nothing.

During this period, I was teaching and researching, fulfilling my service to the university, dutifully taking my meds and long hikes in the bluffs at the town's limit, hungry for some sort of equilibrium, when I dug into the work of Mary Wollstonecraft. I planned to teach an excerpt from her most famous work, *A Vindication of the Rights of Woman,* the following semester in a feminist philosophy course. At the time, I believed that she was simply after women's right to education and citizenship. As I read through this work, however, a more complex picture of her emerged—that of a philosopher whose fiction and nonfiction stemmed in no small part from principles she forged in conversation with the work of other philosophers, especially Jean-Jacques Rousseau.[1] I also discovered a rich philosophy of psychology that spoke to me. I went on to read her fiction, letters, and other treatises. I was amazed to discover that Wollstonecraft was interested in the cultivation of women's personhood—and the obstacles to it. She knew that for women, becoming a person was not necessarily a wholesome, pretty, or pleasurable process, and it could at times make a woman greatly disappointed with herself when, for instance, she found how much her selfhood was not in her control or how she'd delegated the care of her being to others. But without this work of self-examination, woman remained a tool in someone else's hands, enabling the will of her oppressors, complicit in her own captivity.

Somehow, as I traced Wollstonecraft's life and ideas, a silhouette of myself began to emerge from a new understanding of how my own choices had limited my potential and what sorts of freedoms were still available to me.

One windy day in June 1795, Wollstonecraft, her one-year-old daughter, and her nanny, with a small crew of men, pushed off in a boat into rough waters from a port on the eastern shore of England.[2] Wollstonecraft's baby wriggled in her arms as the boat rocked and swayed in the gigantic gray waves of the North Sea.[3] Yet Wollstonecraft would not be deterred by the dangers of the passage. This was an opportunity for her to write about her travels and to capitalize on her reflections by selling her stories. When the jagged shoreline of Sweden finally appeared after days of endless ocean, she began to record her observations.

Wollstonecraft wrote about how traveling as an unattached woman could be unsettling: when she asked for help from a strange man, he pointed her to his small, dark cabin.[4] It could be demeaning: during a dinner conversation, her male host complimented her for asking *"men's questions."*[5] And it could be enraging: when she learned that men in the Swedish village she was visiting stood by unbothered as women washed linens in an icy river, causing their hands to crack and bleed.[6] "The men stand up for the dignity of man, by oppressing the women," she observed.[7] Her heart was heavy when she thought of her daughter, who would one day experience being a woman in the world: "I feel more than a mother's fondness and anxiety, when I reflect on the dependent and oppressed state of her sex," she wrote. "Hapless woman! what a fate is thine!"[8]

From a young age, Wollstonecraft aspired to support herself so she would not need to depend upon a man for her well-being. This was a hope that she had for all women and that she expressed in her philosophical and literary works. By her early thirties, she was already the well-known author of *Rights of Woman* and had achieved her dream of self-sufficiency through her writing.

Wollstonecraft's travels around Scandinavia provided her with an opportunity to unleash her insatiable curiosity and powers of reflection. Her uninhibited and wide-ranging examination of landscapes and lifestyles challenged the philosophy of Rousseau, found observational support for the theory that evolution selects for species and not individuals, and captured astonishing encounters in the natural world, as when her boat drifted over a constellation of sea creatures "like thickened water" that closed at the touch of her paddle.[9]

The other motivation for her trip was more personal. She was chasing down a ship captain on behalf of Gilbert Imlay, the father of her daughter. Imlay had sent Wollstonecraft to Scandinavia both to attend to some business on his behalf (the details of which are unclear) and, also likely, to shake her off.[10] It was a humiliating mission made worse by the fact that only two weeks before her departure, Wollstonecraft had attempted suicide after learning Imlay had cheated on her with a young actress.[11] (A man his age, he said, needed "variety.") Although it wasn't easy, she was willing to forgive Imlay, harboring hopes that her travels would cement her and her daughter's fate to his. But as each day on her trip passed, these hopes dwindled. "I am weary of travelling – yet seem to have no home – no resting place to look to. – I am strangely cast off. – How often, passing through the rocks, I have thought, 'But for this child, I would lay my head on one of them, and never open my eyes again!'"[12]

Being rejected by Imlay was traumatic, as was the realization that a man had the power to make her miserable. In *Rights of Woman*, she'd disparaged women for putting themselves in a position like this, characterizing those who staked their well-being on men as "weak, artificial beings" with a "spaniel-like affection."[13] She warned that "many innocent girls become the dupes of a sincere, affectionate heart"[14] and was disillusioned when this happened to her. She shared these thoughts in a letter to a friend: "It seems to me, that my conduct has always been governed by the strictest principles of justice and truth. – Yet, how wretched have my social feelings, and delicacy of sentiment rendered me!"[15]

The more I read, the more I came to appreciate Wollstonecraft as a fascinating and important part of the Enlightenment story, albeit a part that isn't told in philosophy classes or textbooks.[16] She lived and wrote at a time when significant shifts in science and philosophy were ushering in new standards of objectivity—and, along with them, fresh theories of women's inferiority. Wollstonecraft responded with a bold, unbridled voice of opposition: "I think the female world oppressed; yet the gangrene, which the vices engendered by oppression have produced, is not confined to the morbid part, but pervades society at large."[17] Her aim was to draw awareness to the ways in which social systems and institutions abet the oppression of women, and her hope was for women to live, work, and think as freely as men.

Such a vision had its costs. Wollstonecraft's desire for women's autonomous selfhood made living with her own sense of powerlessness at times insufferable. (She experienced bouts of depression throughout her life and would attempt suicide a second time shortly after her trip to Sweden.) I knew that struggle and felt the pain of recognition as I read about her life: how being a feminist leads to a fractured sense of self. There is the you who you want to be and the you who you are. The you who is free and the you who is subservient. The part of yourself you love and the part you loathe.

Wollstonecraft wrestled with these sides of herself on an epic scale, and her philosophy is remarkably attuned to how a woman's personhood is weakened by social forces.[18] In this way, she anticipates what more recent feminists have also explored. In the 1970s, philosopher Monique Wittig wrote about how aspects of lesbian selfhood and desire are immune to the patriarchal forces that inhibit heterosexual women. She says lesbianism is "beyond the categories of sex (woman and man)," thereby challenging heterosexuality, "a social system which is based on the oppression of women by men and which produces the doctrine of the difference between the sexes to justify this oppression."[19] Then there are other thinkers, such as contemporary scholar and feminist Catharine MacKinnon, who believe it's extremely difficult, if not impossible, for anyone's sexual preferences and identity to escape the grips of heterosexual male supremacy.[20] Wollstonecraft in her most hopeful moments would agree with Wittig that women can resist the harmful effects of conventional erotic relationships, a view possibly informed by Wollstonecraft's own experience at nineteen of falling in love with a woman. Yet like MacKinnon, Wollstonecraft suggests that being single or a lesbian doesn't guarantee freedom, because women's psyches are shaped in a society saturated with patriarchy. Her message is that society must change. Until then, all women must acknowledge their own habitual passivity and subservience if they are ever to overcome them.

Well before she cracked open her first philosophy book, Wollstone-craft had been keen to free herself from the tyranny of men. This tyranny started with her father, an abusive, short-tempered alcoholic.[21] Wollstonecraft was born in London in 1759, the second of seven children and the only child to stand up to her father, taking his blows in place of her mother.[22] Her father was terrible at managing money. He aspired to be a gentleman farmer and moved the family frequently in his effort to achieve that goal—seven times by the time she was nineteen—squandering more money with each move.

Wollstonecraft resented her parents' preference for her older brother, Edward. She felt she had been born into a family that treated her with either indifference or unkindness, and so she spent as much time as she could away from it, either outside in nature romping freely like the boys or in the homes of more supportive families.[23]

Between the ages of ten and fifteen, Wollstonecraft attended school with her sisters, until her father pulled them out and moved the family to London. That was the last formal education she would ever have.[24] All other learning for Wollstonecraft was either on her own or via informal tutorials at the homes of friends. The first such home was that of her friend Jane Arden. Jane's father was a lecturer in empirical science and experimental philosophy, subjects he also taught Jane and Mary.[25] Wollstonecraft was curious and eager to prove herself. Her written English was unpolished, and it embarrassed her when she compared it to Jane's refined fluency. Still, she was determined to improve, and the letters she wrote to Jane provided an opportunity not only to bond with a friend but also to practice her skills. Ever competitive and determined, Wollstonecraft sought opportunities to stand out. In a letter to Jane about her father's tutorials, she wrote, "Pray tell the worthy philosopher, the next time he is so obliging as to give me a lesson on the globes, I hope I shall convince him I am quicker than his daughter at finding out a puzzle, tho' I can't equal her at solving a problem."[26]

At sixteen, she fell into the fold of the Bloods, a poor family that held learning in high esteem.[27] Fanny Blood, who was two years older than Wollstonecraft, excelled at writing and agreed to tutor her.[28] A year later, the Wollstonecrafts moved to Wales, but Mary and Fanny kept in touch. None of their letters have survived. Perhaps they chose to destroy them, hoping to hide from future generations what they could hardly suppress in themselves. Wollstonecraft was in love with Fanny.[29] When Wollstonecraft recounted the first time she saw her, she described a scene most people would find unremarkable—Fanny caring for children—yet for Wollstonecraft the moment was arresting. Her relationship to Fanny was "a friendship so fervent, as for years to have constituted the ruling passion" of her mind. Wollstonecraft saw their physical distance as temporary: "To live with this friend is the height of my ambition."[30]

Not long before meeting Fanny, Wollstonecraft had declared she would never marry. It was a daring and unusual statement, perhaps inspired by her same-sex desires and a wish to avoid exposing herself to the abuse she had suffered as a child. Also contained in this statement was an awareness that in marriage a woman's life is no longer her own. A few years later she wrote, "It is a happy thing to be a mere blank, and to be able to pursue one's own whims, where they lead, without having a husband and half a hundred children at hand to teaze and controul a woman who wishes to be free." Rather than become a wife, she would "endeavour to do better."[31]

This wish extended to all women. In her novel, *Mary, A Fiction*, Wollstonecraft inverts the marriage plot, a type of storyline that was also popular in her day. Rather than overcoming a series of obstacles to marriage, her protagonist strives to overcome the obstacle of marriage itself.[32] The novel turns on Mary's (the protagonist's) realization that she has married a man who does not care about her intellectual and emotional development. This realization makes her mentally and physically ill: "When her husband would take her hand, or mention any thing like love, she would instantly feel a sickness, a faintness at her heart, and wish, involuntarily, that the earth would open and swallow her."[33] The story concludes on a dark and, I think, tragically ironic note, when Mary's freedom from marriage arrives only at her death: "In moments of solitary sadness, a gleam of joy would dart across her mind – She thought she was hastening to that world *where there is neither marrying*, nor giving in marriage."[34]

When Wollstonecraft's mother died in 1782, the family scattered, and Wollstonecraft temporarily moved in with the Bloods.[35] During this time, she observed how Fanny and her mother often toiled through the night, sewing to earn money. This strain only exacerbated Fanny's existing lung condition. Wollstonecraft wanted to save Fanny from this poverty and help restore her health, not to mention keep her close. Fanny confided that she wanted to be free of her family.[36]

But Wollstonecraft wasn't yet sure how to make it work. Eventually, a totally separate problem provided a solution.

In December 1783, Wollstonecraft's younger sister Eliza (who also went by Bess) became severely depressed.[37] The nature of her emotional distress is unclear. Since Eliza had recently had a baby, some historians suggest it was postpartum depression. Others suspect her husband physically abused her or forced her to have sex; neither act was illegal. Whatever the case, Eliza's situation was exacerbated by the fact that divorce was not an option: only four women in the previous two hundred years had successfully requested and gotten a divorce.[38] After a stay in Eliza's home, Wollstonecraft wrote to her sister Everina in alarm: "I don't know what to do – Poor Eliza's situation almost turns my brain – I can't stay and see this continual misery – and to leave her to bear it by herself without any one to comfort her is still more distressing – I would do anything to rescue her from her present situation."[39]

An idea did come. "Those who would save Bess must act and not talk," Wollstonecraft wrote to Everina.[40] One day in mid-January 1784, Wollstonecraft helped her sister escape to an acquaintance's cold, drafty home, where they hid for days.[41] Through intermediaries, Eliza sent letters to her husband. He refused to support her or allow her to see their five-month-old baby, which he legally had the power to do, unless she returned. Sacrificing her own health and safety for access to her child was an awful bargain that she couldn't make. Although it was Eliza's decision to leave, Wollstonecraft was blamed by others for the "monstrous intervention."[42]

Now, three single women—Wollstonecraft, Bess, and Fanny—needed a home and income. Wollstonecraft, who was then twenty-five, came up with the idea of making a living at needlework and painting. Fanny was an excellent illustrator but knew Wollstonecraft's talents and interests lay elsewhere, and she quickly shot down the idea in a letter to Everina: "I am sure she never could endure such drudgery."[43] Wollstonecraft also had the idea of starting a school. Word got out that the sisters needed employment, and a few months later, a wealthy widow, Mrs. Burgh, offered them money.[44] Burgh wanted the women to start a school in Newington Green, a small community of rational dissenters who rejected Anglicanism and the idea of a state-run religion. (For their radicalism, dissenters could not vote, hold public office, enter Oxford, or obtain a degree from Cambridge.) Burgh and other nonconforming Protestants needed teachers for their children. Even though the Wollstonecraft children were raised Anglican, they rarely attended church.[45] Wollstonecraft felt no compunction and accepted the money. Eliza and Fanny joined her, and in three weeks they had twenty students and enough funding to live on their own.[46] Everina and Fanny's brother came to lodge with them too. Wollstonecraft and Fanny were together once again under one roof.

Wollstonecraft began to think about what sort of teaching would be ideal for girls. Burgh's late husband had run an academy of dissenters and published a manual outlining his philosophy of education. His work was steeped in Locke's philosophy, which was widely accepted at the time. When Wollstonecraft read Mr. Burgh's manual, it gave her insight into the language of intellectuals. To her disappointment, Burgh's manual proposed only a meager education for girls, buying into the traditional view that female roles did not require a rigorous education. She would develop an alternative model, and Newington Green would provide an opportune place for her to work out these ideas.

Among her new community's members was Richard Price, a moral philosopher and Unitarian theologian who was also a vocal critic of colonialism and slavery.[47] Price's ideas impressed Wollstonecraft, and although she never embraced rational dissent, she stopped going to Anglican services altogether and endorsed egalitarianism. Wollstonecraft also attended the dissenters' weekly supper clubs to discuss theories. It was here that she sharpened her arguments in favor of a rigorous education for girls.[48]

That girls should be educated was rather uncontroversial at the time. Most people agreed that to become good mothers, girls needed some learning, but there was disagreement about how demanding their studies should be.[49] The latest "evidence" in medical science continued to perpetuate the longstanding view that women were naturally inferior to men. In 1775, a year before the American Declaration of Independence was signed, influential French physician Pierre Roussel said that "the essence of sex . . . is not confined to a single organ but extends, through more or less perceptible nuances, into every part."[50] A widely circulated anatomical drawing of a woman exaggerated features of her anatomy, so that her head resembled a toddler's and her hips an ostrich's—an image that lent itself well to the argument that women were destined to obey men and have babies.[51]

Wollstonecraft would have none of this pseudoscience. Like Astell and Masham before her, she believed men viewed women this way because it benefited them to do so. Rousseau's philosophy helped her formulate the idea that the human psyche is fragile and sensitive to stimuli and that a good education has the power to awaken a person's consciousness and bring about liberation. A bad education would do the opposite. She took these principles and gave them her own twist, arguing that any meaningful cognitive differences between the sexes were due to variations in schooling and experience. She believed that God wanted both sexes to have intellectual autonomy and that it was morally wrong to hinder someone from thinking for themselves. She set to work on a book about the education of girls—a book that would set higher expectations for them than Burgh's manual did, a book that would explain why girls' learning should equal boys'.

While Wollstonecraft insisted that thought wasn't sexed by nature (one day she would write, "It be not philosophical to speak of sex when the soul is mentioned"[52]), from her earliest forays into philosophy, it's clear her thinking was profoundly influenced by her being a woman. Here she anticipated Simone de Beauvoir, who more than 150 years later would argue that "one is not born, but rather becomes, a woman."[53] Wollstonecraft believed that being female didn't present an innate obstacle to thinking but rather that as a thinker, a woman couldn't help but reflect on the ways that women were harmed by social systems. How could she, a female thinker, escape the gravity of the woman question when the world asked it in response to her existence? What creative and intellectual freedom does a woman have under such a persistent weight?

In the meantime, Fanny's lung condition worsened. A man who was courting her had moved to Portugal, and in the belief it would help her health, Fanny followed him south. Wollstonecraft was reluctant to let her go, but she also hoped that the warmer weather would provide an opportunity for Fanny to convalesce. Not long after Fanny arrived in Lisbon, she was married and became pregnant. A few months later, Wollstonecraft took a ship south over stormy seas to be with Fanny during the birth, but when she arrived, she was shocked by the terrible state of her friend's health. It took her a few days to compose herself and write a letter to her sisters. "I am now beginning to awake out of a terrifying dream," she wrote. "Fanny is so worn out her recovery would be almost a resurrection."[54] But the dream—or rather nightmare—wasn't over. A few days after giving birth, Fanny died.

Overcome with grief, Wollstonecraft returned to England to more depressing news. In her absence, her school had failed financially, and she had to close it; the experiment had lasted only two and a half years.[55]

In the free time that followed—and possibly to distract herself from her sorrow—she threw herself into her work. She finished her pedagogical manual, *Thoughts on the Education of Daughters*, and traveled to London to meet with Joseph Johnson, a dissenter and a powerful London publisher who over the course of his career supported such writers as William Blake, Erasmus Darwin, Benjamin Franklin, and Thomas Paine. Johnson, a plainly dressed, short forty-eight-year-old, offered to publish her work for ten pounds.[56] It was a modest sum, but Wollstonecraft was buoyed by the thought of one day supporting herself as a writer.

She looked for work and, in the summer of 1786, took a job as a governess to the Kingsboroughs, the largest landowners in Ireland.[57] She didn't want the position. Waiting on others struck her as servile, but she needed the money. She moved into a room in their Palladian mansion, which sat on over a thousand acres—a setting that was an extravagant embarrassment to the egalitarian sensibility she'd cultivated while at Newington Green. Now among the aristocrats, she observed how the men and women were immersed in a culture of sex complementarity, in which they accentuated their differences in dress and behavior. Wollstonecraft found all of it repulsive. Surrounded by women who spent hours on their looks and feigned ignorance to attract men, she felt "confined . . . to the society of a set of silly females."[58] She managed to keep these opinions to herself at first, and she described initially feeling their warmth: "I am a GREAT favorite in this family." She also unexpectedly discovered joy in her work with the children: "I go to the nursery—*something like* maternal fondness fills my bosom . . . and I discover the kind of happiness I was formed to enjoy."[59]

No matter how real her maternal feelings may have been, she didn't fall prey to the specious argument that her destiny was to raise children. Her sense of purpose lay in what she did once the children were asleep. In the evenings, after the girls were in bed and her duties officially over, Wollstonecraft would return to her chamber and read by candlelight well past midnight.[60] "When I have more strength I read Philosophy – and write – I *hope* you have not forgot that I am an Author," she wrote to her sister Eliza.[61]

These evenings alone with her thoughts accumulated into an identity: she began to see herself as a philosopher. What encouraged this new self-understanding was a novel conception of the imagination that gained traction in the eighteenth century. Locke's theory of the mind, that all ideas arose from sensation and reflection, was by then widely accepted.[62] He had solved a major philosophical problem facing seventeenth-century thinkers: how to reconcile a theory of the mind with Newton's theory that the material universe could be explained according to mechanical laws alone. Locke's genius was to do for the study of human consciousness what Newton did for the physical world. He presented a model that didn't rely on a divine will.[63] For Locke, our minds arrange ideas that we derive from sensation and reflection, but whether those arrangements resemble reality or God's universe, our reason cannot say.

Not everyone was comfortable with how Locke's theory relied little, if at all, on God. In an attempt to link Locke's theory of consciousness to an objective reality, some philosophers argued that the human mind structures subjective data according to a divinely inspired vision.[64] The imagination became not only the faculty that formed images but also one that organized phenomena into transcendent, divine insight.

Now that the imagination had come to play a significant role in theories of knowledge, philosophers had to provide a meaningful distinction between illusions and madness on the one hand and transcendence on the other. The distinction between lower and higher forms of the imagination did just this: the lower order was uninspired and fictitious, whereas the higher order illuminated supreme truths. These supreme truths were also called "the sublime," and the ability to perceive the sublime was labeled "genius."

Just as soon as this theory of genius was born, so were the reasons women were excluded from it. Thinkers from Burke to Rousseau to Kant, each of whom discussed some version of the sublime, argued that women were incapable of apprehending it.[65] Rousseau put it this way:

> Women, in general . . . have no genius. They can succeed in
> little works which require only quick wit, taste, grace, and
> sometimes even a bit of philosophy and reasoning . . . But
> that celestial flame which warms and sets fire to the
> soul, that genius which consumes and devours . . . those

*sublime transports which carry their raptures to the depths
of hearts, will always lack in the writings of women; their
works are all cold and pretty as they are; they may contain
as much wit as you please, never a soul.*[66]

Not everyone agreed with Rousseau. A counternotion held that
genius could reside in the uneducated—in those who were shut out of
the aristocratic and university-educated classes—including females.[67]
This left just enough room for Wollstonecraft to wedge her foot in
the door and present herself, a woman with virtually no education,
as a philosopher with valid insight into reality.[68] It was a door that
she would one day swing wide open for other women.

An intruder on these blissful evenings of reflection was her
employer, Lady Kingsborough. She put pressure on Wollstonecraft
to join her at social gatherings, invitations Wollstonecraft routinely
turned down as she had no interest engaging aristocratic women in
conversation. Wollstonecraft continued to retreat to her room every
evening. This infuriated Lady Kingsborough, who was not accustomed to rejection by an inferior.[69] Lady Kingsborough had another
reason to be unhappy with Wollstonecraft. Her fourteen-year-old
daughter, Margaret, was becoming less docile under Wollstonecraft's
tutelage. (Margaret would come to disown her upper-crust, feminine
destiny, and cross-dress as a man while attending medical school.)[70]
Lady Kingsborough eventually dismissed Wollstonecraft.

Although Wollstonecraft needed money to support herself and
her sisters, the loss of her job came as a relief too.[71] She wrote, "I
long for a little peace and *independence*! Every obligation we receive
from our fellow-creatures is a new shackle, takes from our native
freedom, and debases the mind, makes us mere earthworms – I am
not fond of grovelling!"[72]

Wollstonecraft quietly packed her belongings and went to London. While her sisters believed she was still a governess on summer vacation with the Kingsboroughs, she lugged her bags to her

publisher's door and knocked. When Joseph Johnson opened the door, she handed him several manuscripts, including one for a novel. Johnson took her in and helped her find a place to live. He also agreed to publish her novel and hired her as a reviewer at a monthly journal he'd founded, the *Analytical Review*, which discussed books by social reformers and provided Wollstonecraft with a steady source of income.[73] A few months later, once she was settled and confident she could live and work as a writer, she wrote to Everina that she was "going to be the first of a new genus."[74]

Her work at the *Analytical Review* was an education in itself.[75] Wollstonecraft learned French and German in order to translate excerpts and reviews, which opened her up to philosophical debates and gave her a more intimate understanding of Rousseau, whose brilliant yet sexist philosophy alternately inspired and frustrated her. She reviewed works of science, philosophy, history, fiction, and travel.[76] She learned about debates central to English theology and moral philosophy.[77]

Johnson brought her into his circle of radical intellectual bohemians, which included William Godwin, Henry Fuseli, Thomas Paine, and Mary Hays.[78] Wollstonecraft started to wear her auburn hair down, and simpler clothing, rebellious choices that reflected her commitment to authenticity and her unwillingness to pander to class divisions or the sexual preferences of men.[79] Some in the group saw her decision to literally let her hair down as off-putting, calling her "a philosophical sloven," though another observer found her new look becoming, writing that she had charm and "pleasing" features.[80] She was impressive, intimidating even, and a number of her female contemporaries looked to her as a model intellectual. She was unafraid to speak her mind to wealthier women who sought her editorial advice or to a roomful of men.

Over the next three years, her ideas fermented. She discovered she wanted to explore a new mode of expression. Women were allowed to write novels and education manuals, to translate literature and write book reviews, but she wanted to write political philosophy.

In 1789, Wollstonecraft was galvanized by news of the French Revolution and inspired, as so many other intellectuals were, to challenge the necessity of traditional social hierarchies. Over the course of one month, at age thirty-one, she wrote her first work of philosophy, titled *A Vindication of the Rights of Men*, which deftly attacked the philosophies of Edmund Burke and Jean-Jacques Rousseau. It was an immediate commercial success. Booksellers ran out of copies, and a librarian said that "there is no keeping it long enough to read it leisurely."[81] It also brought her to the attention of influential people, including future US president John Adams, who effused in a letter after reading it that Wollstonecraft was "a Lady of masculine masterly understanding."[82] (Adams's comments express a similar sentiment to those of Wollstonecraft, who, in a review of her contemporary, historian Catharine Macaulay, called her a "masculine and fervid writer"—comments that were female-forward for the time.)

The positive response to her work encouraged Wollstonecraft to embark on another ambitious project: her book *Rights of Woman*. I was moved to tears and laughter when I read this work as a professor, and I think part of my reaction had to do with my age. Wollstonecraft was thirty-two when she wrote this groundbreaking book, and I was twenty-eight when I read it—an age when a woman has experienced enough of life to observe the effects of misogyny on herself and other women. I needed cathartic release, and Wollstonecraft offered an outlet. Her tone in this work is not conversational. It's stentorian. And what she says about male philosophers is racy and delightfully out of place among the niceties of academia.

"Men, indeed, appear to me to act in a very unphilosophical manner when they try to secure the good conduct of women by attempting to keep them always in a state of childhood," she writes in *Rights of Woman*.[83] She says that according to Rousseau, "with respect to the female character, obedience is the grand lesson which ought to be impressed with unrelenting rigour" and "a woman should never, for a moment, feel herself independent, that she should be governed by fear to exercise her *natural* cunning, and made a coquetish slave in order to render her a more alluring object of desire, a *sweeter* companion to man, whenever he chooses to relax himself."[84] I love the final clause: "whenever he chooses to relax himself"! When the most acclaimed male philosophers of her era used women as servants or beautiful objects for their pleasure, she turned the male gaze back on itself: these philosophers were thinking with their penises. (It would be a hundred years before Nietzsche would state that the convictions of even the greatest philosophers are motivated by irrational urges, by the wish to gratify their sexual appetites and to stay in power.) In her assessment of philosophers, Wollstonecraft raised the question of whether men were sufficiently objective to philosophize about women. Women weren't the only ones whose minds and moral sensibilities were warped by patriarchy.

Wollstonecraft took philosophical authority from these men and gave it to herself. "As a philosopher, I read with indignation the plausible epithets which men use to soften their insults," she writes, such as "fair defects" and "amiable weaknesses."[85] She was better suited to philosophize about women, because she was both a philosopher and a woman—a clever inversion of the claim that being a woman disqualified her from doing philosophy. She knew how to think, and she knew how to be a woman in the world, too, an experience that generated in her a sympathetic curiosity for herself and for other women. Men are conditioned to see women as a means, she knew, but she had a greater capacity to consider women as something more. "I have, probably, had an opportunity of observing more girls in their infancy than J. J. Rousseau – I can recollect my own feelings, and I have looked steadily around me," she writes.[86] "That woman is naturally weak, or degraded by a concurrence of circumstances, is, I think, clear."[87] She says women's way of being is "produced by oppression" and in another passage that it is "a natural consequence of their education and station in society."[88] These are thoughts she had expressed in her education manual, but now she added more nuance.

Wollstonecraft argued that our sense of morality, our ability to reason, and the objects we desire are learned when we are young, through:

> an habitual association of ideas, that grows "with our growth," . . . [and] can seldom be disentangled by reason. One idea calls up another, its old associate, and memory, faithful to the first impressions . . . retraces them with mechanical exactness.[89]

Wollstonecraft held that for women, the association of ideas is particularly troublesome, because they live in a culture that regularly encourages them to see themselves as inferior to men and as their servants.[90] As humans they grow up seeking pleasure, which, as women, they learn to get by pleasing men. If women appear weak, it's because the system makes them so.

She said that women's servile traits would disappear "when they are allowed to be free in a physical, moral, and civil sense."[91] To correct for this, society needs to be restructured so that there is equality: "I love man as my fellow; but his scepter, real, or usurped, extends not to me."[92] She also believed the inverse to be true: "I do not wish [women] to have power over men; but over themselves."[93]

She did not turn to the political tradition of Hobbes, modified by Locke, who argued that members of society were brought together by mutual advantage. Instead, she agreed again with Rousseau, who argued that the best, freest society requires citizens who have sympathy for the suffering of others, whom they would help whether it was advantageous to them or not. Wollstonecraft wanted men to care about the suffering of women, to look beyond the gain women's servility provided and wish instead for their self-sovereignty. Once society allowed that women were "rational creatures" who "ought to endeavour to acquire human virtues (or perfections) by the *same* means as men, instead of being educated like a fanciful kind of *half being* – one of Rousseau's "wild chimeras" – they would see that God expects many things of women.[94]

Wollstonecraft said her imagination allowed her to perceive that God intended each married woman to be "an active citizen . . . equally intent to manage her family, educate her children, and assist her neighbours."[95] She imagined women as doctors, property holders, and business owners as well.[96]

Such an egalitarian vision made living with the constraints of the present unappealing to her: "I think, and think," she writes, "and these reveries do not tend to fit me for enjoying the *common* pleasures of this world."[97]

Setting aside the religious dimension of her thought, there are aspects of her philosophy that speak to secular women today. She wanted to articulate the form of women's loss, the invisible ways women are made mute, uncertain, weak, the various ways institutions shape sexist habits of thought and feeling. She wanted women to take notice: to observe how culture teaches them that their only power lies in their sex appeal, and that they are otherwise to be followers rather than leaders, objects rather than subjective thinkers. She asked women to reflect: when you're not trying, where does habit take you—what principles organize your day—who do you serve? If you're unnerved by what you discover, she reminds you to envision something more for yourself. The feminist imagination reveals that you are not only what you are, but also what you can be.

Not long after Wollstonecraft wrote about how she wanted women to adopt male freedoms and ambitions—things she wanted for herself too—she acknowledged that she was a creature of the world with a sexual appetite and fell into a series of relationships with men. What she didn't anticipate was how these romantic flights, taken in a culture of female oppression, would each in their own way contribute to both her well-being and her self-loathing, and—in the worst moments—her despair.

Enter Gilbert Imlay. After the publication of *Rights of Woman*, Wollstonecraft traveled to Paris. She went there to start work on a book about the French Revolution—and to get over a recent heartbreak. She had fallen for the painter Henry Fuseli, who she believed was in love with her as well. They spent many hours together discussing art and philosophy, and Wollstonecraft formed an intense bond with him.[98] She wrote that she had never known a man "possessed of those noble qualities, that grandeur of soul, that quickness of comprehension, and lively sympathy."[99] It's possible they were having an affair, and she did propose moving in with him and his wife, an experimental ménage à trois that the couple rejected.[100] Wollstonecraft hoped that Paris would help her recover from her rejection.

Once there, she met Imlay, an American entrepreneur from Kentucky who had written a book about the United States. He was outwardly supportive of equality and women's rights. He and Wollstonecraft started to spend time together, taking tea and walking around Paris, sharing ideas. Things soon became serious, and by the late spring, Imlay had declared his love and expressed his wish that Wollstonecraft would move with him one day to America. Soon after, they returned to his apartment and had sex—her first time.[101] Wollstonecraft believed that this relationship was the birth of something new not only for her but also for womankind: a romantic partnership between equals bound together not by law but by affection.[102] She appreciated the power of sexuality to draw couples together and believed it should be celebrated, not stigmatized, as long as it was governed by reason. She did not see sex as an inherent evil. She wrote, "It is not against strong, persevering passions; but romantic wavering feelings that I wish to guard the female heart by exercising the understanding."[103] At a party, when a Frenchwoman mentioned proudly to her that she had no sexual appetite, Wollstone-craft responded, *"Tant pis pour vous"*—too bad for you.[104]

Not long after Wollstonecraft arrived in Paris, the revolution took a turn, and England and France were at war. British citizens in Paris were suspected of being spies. To be safe, in June 1793 Woll-stonecraft rented a small cottage in Neuilly, four miles outside the walls of Paris. It was managed by an elderly caretaker, who warned her of "horrible robberies and murders" in the nearby forest.[105] This didn't stop Wollstonecraft from taking long walks there on her own to clear her mind. Once she made it over ten miles to Versailles and strolled through the abandoned palace.[106] Her caretaker had the habit of insinuating himself into her life by making her bed and bringing her grapes—chores he refused to do when Imlay was visiting from Paris. That fall, as the Reign of Terror began, Wollstonecraft discov-ered she was pregnant.

She moved into Imlay's apartment, where she continued her writing. Though he traveled a lot for work, they planned to raise their child together and move into a home in Le Havre, a port city where he was conducting business. It was scandalous for an unmarried woman to be pregnant, and once Wollstonecraft started showing, she signed her letters "Madame Imlay" to stem gossip. Although they never officially wed, she and Imlay declared themselves to be married at the American embassy. The benefit was, because of this closer association with the Americans, the French were less likely to see her as a political enemy.[107]

In 1793, Paris was run by a radical political group known as the Jacobins, who declared the more moderate revolutionaries to be ene-mies and sent them to the guillotine. As Wollstonecraft walked along the streets of Paris in the aftermath of these executions, the edges of her dress absorbed the blood that pooled on cobblestones. She was disgusted by how the revolution, once so promising, had turned cruel and gruesome. This was not what she had imagined when she had defended it. The Jacobins were fiercely against women's equality and took inspiration from Rousseau's concept of woman as subordinate and servile. They took back the promise of women's rights that had formed part of the rhetoric of the early revolution and that was one of the reasons Wollstonecraft had been inspired by the cause.[108] Within the year, Olympe de Gouges, French author of the *Declaration of the Rights of Woman and of the Female Citizen*, published a year before Wollstonecraft's *Rights of Woman*, would be sent to the guillotine—but not before her clothes were torn off and her lower parts exposed and inspected to see if she had the genitals of a man.[109]

It was not safe for Wollstonecraft in Paris, but still she tarried. She did not want to leave Imlay. By December 1793, he was again away on business, and she wrote, "Am I to see you this week, or this month? – I do not know what you are about – for, as you did not tell me."[110] She told him not to let business keep him away for too long. "Be not too anxious to get money! – for nothing worth having is to be purchased."[111] January arrived and he was still absent. Wollstonecraft grew more impatient. She didn't care for his flowery words. She wanted him around: "I do not want to be loved like a goddess; but I wish to be necessary to you."[112]

In January 1794, she traveled to Le Havre to join Imlay and, in May, gave birth to their daughter, whom she named Fanny. Soon after, Imlay left again, this time for London, promising to rejoin them soon, and Wollstonecraft and Fanny returned to Paris. Once more, she awaited Imlay's return and wrote him:

> *I have been playing and laughing with the little girl so long, that I cannot take up my pen to address you without emotion. Pressing her to my bosom, she looked so like you (entre nous, your best looks, for I do not admire your commercial face) every nerve seemed to vibrate to the touch, and I began to think that there was something in the assertion of man and wife being one.*[113]

But Imlay did not return as he had sworn. And Wollstonecraft did not want to raise Fanny without him.[114] By the following April, with Imlay still abroad, she lost patience. If he would not travel to her and Fanny in Paris, then she and Fanny would travel to see him in London. She weaned Fanny for the occasion, as medical practice held that sex tainted breastmilk. Imlay had a furnished house waiting for her and Fanny, but stayed in a nearby hotel, telling Wollstonecraft it was for purposes of business. Once she was settled, he did not go to see her. And then she found out: Imlay was sleeping with someone else.[115] The news overwhelmed her. His unwillingness to commit to her meant that she would be a social outcast. On May 22, 1795, Wollstonecraft sent Imlay a note by foot messenger and then overdosed on laudanum, falling into a coma. Imlay came and resuscitated her.

After her suicide attempt, she was embarrassed and wrote to Imlay: "I have very involuntarily interrupted your peace . . . I will avoid conversations, which only tend to harass your feelings."[116] Imlay recommitted to her, asking her to take that trip to Scandinavia for him.[117] When she returned from abroad, she discovered that he was with a new woman. She threatened suicide again: "I shall plunge into the Thames where there is the least chance of my being snatched from the death I seek . . . In the midst of business and sensual pleasure, I shall appear before you, the victim of your deviation from rectitude."[118] Then she went to a quiet bridge outside of London, tied rocks to her legs, and tipped over into the river. To her consternation, bystanders pulled her out and revived her. Months later, she finally gave up on Imlay and told him: "It is now finished."[119] She would raise Fanny on her own.

Wollstonecraft was bruised but was slowly recovering and started life again by rekindling relationships with old friends. That year (1796) Mary Hays, part of the original group of intellectual bohemians Wollstonecraft had met before she'd left for Paris, brought her back into the fold. Hays hosted gatherings at her home in Hatton Garden, and once more Wollstonecraft was surrounded by a community of

vibrant artists and intellectuals. One of these friends, William Godwin, a philosopher, was particularly interested in getting to know her
more. The first time they met, things hadn't gone well. This was five
years earlier, after the success of *A Vindication of the Rights of Men*.
Hays had invited them to dine at her home along with another guest,
Thomas Paine, who had written the famous pamphlet that helped
inspire the American Revolution. Godwin wrote that Wollstonecraft
had dominated the conversation; he had been keen to talk to Paine,
who ended up hardly speaking. Godwin wasn't interested in what
Wollstonecraft had to say. In fact, he'd read Wollstonecraft's book
and was turned off.

> *I had barely looked into her [book], and been displeased,*
> *as literary men are apt to be, with a few offenses against*
> *grammar and other minute points of composition. I had*
> *therefore little curiosity to see Mrs. Wollstonecraft.*[120]

It's uncertain whether he ever shared those specific words with her.
When I read them in the context of Loofbourow's concept of the "male
glance," I thought how dismissively Godwin had originally treated
Wollstonecraft. His admission that he'd "barely looked into" *Rights
of Men* and that the grammatical errors—these few offenses—had
prevented him from taking the rest of the work seriously, was just
too much. I didn't like this early Godwin.

But then I read their correspondence, and a more complicated
picture emerged. It would be far from the last time he would patronize
her, but Wollstonecraft and Godwin went on to have a healthier affair
than she'd ever had before—a reminder of the trickiness in diagnos-
ing misogyny and sexism in patriarchy, when the same individual
can be both a woman's supporter and her detractor.

After Hays's dinner in 1796, Wollstonecraft and Godwin started
a friendly correspondence that soon developed into something
more. Godwin confessed that he had fallen for her on reading her

Letters Written During a Short Residence in Sweden, Norway, and Denmark, which he declared a work of genius that brought out her vulnerabilities—a "softness" and "gentleness"—qualities he much preferred to the "harshness and ruggedness of character, that diversify her *Vindication of the Rights of Woman*."[121] As she started to fall for Godwin, she feared being made a fool: "I perceive that I shall be a child to the end of the chapter."[122]

Godwin had a difficult time comprehending how Wollstonecraft, a woman of extraordinary intelligence, could have fallen for Imlay. He attributed it to a lapse in judgment: "She ventured not to examine with too curious a research into the soundness of her expectation."[123] But if he had attended to her *Rights of Woman* more closely, he would have understood. There she explained that a woman's romantic desire, fashioned in an environment of inequality, made it difficult for her to think in her best interest.

By summer, she and Godwin had become serious about each other. They corresponded multiple times a day and dined together in the evenings. They shared their work and discussed philosophy and literature. They also started to have sex. One day, when she had written to him expressing insecurity about the prior evening they'd spent together and wondering if she should have been more sexually modest, he wrote, "Humble! for heaven's sake, be proud, be arrogant!"[124]

At first they decided not to marry. Godwin was philosophically against it, believing marriage to be an oppressive institution. But as they came to appreciate the full scale of the censure and ostracism that were sure to come, they decided to do it.[125] They rented a home together but also kept separate lodgings, Godwin staying in his house and Wollstonecraft in hers. "We were both of us of opinion, that it was possible for two persons to be too uniformly in each other's society," Godwin wrote.[126] Godwin had a small house twenty doors down from Wollstonecraft and Fanny. Although Fanny spent most of her time with her mother, she also spent time with Godwin, who treated her as his own daughter. Wollstonecraft sent notes to him with instructions like "Do not give Fanny a cake to day. I am afraid she staid too long with you yesterday."[127]

Godwin and Wollstonecraft were a progressive couple, permitting each other to meet alone with members of the opposite sex, something then taboo. "A husband is a convenient part of the furniture of a house, unless [he] be a clumsy fixture. I wish you, from my soul, to be riveted in my heart; but I do not desire to have you always at my elbow – though at this moment I did not care if you were," she wrote.[128] Their separate households were generally a wonderful thing for both of them, except for the period during which Miss Pinkerton, a young, beautiful, unmarried woman, dined with Godwin on multiple occasions. Godwin insisted it was platonic, but Wollstonecraft's former insecurities rose to the surface: "My old wounds bleed afresh – What did not blind confidence, and unsuspecting truth, lead me to . . . But enough of the effusions of a sick heart . . . The weather looks cloudy; but it is not necessary immediately to decide."[129] Godwin agreed to not see Miss Pinkerton again.

That same year, Wollstonecraft started work on a new novel, *The Wrongs of Woman: or, Maria*. It was intended to be a follow-up to the *Rights of Woman*, a further exploration into the ways society makes it difficult, if not impossible, for a woman to live a happy, autonomous life. It was pioneering. Like her first novel, it featured a female protagonist who struggled in a profoundly inhibitive marriage. But in this second novel, Wollstonecraft included a working-class character named Jemima to illustrate "the wrongs of different classes of women equally oppressive, though from the difference of education, necessarily various."[130] When the wealthy female protagonist, Maria, asks Jemima for help, Jemima replies, "What should induce me to be the champion for suffering humanity – Who ever risked any thing for me?"[131] Although Jemima eventually comes to Maria's aid, Wollstonecraft's refusal to treat Jemima's support of her protagonist as a given is a powerful critique of social class hierarchies. Wollstonecraft was particularly drawn to portraying the emotional and psychological trauma of being a woman in a man's world. The book was intended for women, to help them assess their own lives and faculties and begin to discover what parts of themselves are the result of oppression and what parts are not.

The novel was intended for men as well. Wollstonecraft's aim was to encourage them to sympathize with the plight of women and care enough to help change it. She began to see the limits of this project when she shared drafts of it with two men, her friend George Dyson and Godwin. Dyson's comments angered her, and Godwin's sent her into despair.

Dyson apparently didn't understand why Maria, the protagonist, struggled or how her husband stifled her, which shocked Wollstonecraft and seemed to prove her point that what plagued society was men's inability to feel compassion for women's subjection. She wrote him:

> I am vexed and surprised at your not thinking the situation of Maria sufficiently important, and can only account for this want of – shall I say it? delicacy of feeling, by recollecting that you are a man – For my part I cannot suppose any situation more distressing than for a woman of sensibility with an improving mind to be bound, to such a man as I have described, for life – obliged to renounce all the humanizing affections, and to avoid cultivating her taste lest her perception of grace, and refinement of sentiment should sharpen to agony the pangs of disappointment . . . [Y]et you do not seem to be disgusted with him!!!
>
> These appear to me (matrimonial despotism of heart & conduct) to be the particular wrongs of woman; because they degrade the mind . . . [I]t is the delineation of finer sensations which, in my opinion, constitutes the merit of our best novels, this is what I have in view.[132]

Godwin also overlooked the groundbreaking themes in her novel. Instead he focused on mechanics and told her the writing was ungrammatical. This was simply too much for Wollstonecraft to take. The next day, she could barely get out of bed. She had been, she wrote:

> Labouring all the morning, in vain, to overcome an oppression of spirits, which some things you uttered yesterday, produced; I will try if I can shake it off by describing to you the nature of the feelings you excited.
>
> I allude to what you remarked, relative to my manner of writing – that there was a radical defect in it – a worm in the bud – &c What is to be done, I must either disregard your opinion, think it unjust, or throw down my pen in despair; and that would be tantamount to resigning existence; for at fifteen I resolved never to marry from interested motives, or to endure a life of dependence.[133]

She went on to say she hadn't been able to write anything since. She'd tried to convince herself that his opinion was not accurate, reminding herself that she had already attained great literary success. Still, she couldn't shake the desire to stick her head in a hole. "I am almost afraid to go into company."[134]

Days later, she had recovered from Godwin's comments. She told him that she wanted to start grammar instruction. It's a setup that I find humiliating: she was a world-renowned author, a former writer for a serious journal, brought to heel by a man who told her she needed grammar lessons. Godwin knew that men used grammar as a way to dismiss women's writing out of hand, and perhaps he was trying to protect her from criticism to come. If this was the case, his intentions didn't come across well. There is something to be said for Wollstonecraft, who was willing to still learn and cultivate her writing skills—a willingness to see one's faults and improve is a virtue. But since the reverse of this situation was at that time unimaginable—a world-class male author getting grammar lessons from a female author—then it was potentially toxic and self-debasing for a woman such as Wollstonecraft to go forward with her plan. Still, she tried to keep the situation light and romantic: "Fancy, at this moment, has turned a conjunction into a kiss."[135]

That December she became pregnant.

For months she worked on her novel, but despite her diligence, it was still in process as she went into labor. On August 30, 1797, a midwife was called. "I have no doubt of seeing the animal to day," she wrote Godwin.[136] She asked Godwin to send some distraction: "I wish I had a novel, or some book of sheer amusement, to excite curiosity, and while away the time – Have you any thing of the kind?"[137]

If he sent something along, she probably didn't read it. It was a difficult birth. According to custom, Godwin stayed away. The baby was born that night at 11:20 p.m., a girl, who was named Mary. At 2:00 a.m., the midwife reported that things were not going well. Wollstonecraft had not birthed the placenta. A doctor was sent for. At the time there were no sanitary standards, and the doctor, fresh from the hospital where he had touched sick and dead bodies, came and stuck his hands inside her birth canal to pull out most of the placenta, which came out in bloody pieces. When Godwin was finally allowed to see Wollstonecraft, she told him that she had "never known what bodily pain was before."[138] After little success with the first doctor, they called in another, who performed more invasive work to remove the rest of the placenta. Wollstonecraft came down with a fever and chills and bouts of uncontrollable shaking—signs of a serious infection. She died ten days after she birthed Mary, whom Godwin would raise and who would one day be renowned as Mary Shelley, author of *Frankenstein*.

Although some of her contemporaries were eager to burnish Wollstonecraft's legacy, she quickly fell out of favor in intellectual and literary circles. Godwin published her unfinished novel, which, because it detailed the protagonist's sexual relationships with men, was criticized for promoting sexual license.[139] Not helping matters, Godwin's memoir of Wollstonecraft, published a year after her death, also described her embrace of her own sexuality as healthy and natural. The thought of women relishing sex was scandalous, and critics, including women, denounced Wollstonecraft.[140] The same month that Wollstonecraft died, one of the Kingsborough daughters she'd tutored ran away from home at age sixteen after an affair with, and subsequent pregnancy by, a married man of thirty. Mr. Kingsborough shot and killed his daughter's paramour, a crime for which he was put on trial. Nevertheless, it was Wollstonecraft whom critics identified as the true perpetrator: she had corrupted the girl through her philosophy of sex positivity and women's liberation.[141]

Godwin described Wollstonecraft's literary contributions in terms more romantic than philosophical, placing her in the pantheon of Romantic poets and artists by referring to her as a Young Werther, à la Goethe's *The Sorrows of Young Werther*:

> *We not unfrequently meet with persons, endowed with the most exquisite and delicious sensibility, whose minds seem almost of too fine a texture to encounter the vicissitudes of human affairs, to whom pleasure is transport, and disappointment is agony indescribable. This character is finely pourtrayed by the author of the Sorrows of Werter. Mary was in this respect a female Werter.*[142]

Yet she was also a philosopher. Godwin could have called her a female Rousseau, because Rousseau was her favorite thinker and because, like him, she wrote novels, autobiographical fiction, and philosophical works. But this is not how Godwin, a self-described philosopher who also wrote novels, thought of her, and it is not how she is remembered today. Her work is read, but mostly in English studies and women's studies. Rarely in philosophy.

Virginia Woolf came across Wollstonecraft in her research on remarkable women and wrote an essay about her. Woolf says, "The reformer's love of humanity, which has so much hatred in it as well as love, fermented within her."[143] What Woolf appreciates about Wollstonecraft—and what I do too—is her complexity. Wollstonecraft was eager to birth a new world of equity and freedom, where women of all backgrounds are free from oppression, a place "of their own creating," formed through an effort that comes as much from love as from vexation.

Woolf wrote elsewhere about anger as an emotion that was ruinous yet inevitable for women creating art under conditions of subjection: "It was a thousand pities that the woman who could write like that, whose mind was tuned to nature and reflection, should have been forced to anger and bitterness. But how could she have helped herself?" I know what Woolf means. If the world were fair and women were treated well, it would be easier for some of us to focus on other subjects, such as metaphysics, rather than on our unjust situation.

We're not there yet, however, and this was Wollstonecraft's point. I tend to think that if you're a woman and you care about your freedom, you cannot help but harbor some anger and frustration. Whether it's expressed in a thought to yourself or in an essay, to think like a woman, to produce and create like a woman, often involves anger. It's a feature of a woman's psyche as she comes into her own in a world that (still) does not want her to.

It was this lesson from Wollstonecraft, the honoring of my own anger and of how it operated to protect my sense of self-worth, that stuck with me that year when I'd been studying her texts in earnest. And the following summer, it gave me courage to shift the course of my life.

Heroes

One balmy July evening, I was studying at a wooden desk in the dorm room I was sharing with Alex. We were one week into a seven-week immersive language program at a college in Vermont where we hoped to learn basic French to expand our own research projects. We'd been married for four years, and although we worked on a college campus, we hadn't been in a dorm room since we were undergraduates. We pushed the two twin beds together, threw a blanket on top, and unpacked our books and personal items, including some philosophy books in French and Alex's oxblood leather satchel. No matter what changes we introduced, it still looked like any other dorm room: a space designed for the young and unattached, a fact that only underscored our awkwardness as a couple.

The year before, we'd sold our house so we could afford to travel and do things like this program. Our apartment in Iowa, which sat empty while we were in Vermont, was situated at the front of a Victorian home with twelve-foot ceilings and tall windows. It was the only habitable unit in the building, and the rest of the structure, which was the bulk of it, sat unrenovated and unused, except by the creatures we heard pawing around on the other side of the wall. After dinner, I would walk through the side yard, past the vacant part of the house, and around to the back, where the grass grew tall and unruly. Here I dumped food scraps into a compost pile that I stirred with a stick to keep it from going rogue, which is what would happen, I'd read, if I wasn't mindful. Given half a chance, a few wild microbes could easily overtake the ecosystem and alter the temperature, color, and smell of the whole mass. Now that we were away, and a week had passed since I'd last tended the pile, I imagined that this change had already occurred and that when we returned home in six weeks, we would find the tame, loamy pile transformed into a neon, anaerobic sludge or a heap of inert earth.

I was about to turn around and share this fear with Alex, who was studying at a desk behind me, but I had no idea how to express such notions in French. When the program started, Alex and I had signed a language pledge vowing to talk only in French until the program ended, so we communicated by miming or uttering single-word sentences, such as "*Manger*," while pointing in the direction of the cafeteria, or "*Bibliothéque*," indicating a wish to study outside of our room. Anything more complicated than that simply wasn't said aloud, including most of my anxieties and insecurities and the validations that Alex normally provided in return. It was a relief for him, I imagined. And it was an easier adjustment for me than I'd expected. To my surprise, I wasn't lost without Alex's input. I was even happy. I filled most of my time with French. I spent hours on my own, conjugating, memorizing, and trying to string together complete sentences, or with new friends from the program. I started to feel a joy and fullness I hadn't felt in years.

At my desk, I was reading a children's story in French about a wily elementary-school boy. It was slow going—I had to look up almost every word—moving between the book and the dictionary, and I was easily distracted by the music on my headphones. Looking out the window to my right, I saw in the distance an ancient stand of plane trees, behind which stretched green acres. The color, together with the gesture of looking through a window, reminded me of a moment nine years earlier that I hadn't thought about until then. I had just graduated from college and had been dating Alex for a few years when I decided to travel alone in India. At one point, I was on a train from Delhi to Jodhpur looking through the window after having finished *The Great Gatsby*. Toward the end of the book Gatsby looks across the harbor at a green light that had once been symbolic of a life he had longed to have, and that he had used to orient himself in the world, but which now was losing its powers of enchantment. I thought to myself then that all life is suffering and that the trick is to find the suffering that's worth longing for. The train was passing through the Thar Desert, the barren land occasionally punctuated by a solitary khejri tree rooted in the dry soil. Just before this train trip, I had been in a hospital in Delhi for two weeks recovering from an allergic reaction to an antibiotic. I only knew a few other travelers, so I spent most days in the hospital by myself. One night I woke to find I'd fainted on the floor. My first sight: the glass IV dripping fluid into my arm. I felt simultaneously the ocean of life and my irrelevancy in it. After the nurse came and helped me back to bed, I lay wide awake and thought to myself that when I was released from the hospital, I wouldn't leave India right away and return to Iowa or to Alex. Instead I'd stay on and travel for a few more weeks, even though I was physically weak. Gazing at the passing desert, heading deeper into unknown terrain, I wanted nothing more than to be on my own. Now, from my desk in Vermont, looking out at the green arboreal light, I wondered whether I was facing the future that would make suffering worth it. *I wasn't*, I thought, startling myself. And then I realized what I'd done: how quickly I'd sidelined myself, how easily I'd entered into a state of passivity. I was sad. I was livid.

Just then I heard Alex say something behind me. I removed my headphones and turned around to face him.

"*Manger?*" He pointed to his watch, indicating he'd like to go in thirty minutes.

I nodded. Now I sat frustrated and confused about what to do with my revelation. I tried to refocus my attention on the story I was reading. I could just make out that a teacher was attempting to organize her class for a photo, but the students were uncontrollable.

Once she got children in one section of the risers to pay attention, children in another section would slip out of place.

One morning, during the second week of French class, a student stood up and encouraged us to join her at the French language program costume ball on Friday—in two days. Her name was Zuzanna. She was wearing a white tank top and an ice cube necklace, and she seemed neither to notice how beautiful she was nor to care much about how others looked or carried themselves. This made her less intimidating and was why she was so good at getting people together. You got the sense that all she needed from any person was a willingness to come along. She was beguiling, and most of the students didn't resist. The week before, when she'd announced a similar event, I'd rebuffed her and studied in the library, but this week she wouldn't have it. "*Viens. Viens!*" she persisted. "*Peut-être,*" I told her.

That day in class our instructor asked us to pair up. I was seated as usual next to Alex, but since we had been partners for the last exercise, we each chose someone new. Mine was Orhan, a Chicago-based medical student from Istanbul. Our task was to furnish an imaginary apartment. Orhan and I were both committed to learning French but eager to mock the exercise to keep it interesting. We would get an apartment with three stories: one floor for each of us and then a third for our plant collection. We would have no cats because we were dog people. We were old roommates from college who shared the same name, "Fédéric," and coincidentally each of us had become dentists in Paris. And in our living room we would have only one armchair, a *fauteuil*, a word we couldn't pronounce without laughing at ourselves. That was how a tedious activity flew by, and the next day when we were tasked with yet another boring exercise, we picked each other as partners again.

This time we had to write a survey to interview people, but we first had to practice on each other. I learned that he was twenty-seven, five years younger than me, and that, like me, he adored New Order and Joy Division. That he loved his split-toe Nikes, shoes I couldn't take seriously. That when he returned to Turkey, he would gift his mother with an expensive jar of La Mer lotion, and that, after his medical residency he would spend a year fixing the cleft palates of children in Africa. That he had recently been in Costa Rica with his then-girlfriend. He had a lanky build, black hair, and olive skin and smelled faintly of fresh soap and cologne. *Another new friend in language camp*, I thought. I also had the fleeting idea that if things were different, I would try to be closer to him—with the door closed.

I perceived other married people in the program to be less disciplined than I was. One classmate, Sarah, had been married for a year, but she openly criticized her husband, who was home in Connecticut. She spent her free hours with another student in the class, Rich, a muscular man of twenty-two. She insisted her marriage was over, and I accepted her flirtations as benign. Another classmate, John, whose wife was home in Washington, had a crush on a woman in another language class. He spoke highly of his wife with me but then would spend evenings with the other woman. I imagined him returning to his wife as if nothing had ever happened over the summer. I couldn't comprehend the duplicity. *Asshole*, I thought.

The next day in class, Orhan sat across the room from me. I wanted him near and felt disappointed he wasn't. That's when I started to worry.

On Friday, Zuzanna convinced me to go to the costume ball. I was secretly happy to learn that Orhan was going too. Alex would be at the library and said he might join us later. An hour before the ball, Zuzanna pulled me into her room with Sarah. They were playing music and teasing hair, and they seamlessly incorporated me into the ritual. They stood behind me in the mirror and I observed them, each an inch taller than me with glitter-streaked cheekbones. We hardly spoke, relying mostly on gestures, communicating, I imagined, as prehistoric humans once did. As they worked on me, I felt their hands fixing my hair, their fingers applying my makeup, their repeated gentle touches—each alone a mere gesture, yet each a primitive expression of acceptance as well—together forming a succession through time and space like a rope, pulling me back into a community. I hadn't realized how lonely I had been until then. No matter how much Alex told me that I belonged, I never quite felt I did. I began to realize that perhaps the problem was that I did not belong with him.

Zuzanna placed a medal made of red foam and gold glitter strung with red ribbon around my neck, completing my costume of a victorious track star. My smile was bright and I laughed, and somehow the world started to feel like an intoxicating promise again. As I looked in the mirror and caught my smile, I felt ignited. And then a twinge. The feeling was clear and distinct. I didn't want Alex to join me that night. I didn't want to be with him anymore.

Days later, on a scorching hot morning, I stood on a sidewalk half a block away from the building that held French class, phone to my ear, my head bowed as the sun cooked the nape of my neck. On the other end of the line, my therapist was telling me to wait and not be hasty. She said I should let the program end and see how I felt back in Iowa once I returned to my job and the rest of my life. I was looking down at a holly bush whose leaves were wilting in the heat. I was angry she wasn't hearing me; I felt like she was trying to talk me out of a decision I had already made. As she spoke, I knew that something fundamental had shifted in me. The change had been rapid, a series of mini eruptions, and then it was over and I was different. The thought of reversing course and reintegrating myself into my old life seemed inconceivable, like death. The sentiments that had once bound me to Alex and to our life were no longer there.

"I'll try to hold off," I told her.

I hated being dishonest with Alex. I also feared telling him how I felt. To devastate a person who loved and cared for me because I was devastated by our relationship was a twisted moral calculus, and yet I couldn't muster the feelings necessary to live our life together anymore. I was pining for Orhan but refused to act on my feelings while I was still with Alex. Keeping this a secret made me feel worse than I already did.

After another week, I couldn't do it any longer. I found Alex in the library and asked him if we could talk. We walked outside to the middle of the quad. There on the lawn, as we sat in Adirondack chairs, I ended our marriage. I didn't mention Orhan, not only because Orhan himself had no idea how I felt but also because I reasoned he was a catalyst and not the cause. I did talk about how I struggled to be my own person in our relationship, despite trying for years.

Alex didn't protest. I wondered if it was because he could tell that I was determined or because he was in shock. We agreed to finish the final weeks of the French program separately. I moved out of our dorm room. A new friend in the program, Stephanie, from New York City, said I could stay with her. The next day, the director kindly offered me a room of my own.

A part of me would like to say that the momentousness of this decision made me want to stay inside that night, to wrap myself in a blanket and absorb the gravity of what I'd done. But I wanted nothing more than to be out. I wanted to find Zuzanna, to see Orhan.

Zuzanna had organized an all-class trip into town that evening, and on the way to a bar, I told her in English about the separation. She took my hand and Sarah's and pulled us to the front of the group. On our way into town, a light rain fell, and as I looked behind me to see how the others were doing, I spotted Alex at the back of the group. I caught my breath. I let go of Zuzanna's hand and hung back until I was next to him. I asked how he was, and he replied that his wool sweater was getting damp from the rain. Under the streetlights, I saw it was covered in tiny droplets of water that it resisted absorbing. I wanted to run my palm across its surface to brush the water off. When we first started dating I convinced him one night to walk with me outside in a drizzle that suddenly turned into a downpour. We ran back to his apartment, laughing, and stripped off our wet clothes. Now, his complaint about the rain annoyed me, and I was eager to return to the others. I couldn't comprehend why Alex wanted to be here; he hadn't shown much interest in his classmates before. I angrily thought that he didn't believe my intentions or that he was here to change my mind. But he was quiet. It occurred to me that maybe he was unsure what to do except follow the person who had followed him for years. I suggested he return to his room to pat his sweater dry with a towel. He said he would see and then we said goodbye and I joined the group. I lost track of him after that. I was relieved.

What does this say about my character? Who am I to leave a loved one in a wool sweater in the rain? What sort of person am I to then go out to a bar where I would sing and laugh harder than I had in a decade? What moral grounds did I have for such a rupture? What kind of self-assertion is birthed in such violence?

A few weeks later, in the apartment we had shared in Iowa, we signed the divorce papers. A friend of ours was a divorce lawyer and drew up the paperwork quickly. Outside, the leaves were starting to turn, and except for an occasional passing car, it was almost as still as it was in the apartment. We sat across from each other at our small coffee table, on a red velvet sofa set my parents had bought when I was five and had passed on to us a few years before. In my guilt, I signed them away to Alex in the divorce, along with all the other furniture, most of our kitchen utensils, and the car. I wanted to alleviate as much of his pain as possible, and also my own.

I moved back in with my parents, who lived eighty miles away. They lent me a small stick-shift convertible that I drove that fall through the farmland to the college where Alex and I taught. When I wasn't commuting, I was at home with them, watching TV, eating my mother's home-cooked meals, walking the dog on the golf course in the frost, like I had done as a teenager. They were supportive, opening their home to me again, but I knew that my decision was a sore point for them, particularly for my mom. She wanted me to be happy, but she also recognized that Alex's whole life was being uprooted for that happiness. She didn't put it that way. She just told me that she loved him, and that was enough to remind me that Alex and I weren't the only ones affected by what I'd done.

In moments like this, I thought of Wollstonecraft, whose opus was devoted to raising awareness of the injustice of the routine crumpling of a woman's autonomous selfhood for the sake of a man. Wollstonecraft believed that a marriage needn't be abusive to be bad, and that the harm caused to a woman's psychic and intellectual well-being was reason enough to break it off. It was a brave move for her to pit a woman's selfhood against the harm caused to a husband, family, or community and to not even submit that they were moral equivalents. I agreed, but it was hard to feel entirely proud of my choice.

One night I sat on a big plush chair in my parents' room, hanging out with them. Their Labrador retriever, Tucker, whose name, in my mother's view, too closely resembled another word, lay in front of the TV. An episode of *Law & Order* was on, and during a commercial break, my parents asked what my plan was for after the fall semester. Leaving Alex was complicated by the fact that we worked at the same place. I had spoken with the dean, who assured me we could both keep our jobs, but our circle of friends was small, as was the town itself. I couldn't imagine building a new community for myself, so I resigned from my tenure-track position in philosophy without any alternatives in the offing.

"Where will you live and work?" my dad asked.

I told him that my friend Stephanie from the French language program had invited me to visit her in Brooklyn to see if I liked it there. My dad raised his eyebrows. I said that the benefit was the many colleges in the area and that I might find an adjunct teaching gig for the short term. I was also toying with the idea of moving to Portland, Oregon, to be near my sisters. Or maybe Chicago, I added.

"Chicago? Why Chicago?" he asked. This was when I told them about Orhan.

"What?!" they said.

"Was he the reason for your divorce?" my mother asked, turning down the volume on *Law & Order*.

"No. We're still in touch, but I'm not sure what will happen."

I didn't tell them how after my separation, I found Orhan on the way to class, pulled him to the side, and told him, in French, that I was single and I wanted him. Or how he looked at me and told me he felt the same. Later that evening, I asked him to visit me in my room, and he did. That was the first of several nights we spent together before the program ended a week later. We said we would keep in touch, and I imagined there would be another chance for us to be together again.

I didn't tell my parents how on my long, solitary drives to and from work, I would daydream about Orhan. I imagined meeting his mother, whom I would try to win over. Orhan, of course, had no idea about any of this. All he knew was that I had a strong physical attraction to him.

"Does he know how you feel about him?" my dad asked.

"Not really," I said. Orhan and I (ludicrously) never broke the language pledge, even after the program ended. Plus, I was having a hard time getting in touch with him. He was with his brother sailing the southern coast of France. He wouldn't return my calls or emails for days, and then always had an excuse ready. When he got back to Chicago in early September to begin his residency, he had more excuses for why he wasn't available. My dad was quick to suspect something was amiss, but it took me until early October to take the hint. After he canceled another phone call, this time with the excuse that he wanted to see the latest Batman movie, I finally got the message.

I was faced with myself, and what I saw repulsed me. Just as soon as I'd peeled my future from Alex's, I'd rebonded it to another man's. After years of suffering from not taking charge of my own life, my default wasn't to construct my own future but rather to insert myself into another man's destiny. How easily I had betrayed my dreams and future for some guy—in this case, one I hardly knew. I didn't need a man to stifle me, I thought. I could do it all on my own.

Once again, despite my best efforts, I was falling into the role of the sidekick. From a young age, I'd dreamed of one day becoming an independent woman like Melanie Griffith's character in the film *Working Girl*. In this vision, I am surrounded by skyscrapers, adjusting my suit while hailing a taxi. My life has professional direction and purpose. But in another daydream, I am the girlfriend to a man who's gorgeous and fascinating. He picks me up in his car, and my eyes are on him. He's the protagonist of the story of our lives, and I am Sloane in *Ferris Bueller's Day Off* or Lori in *Explorers*. The feminist film theorist Laura Mulvey writes about this phenomenon: "The female spectator may find herself secretly, unconsciously almost, enjoying the freedom of action and control over the diegetic world that identification with a hero provides."[1] A part of me enjoyed playing the secondary role. If I couldn't be the hero, I took pleasure in my proximity to him.

I meditated on Wollstonecraft, who championed women's freedom yet was susceptible to Imlay's whims for years. I considered her words: "Men," she said, "have too much occupied the thoughts of women; and this association has so entangled love with all their motives of action; and, to harp a little on an old string, having been solely employed either to prepare themselves to excite love, or actually putting their lessons in practice, they cannot live without love."[2] I realized this was true of me. I also saw my knee-jerk submissiveness as a warning of what could happen if I wasn't extra vigilant.

As Wollstonecraft made clear in her first novel, a woman's journey to self-actualization isn't about finding a husband but rather about avoiding the pitfalls in society that make it hard for her to live and think for herself. The aim of her second, unfinished novel, *The Wrongs of Woman*, is to show that women have available to them a fulfilling life experience that has nothing to do with a man. At one point in the novel, the female protagonist says:

> *"Was it possible? Was I, indeed, free?" – Yes; free I termed myself, when I decidedly perceived the conduct I ought to adopt. How I had panted for liberty – liberty, that I would have purchased at any price, but that of my own esteem! I rose, and shook myself; opened the window, and methought the air never smelled so sweet . . . my imagination collected, in visions sublimely terrible, or soothingly beautiful, an immense variety of the endless images, which nature affords, and fancy combines, of the grand and fair.*[3]

I realized that I wanted this freedom from the marriage plot—to not have it be the defining feature of my life, to experience the thrill and hope of a major detour. More importantly, I was to unleash my mind and imagination. I grasped an additional meaning in Wollstonecraft's words: the only one who can ultimately save you is you.

And so, in mid-October, I visited New York City, secured an adjunct teaching position that would start in January, and made a plan to move there before the start of the semester.

I was leaving behind a solid job, a community, and a good, kindhearted partner. Now that I was the agent of my life, I would be fully responsible for any failures. I felt terrified and alive.

Into the Hands of Virginia Woolf

I rented a bedroom in a shared apartment, a fifth-floor walk-up on Second Avenue. My room was small but had large windows, and I could see the street below and the rooftops across the way. My mattress was on a makeshift loft under which was most of the room's floor space. There I kept my suitcase, which doubled as a dresser, and a small wooden chair on which I kept my briefcase, books, and pens. The kitchen attracted cockroaches of different sizes, which appeared in waves after a disturbance on the other side of the wall. In the bathroom hung two small ink drawings, one of a man pissing standing up and another of him sitting down. Choose your pleasure, it seemed to say. My roommate, Freddie, was a gregarious medical student, and when he wasn't working a shift or out with his boyfriend, we'd order takeout from East Village Thai and watch reality TV on the shabby couch in the living room. Otherwise, I had the place to myself. I was happy. In the evening the avenue below quivered with conversations and shrieks of laughter.

I longed to discover the sort of person I was—the sort of thinker—now that I wasn't seeing myself through the lens of a man.

I got so much satisfaction from basic activities, like going to the store and buying whatever I wanted to eat, making friends with people I liked, picking out used books that interested me. Small things, childish even. I strolled through the Lower East Side for hours

admiring the details of buildings, people, and stores; I struck up
conversations with strangers and made new friends. I lingered on
faces in the subway to the point that it was almost rude. It was hard
to stop. Now that my subjectivity was on the loose, my days felt slow
and rich, as if anything could yield the miracle of meaning. The
existentialists wrote about the angst following the realization that we
have no guide but ourselves in this life, and although I felt some of
that anxiety, I was elated as well. I was filling a primal, psychic need
to experience myself.

Weekday mornings I went to work at a university in Jamaica,
Queens, a diverse middle-class neighborhood. To get there, I took
the F train to the second-to-last stop, where retail shops gave way to
homes with yards, and walked up a long hill to campus. From the
top I could see the towers of Manhattan in the distance. The chair
of the department, Jim, a tall man in his fifties with a kind face, was
impressed with my teaching recommendations and years of experience, and offered me three courses, the maximum number an adjunct
could teach per semester. I felt irrepressible. My heart filled with
pride. I had gotten this job on my own—without any help from Alex.

Teaching days were my greatest joys. Most of my students were
students of color and the first in their families to attend college. I
taught the philosophy of the human person and feminist philosophy.
Halfway through the semester, Jim told me about a full-time job that
would open up in about a year in the department. It was a four-year
contract with health insurance that he wanted to offer to me when
the time came, but he wanted me to know it wasn't renewable. After
the stock market crash the year before, the department had been
forced by administrators to scale back in size. Nearly half the students
were on financial aid, and the university didn't have a large endow-
ment. When professors retired from their tenured positions, the dean
was not filling those positions but instead hiring adjunct staff with
limited-term contracts. The philosophy department needed teachers
for their classes, and bowing to institutional pressure, Jim hired more

adjuncts. I realized that was partly how I had found a teaching job on such short notice. Jim hated the situation and rubbed his eyes with his palms in frustration. Nevertheless, the four-year full-time job sounded incredible to me. It meant I could stay in the city for at least the next few years; I had enough in my savings account to get me through until the four-year job opened up. I told Jim I wanted the contract when it became available.

Of course, I was also only delaying the inevitable. Once the contract ended, I would go on the job market for a post that was unlikely to be in or near New York City. I would be competing with hundreds of other applicants from excellent universities, applicants who had rave recommendation letters and whose areas of research were far more in demand than mine: early modern women philosophers. I was coming to terms with a fact of my profession that I had happily ignored until I'd resigned my tenure-track job in Iowa: the job market was grim, and I would most likely need to find another line of work.

Still, I wasn't quite ready to give up.

In a last-ditch effort to secure a future in professional philosophy, I wrote to my advisers in my graduate program and let them know I was interested in any leads for job opportunities. I needed to build up my curriculum vitae in order to be competitive. One adviser did eventually reach out. He emailed to say he was writing an article for a top publisher and wanted to include a discussion of Astell. He was using a similar framework to the one I'd used in my dissertation, though he didn't refer to my work.

"Does it make sense?" he asked me. My heart leapt into my throat. I thought, *He wants to know what I think. I'm not the idiot I suspected I was in my darkest moments.* I wrote to him immediately, affirming that his idea made sense. I told him I was happy to help.

Then I grew skeptical. I reread the email and noticed that the attached proposal for his paper, which he'd already sent to the publisher, stated his intention to include Astell. The thought crossed my mind that perhaps he wasn't asking for clarification so much as for permission. I clicked on his web page and saw he'd recently held a conference on early modern women philosophers. He hadn't invited me, although I was a short train trip away and other junior scholars had attended. Going to the conference would have been a great boost for my curriculum vitae and a chance to network with other scholars in my field. He'd given up on me before I'd given up on myself. So I wrote to him, carefully wording my reply: "If my dissertation has somehow inspired your work, would you consider giving me credit or taking me on as a co-contributor?" He didn't respond. When his article came out, he didn't include Astell. Those whom I needed to take me seriously weren't, and the one person who was, Jim, couldn't do much to help.

On teaching days, once class ended, I headed to the campus library to develop my scholarship. My fascination with early women philosophers had led me to look into contemporary feminist thought. The past few years I'd been reading and teaching more feminist philosophy, in awe of the incredible depth and breadth of the field, which spoke expressly to the confusion and loss of confidence I'd felt over the years.

Nonetheless I remained captivated by early women philosophers. I knew them intimately, and the more I read, the more meaning I derived from their texts. The struggle to bring myself into focus as a woman thinker had taken on a greater historical dimension. A part of me became clearer to myself when I attended to the expanding circle of women thinkers of the past. Insofar as I identified as a woman, the story of how they addressed their predicaments as women was part of my story of myself.

I discovered that the questions I was interested in weren't the ones that editors of philosophy journals tended to care about. I was framing my ideas in a personal way—and not in a way you would find in traditional scholarship. My desire to know myself as a thinking woman and to express my self-discoveries in written form was crucial

to my endeavor. I didn't want to disconnect my story from those of
the female philosophers who had come before me or from the long
tradition of feminist scholarship. There was an interconnectedness
there, and when I tried to separate myself out, I also seemed to undo
my motivation for the project altogether.

At the same time, I began to think that the pressure to remove
myself from my philosophical work was symptomatic of the habitual
suppression of women's voices and concerns in mainstream philosophy. Was it possible that academia wasn't the best place for me to continue to develop as a thinker? That my personal quest to know myself
as a woman intellectual and my appreciation for early women philosophers would bear fruit only outside the bounds of the academy?

The twentieth-century English philosopher and novelist Iris
Murdoch was fascinated by philosophy and literature—both "truth-
seeking activities" but with important differences. "Philosophical
writing is not self-expression, it involves a disciplined removal of the
personal voice," she said. Whereas literature is inextricably bound to
the lives of people: "When we return home and 'tell our day,' we are
artfully shaping material into story form."[1] Murdoch gave an example
for emphasis: "You could read all the works of Kant with impassioned
interest, and at the end of it have very little idea what Kant was like
internally, as a human being." I knew what she meant—this imper-
sonal viewpoint was consonant with my philosophical training. But
I was exploring a psychic and intellectual geography that was taking
me further from professional philosophy as I knew it and into a
strange hybrid land of philosophy and personal narrative that seemed
more authentic and moving than my purely scholarly work. Once I
acknowledged that a future in academia wasn't likely—a truth that
brought me great sadness—I was freed up to pursue my inquiry
wholeheartedly and follow it wherever it took me, something that
also brought me not exactly happiness but satisfaction.

Not knowing where my research and introspection would ultimately lead me, I continued taking notes. I was interested in how

early women philosophers had not been completely lost to history despite their omission from the canon. How, after centuries, had their works wended their way into the hands of other thinkers and writers, such as Virginia Woolf? The answer became clearer to me after I learned the story of George Ballard.

Ballard was an eighteenth-century English historian from Gloucestershire whose obsession with the past had begun as a hobby.[2] As a boy, he collected old coins and stayed up late into the night studying them by candlelight. As a teenager, he joined a loose network of like-minded armchair antiquarians. They shared stories about the treasures they unearthed and relished how each discovery transformed, however slightly, their understanding of their country's history.

When he was around twenty, Ballard was hired by a wealthy landowner, Richard Graves, who paid him to comb the land for ancient Greek and Roman coins. He loved the hunt and was good at it. Overall, he walked nearly fifteen hundred miles and turned up over five hundred coins. To deepen his understanding of history, he taught himself Latin and Anglo-Saxon. When he turned twenty-one, he asked Graves and some other wealthy patrons whether he should apply to Oxford to study antiquities. They strongly urged against it, their main reason being that Ballard and his family did not have enough money for tuition. His father, a chandler who sold wax, soap, and candles, had died when Ballard was four years old, and his mother earned a meager living as a village midwife. Ballard, who was a dressmaker, continued in his trade to supplement what he earned hunting for antiquities. To save money on rent, he lived with his mother, and together they served the local women: "Mrs. Ballard delivered their babies and George Ballard made their dresses."[3]

In 1735, his amateur skills were put to the test. A new vicar announced his plans to raze a local church. Ballard was offended by the vicar's lack of historical and aesthetic sensibility: "What can infuse such Monstrous Barbarisme into his Capricious Brains to Demolish such an Elegant Monument?" Ballard decided to try to save the church. He summoned his knack for cataloguing, cultivated over years of numismatics, and made a careful inventory of the church's artistic features. Then he composed a passionate letter, in which he implored an influential landowner to stop the "scandalous proceeding." It worked, and the church was preserved.

Ballard, now twenty-nine years old, came away from this experience with a newfound confidence.[4] This encouraged him to embark on a new, more daring project that came to him unexpectedly. He was altering the dress of a client who knew about his penchant for history and so recommended he get in touch with a friend of hers who shared that penchant. This friend was Elizabeth Elstob, a former scholar of Saxon history and literature affiliated with Oxford. At the height of her career, Elstob had been responsible for the translation of many Saxon works into English, but her luck had changed. Her brother and co-researcher had died, and now, as a female scholar working alone, she struggled to secure funding. Even at the height of her academic research, she faced questions about her authorship: "I have been askt . . . more than once, whether this Performance was all my own."[5] She was past middle age and had nearly given up on her dreams for academic greatness. She was teaching English to schoolchildren.

When Ballard met Elstob for the first time, he was greeted by an exhausted woman who confessed to have scant energy left for research. She described herself with "no time to do anything till six at night when I have done the Duty of the day and am then frequently so fatigu'd that I am oblig'd to lye down for an hour or two to rest my self and recover my Spirits." But Elstob enjoyed talking with Ballard. The two continued to meet and exchange letters, bonding over their status on the margins of scholarship, and their friendship deepened.

Elstob spoke about her struggle to flourish in a profession dominated by men who did not take her seriously. When she felt deflated by her male colleagues, she read through the journal in which she'd collected short biographies of ambitious women of England. She would immediately feel better thinking about the stories of other smart women who somehow found a way to create.

Through his friendship with Elstob, Ballard became interested in forgotten British women writers. "I know not how it hath happened," he said, "that very many ingenious women of this nation, who were really possess'd of a great share of learning, and have, no doubt, in their time been famous for it, are not only unknown to the publick in general, but have been passed by in silence by our greatest biographers." He decided to write their biographies to prevent their loss from history. Elstob helped him find a publisher.

Ballard told his friends that they lived in the age of biography, and he believed that his book would be an exemplar of the genre. He recruited some of his friends to search for details about the ingenious women in libraries, letters, and interviews. Damaris Masham and Mary Astell were among the women he wrote about in his book.

By 1749, Ballard had devoted thirteen years to his tome. His friends started calling him St. George for his defense of the women of England. He had proven to members of Oxford that he was a serious historian, despite spending most of his time tailoring dresses and making hats. He was offered a job as a librarian at the Bodleian Library and housing at Magdalen College. Now he could devote himself to his project, and within a year he had completed a full draft of his manuscript. What excited him most was the thought of introducing these brilliant women to the world. He also couldn't help casting judgment on those who had overlooked them. For example, in the chapter about Masham, just after he introduces her critique of patriarchy, he gets bristly:

> These are some of the many Observations which the Virtu-
> ous and excellently knowing Lady then made on the Tyr-
> ranick Insolence, Oppressive and Monopolizing Tempers
> of the generallity of the Gentlemen at that Time: And this

Erroneous and Pityful way of thinking is still as preva-
lent as ever; for I don't find that their Judgments are in
the least Reform'd . . . Nay, even many of those Gentle-
men who admire Female Literature . . . will nevertheless
generally close their Encomiums with this genteel (tho
perhaps undesign'd) Sarcasm; that they Acted above their
Sex. Complaisantly spoken indeed! Well, be it so, and I
heartily wish that they would act above theirs, and we
should soon see the World more Happy and Wise.[6]

I rubbed my eyes and reread that section many times. How refreshing and wonderful to hear such a defense of women from a man! And what delicious bitterness! What scrumptious anger!

The male writers he shared a draft with didn't feel the same way he did. In fact, they were offended. They recommended he strike this passage on Masham and similar passages. Ballard aspired to be remembered as a significant contributor to the art of biography, but without his passionate remarks he felt the essence of his work was lost. "Many are the Attacks I have met with from a great variety of Gentlemen," he wrote. "To be reproached by those who have long labour'd in the Republic of Letters . . . is like receiving Wounds in the Houses of one's friends."[7] Still, he wanted to publish his book and so he bowed to pressure and excised the passages in which he offered strong defenses of women. In 1752, he published *Memoirs of Several Ladies of Great Britain, Who Have Been Celebrated for Their Writings or Skill in the Learned Languages, Arts and Sciences.* To his disappointment, it did not sell well outside his immediate circle of supporters. Ballard's health had started to deteriorate, and three years later he died.[8] A friend reported that it was because of a "too intense application to his studies."[9]

I learned that Ballard was one of many writers, a number of them men, who sought to shore up women thinkers and secure a place for them in history. Their works included Charles Gerbier's *The*

Praise of Worthy Women (1651); John Shirley's *The Illustrious History of Women* (1686); Gille Ménage's *A History of Women Philosophers* (1690); Rev. John Duncombe's poem "Feminiad" (1751); William Alexander's two-volume *The History of Women from the Earliest Antiquity, to the Present Time* . . . (1783); and Mary Hays's six-volume *Female Biography, or, Memoirs of Illustrious and Celebrated Women of All Ages and Countries* (1803). One of my favorite champions of women authors was Elizabeth Ogilvy Benger, who in 1791, as a girl of thirteen, wrote an epic poem to "celebrate the female writers" and prevent them from "fading laurels." It's possible Benger was drawing on Ballard's work when she wrote this passage: "Astill and Mashham female learning fir'd, / Their bright example every breast inspir'd."[10] Virginia Woolf read some of these sources, or, like Ballard, came across them indirectly through other obscure sources, and added them to her own collection of biographies of women writers from the past.[11]

Despite these writers' best efforts, most people still don't know the women they wrote about. Many things fuel the suppression of women's voices and make it a challenge to keep them in our collective memory. In her 1983 book *How to Suppress Women's Writing*, Joanna Russ mentions the denial of agency, double standards, false categorizing, and anomalousness, to name just a few.[12] But in the field of philosophy, I realized, there was an additional obstacle to honoring women's contributions. That was the conception of philosophy itself. The history of philosophy that I learned about in my college classes was, for the most part, a limited narrative that a few individuals in the nineteenth century decided would define philosophy: the rise of Kant and how the problem of knowledge came to be the central problem of philosophy.

Of course, many pre-Kantian thinkers did not fit nicely into this new framework. Some were interested in questions of the good life and self-cultivation, topics that Kant relegated to the field of "moral anthropology." The historian Johann Jakob Brucker had included Asian, African, and Native American philosophies in volume one of his 1742 history of philosophy. (The Greeks showed up in volume two.) These ideas were expressly omitted from Kantian-inspired histories.[13] Women philosophers were also excluded, certainly because of sexism but also because the topic of the condition of women wasn't considered to be philosophical on Kantian grounds.

This "it began with Kant" history of philosophy came to dominate in universities across Europe and still influences how philosophy courses, textbooks, and scholars consider the history of philosophy today. There are incredible scholars working to rectify the wrongs of the canon, for instance by reintroducing women and people of color back into it; it's a fascinating time to investigate the history of the discipline.

My investigation revealed to me something I didn't expect: the female gaze is not a twentieth-century invention. It did not start with the suffragists, it did not begin with Mary Wollstonecraft, and it is definitely not unique to the West. It's at least as old as philosophy itself. Women philosophers were not late to the scene; it seems they were there from the start, and they had much to say about their oppressive condition. It's a fact hard to appreciate, because for most of history the burden of acquiring and sharing knowledge of women thinkers rested on the individual, the enthusiast, the eccentric.

Fortunately, this is changing. Scholars in critical studies programs that emerged in the latter half of the twentieth century, with support from institutions of higher learning, have created a rich body of knowledge about women thinkers that continues to grow—even though critical lines of inquiry are still not embraced by many practitioners of philosophy.

It's not that there have been no women. It's not that no one has cared. Many people have. Some men have. That's what I found so unnerving: women philosophers weren't exactly forgotten; they were just never integrated into the canon. It's a failure of imagination and morality on the part of certain historians because these women were not isolated; they were a part of the conversation about the social and philosophical issues of their day. For too long we have ignored the dissenting voices that complicate the canon. The men of the Enlightenment were brave thinkers challenging traditional modes of thought, but the women of the Enlightenment were also brave, highlighting the ways in which men's thinking fell short of their own ideals. The reward for such courageous thinking shouldn't be a precarious spot in history.

Some evenings after I got home from teaching in Queens, I'd sit on my loft bed and spread my notes about women philosophers out before me. I felt a strange thrill in the gesture, just like I imagined Elstob experiencing hundreds of years before. I wondered what it would have been like to have heard the stories of these women thinkers earlier in my life. To have absorbed their great diversity of responses to the phenomenon of being a woman from when I was first exposed to art, literature, and philosophy. Would my life have been different? Would I have cared less about dominant cultural codes that taught me my autonomous selfhood didn't matter much? Would I know what it means to think like a woman?

Bedtime Stories

Very little is known about philosopher Gārgī Vācaknavī, who lived in India twenty-eight hundred years ago. Some things I want to know: When did she first notice her hunger for abstraction? Did she study with her father the sage? Did the "woman question," in some distant yet familiar form, haunt her psyche, too?

Her story, reported in an ancient text, goes something like this.[1] King Janaka, the Hindu king of Videha, invited the brightest minds of his kingdom to his court for a debate, promising to reward the wisest with the prize of gold and a thousand cows. Gārgī was among the guests and the only woman of the sizeable gathering invited to speak. At the start, Yājñavalkya, a famed Hindu philosopher, who said he was the superior debater, claimed the prize for himself without ever debating, which angered the other sages and kicked off a fierce debate. Each sage took a turn arguing against him but dropped away in defeat. Only Gārgī was able to hold her own.

She was fascinated by the nature of reality and suspected that water underpinned everything. (Over a century later, the first Greek philosopher, Thales, proposed a similar idea.) She was also concerned that such a belief could slip into infinite regress: What substance supported water, and in turn, what substance supported that? She asked Yājñavalkya this question, and then another. Yājñavalkya shot back: "Gārgī, do not ask too many questions, or your head will shatter apart."[2] She questioned him further.

What's interesting is that Gārgī, clearly the superior debater, did not take the prize. Perhaps she understood that because she was a woman, the award was never hers to have.[3] At the end of the debate, Gārgī turned to the other sages and declared Yājñavalkya the winner—a gesture that when seen from a certain angle placed her in the superior position of judge. She told the sages: "None of you will defeat him." But perhaps she thought she had.

Another woman of renown in King Janaka's time was Sulabhā, a Hindu nun known for her mastery of rhetoric and yoga who wandered the land on her own in pursuit of truth and freedom—an existence she much preferred to marriage.[4] She believed there was no difference between men's and women's minds and that women could also be sages.[5] When she heard that Janaka believed himself to be wise, she had her doubts. So she traveled to meet him and learn for herself.

Upon her arrival at court, she addressed Janaka: "Most excellent seer in the Kuru line of kings! Who has acquired the training using understanding alone, without giving up the householding life? Tell me the true principles of Absolute Freedom."[6] For Sulabhā, wisdom was a form of spiritual freedom that required a state of detachment, and it was unclear how such freedom could coexist with power. Janaka told her he'd studied with a great sage who taught him how to be both free from the world and in control of it, an argument that did not persuade Sulabhā. This only angered the king, who questioned whether her claim to freedom was due to insight, as she professed. "Or maybe you are on your own, free of a husband through some fault of your own," he said. He added that her yoga, which she was practicing as he spoke, perturbed him.

Now Sulabhā had the answer she sought. That she could disturb Janaka so easily was evidence he was not free or wise. And as for her lack of husband, she said, "Since there was no husband suitable to me, I was trained in the rules for gaining Absolute Freedom." She thanked Janaka for his time and promised to depart in the morning after a good night's sleep. Alone.

Around the start of the sixth century BCE, while some of the first Greek male philosophers were putting forth their ideas, Cleobulina of Rhodes accepted the job of soaping and scrubbing men's calloused and warty feet. It was a calculated move on her part. These feet belonged to the thinkers who came to the home of her father, one of the "seven sages of Greece," and this was her opportunity to discuss philosophy while fulfilling her female duties.[7] Her mind grew sharp as she lathered toes and exchanged ideas about reality. She eventually wrote a work of mind-bending riddles that would be celebrated for hundreds of years and that Aristotle would admire.[8]

In the third century BCE, the Pythagorean philosopher Phintys defended women's right to study philosophy. "Now, perhaps many think it is not fitting for a woman to philosophize, just as it is not fitting for her to ride horses or speak in public," she said. "I say that courage and justice and wisdom are common to both sexes."[9]

Other fragments believed to be written by Pythagorean women philosophers suggest they didn't challenge traditional gender roles so much as double down on them.[10] They wrote that a woman is to be a good wife: she is modest (even her elbow is covered), raises the children, isn't adulterous, yet endures her husband's regular visits to prostitutes.

It seems, then, the Pythagorean women were welcome to express their thoughts—as long as they conformed to the male prerogative.

Aspasia was a prominent member of Athenian society in the fifth century BCE and consort to Athenian general and statesman Pericles.

Originally from Miletus, Aspasia was a resident alien in Athens, a status that prevented her from legally marrying Pericles, and so to make herself acceptable to elite society, she adopted the title of hetaira, a high-class prostitute.[11] Ancient and modern historians get tangled up in questions of whether she was in fact a courtesan or if she ran a harem. But I find her fascinating for additional reasons. She taught rhetoric, and one of her more famous students was Socrates.[12] She described the natural world without reference to deities. Because of this, she may have been put on trial for questioning the gods' authority—years before Socrates faced a similar charge.[13]

Diotima was another teacher of Socrates and appears in Plato's dialogue the *Symposium*. Socrates says her thinking inspired his own about love, knowledge, and immortality. Still, some historians tell us that she did not exist, which, if true, would make her the only fictional person Plato created.[14]

Around 375 BCE, in the lush valley of the ancient Greek city Cyrene (in what is modern Libya), lived a woman called Arete. Her father was a student of Socrates who opened his own school of philosophy, which Arete eventually took over. She taught theories of nature and morality to more than one hundred students and wrote forty works of philosophy, although nothing of her writing remains.[15] It's a shame. I wonder how much of her intellectual vision was like her father's, which advocated indulgence in immediate pleasures, including having sex with prostitutes.[16]

Did Arete acknowledge the ethical dilemma of what to do if the immediate pleasures of the courtesan were in direct conflict with those of her john? Or perhaps women's subjectivity flowed past her, just as it had flowed past her father, invisibly, as air.

*   *   *

After reading Plato's *Republic*, Axiothea left her home in the Spartan-ruled mountain valley of Phlius to study with Plato. Around the same time, another woman, Lasthenia, left her home in the highlands of Arcadia to do the same. There are no records of their ideas or whether they composed original works. What impressed ancient historians was that they were allowed into Plato's Academy and that they wore men's clothes.[17]

In the third century BCE in Greece, the philosopher Hipparchia fell in love with the Cynic philosopher Crates, telling her parents she would kill herself if they wouldn't let her marry him. Crates warned Hipparchia that he had no wealth and could only offer her the life of a philosopher.[18] She wanted that life, even though it entailed justifying herself to ornery men at dinner symposiums. To one such drunk interlocutor, a man who could not keep up with her argumentation and so resorted to criticizing her housework while lifting up her tunic, she said, "Do you think I have done wrong to spend on the getting of knowledge all the time which, because of my sex, I was supposed to waste at the loom?"[19]

In 310 CE, a century or so before western Mediterranean civilization would dip into an age of relative darkness, lived a woman named Sosipatra.[20] She was the rare woman philosopher who was also a mother. (The next mother-philosopher in the West that we know about is Heloise, who lived eight hundred years later.)

After her husband left or died—the ancient sources aren't clear which—Sosipatra raised her three sons alone in Pergamum, a vibrant city sixteen miles from the coast of the Aegean Sea. There, in the comfort of her own home, she founded a school of philosophy and taught theories of the soul and immortality.[21]

* * *

Hypatia, who was born in the late fourth century, was known to be the most brilliant person in all of Alexandria, eclipsing her father, a well-respected mathematician. She chose to be unmarried so she could devote herself to studying and teaching mathematics and philosophy, a decision which some men had trouble respecting.[22] What was a woman to do in this situation? To one pesky suitor Hypatia offered her menstrual rag rather than her hand.

She was fascinated by the geometry of ellipses, composed elegant long-division solutions to astronomical problems, and refined an early version of the astrolabe.[23] As a Neoplatonist philosopher, she believed the ideal world was more real than the material world. Such a view did not keep her from offering political advice. She counseled powerful men to seek discourse over violence in a city fraught with tension between Christian, Jewish, and pagan factions. This was to be her undoing.

In 415 a mob skinned her alive with oyster shells, pulled out her eyes, and dragged her body through the streets. When news of this cruelty reached the rest of the Roman Empire, people were horrified. Ever since, historians have tried to make sense of it: Was she the victim of a crossfire between dueling political factions? Was her death prompted by a hatred and fear of what she symbolized: elitism and paganism? Was the mob ignorant, confusing her astronomy for witchery? Or was it that she was a smart woman with political influence and so seen as a threat to social order?

In the early 700s in Basra, a port city in what is today Iraq, lived Rabia al-Adawiyya, a popular Sufi who taught her theories from her home.[24] Although she did not write down any of her ideas, her followers did, capturing her delightful irreverence.

She insisted that there was no need to cover her face and body as women were expected to do, because there weren't any real men around.[25] To one suitor who asked her to marry him, she responded:

"O sensual one. Seek another sensual like thyself. Hast thou seen any sign of desire in me?" To another: "God can give me all you offer and even double it." Her rejection of marriage—she remained single her whole life—issued from her philosophical commitments.[26] The purpose of life was to unify with God and obliterate the self as much as possible. She said, "The marriage contract is bound to a 'being.' But here 'being' is absent. Of myself I am unaware; alone through Him I am, and under the shadow of His will I exist. My husband must be sought from Him."[27]

She pushed aside the belief shared by many of her male contemporaries that one should fear God. Instead, she promoted a wholly different orientation to the divine, one motivated by a loving passion: "I expect to keep focused on savoring [God's] memory and to free myself from everything else."[28]

One thousand years ago in Japan, a woman, born into the weakest branch of one of the most powerful families, received the coveted position of court lady.[29] Her job was to teach the empress about literature. The other court ladies believed her to be odd: she was pretentious, awkward, and judgmental, and in conversation she was perplexingly meek. Yet she wrote the most incredible stories—some that pleased even the emperor, especially *The Tale of Genji*. It was one of the world's first novels, predating *Don Quixote* by six hundred years, and is still considered a masterpiece. The author's full name is unknown, but she is called Murasaki Shikibu, or Lady Murasaki, after one of her characters. Read one way, *The Tale of Genji* is a story of palace intrigue about the prince and his sexual exploits. Read another, it's a story about the women Prince Genji encounters who often feel "like bits of driftwood" in a male-dominated society. Through reflection on experience and Buddhist philosophy, they discover truths about love and beauty that give them more control over their lives.

* * *

In 1106, at the age of eight, Hildegard of Bingen joined a convent near the Rhine after God told her to.[30] It was one of many visions that came to her over the years, and she used this authority to justify her intellectual life. By the age of forty-two, she reported that because of these visions, she "understood the writings of the prophets, the Gospels, and the other saints, and of certain philosophers, without any human instruction."[31] She wrote multivolume treatises on philosophy, medicine, and the natural world, including the first known account of the female orgasm: "the woman's sexual organs contract . . . in the same way as a strong man can hold something enclosed in his fist."[32] She composed beautiful, eerie chants as well. Hildegard also held that women were men's inferiors, a consequence of Eve's original sin. Yet she believed a woman could overcome this difference. All she had to do was learn—and here she was specific—not from men but from God.

Some men who otherwise didn't believe in the value of women's ideas took Hildegard's insights seriously, convinced that she had direct access to divine knowledge. So when, for example, she told her abbot that "the living light" instructed her to leave and start her own monastery, he relented.

Not all men were as open to her ways. There is a story that at age seventy-six Hildegard traveled by cart to Paris to convince the bishop to integrate her writings into university courses. It didn't work. The universities were consumed by the ideas of Aristotle and his medieval followers.[33]

In the low plain cities of northern Europe in the 1200s emerged strange communities never seen before. Known as beguinages, they were urban collectives for women who wished to escape marriage and devote themselves to a lay religious life. They were self-governed and committed to their members' education. The members, known as beguines, taught one another useful skills including how to read and write and ponder theological ideas. Unlike nuns in convents, beguines were free to leave and marry if they wished. They earned the respect of their local communities because of their commitment to helping the poor. Their existence might be said to be idyllic, except for the occasional infighting and the threat of rape by local men.[34] And the highest spiritual authority in the land, the Catholic Church, pretty much left them alone. Until it didn't.

Some beguines were philosophical, cultivating a new spiritual and intellectual attitude, and, notably, one that departed from church practice.[35] Mechthild of Magdeburg and Hadewijch of Brabant encouraged an informal approach to God without the mediation of clerics. They wrote about Christianity in their mother tongues and allowed women to preach. More controversial was their belief that the ultimate aim of Christian life wasn't to be a virtuous person before God but to lose one's self entirely in Him—to have one's essence to literally disintegrate into the divine essence. "I melted into him and nothing of myself remained," Hadewijch wrote; she wanted "to be God with God." It was audacious and suggested that the beguines had access to a higher form of knowledge than church authorities.[36] Some beguines felt no need to hide this fact either. In an exchange between a beguine and a French church master, the beguine asserted her superiority: "You glow, we take fire. / You assume, we know."[37]

The long decline of the beguines began around 1310, when one of their members, Marguerite Porete, was burned at the stake. Court records report she refused to obey officials' demands that she condemn her ideas. Her book *The Mirror of Simple Souls* was a powerful expression of the beguine idea of folding into God. After Porete's death, the beguines were policed by the church, and membership dropped significantly by the end of the fourteenth century—although not to zero. In 2013 the last beguine died of natural causes in Ghent.[38]

* * *

During the late 1300s and early 1400s, Julian of Norwich, an English mystic, spent her days in a tiny, damp cell attached to her local church. Here she contemplated God and had strange visions. She was convinced they illuminated things that other people should know—things she hoped her *Revelations of Divine Love* would clarify. One of her radical insights: "Jesus Christ . . . is our true Mother."[39]

Birgitta Birgersdotter, born into a Swedish noble family, married at age thirteen and had eight children.[40] After her husband died, in 1344, Jesus appeared to her saying that she was now his bride. She agreed. But it was Jesus's mother, Mary, who walked Birgitta through many of her seven hundred revelations.

Birgitta learned from Mary what divine conception felt like, how it had created in Mary an epistemic shift, making her wiser about everything.[41] Soon Birgitta was again pregnant, but this time with the "word of God." Now full with child of a sort, she had knowledge and authority that men didn't. She was unafraid of controversy and argued against slavery and the Avignon papacy. The pope in Italy, pleased with her message, gave her permission to open her own monastery in Sweden and, after her death years later, canonized her. Her legacy persisted into the Renaissance, inspiring art and philosophy, but it waned during the Reformation, when Martin Luther is rumored to have dismissed her as "Crazy Birgitta."[42]

In 1389, when Christine de Pizan's husband died, leaving her alone with their three children and minimal inheritance, she set out to write for a living. With the support of her French patrons, she wrote over twenty books on a wide range of subjects, including works of political philosophy and biographies of Charles V and Joan of Arc.[43] She was especially drawn to the woman question and wrote about it in *The Book of the City of Ladies.*

In this work, a fictional Christine discovers a book showcasing the sexist ideas of philosophers and poets. After she finishes reading it, she notices "a great unhappiness and sadness welled up in my heart, for I detested myself and the entire feminine sex, as though we were monstrosities in nature."[44] What snaps her out of her funk are three benevolent apparitions, including Lady Reason, who appear with a solution to keep Christine from despair.

Lady Reason tasks Christine with writing a book on the lives and ideas of spectacular women—Sappho, Minerva, Esther, Mary Magdalene, Clotilde, and others. Like a city, this book will be a populated place, an intellectual refuge where women can visit (in this case, in their minds) and be inspired by other women's examples, so they will never again forget themselves in the sea of men's disparaging words. Lady Reason tells Christine that this city will be "extremely beautiful, without equal, and of perpetual duration in the world."

Pizan was celebrated in her day, and her manuscripts were housed in libraries in France, Brussels, and London. During the Renaissance, her work was translated into English, and copies found their way into the hands of Queen Elizabeth I of England and the philosopher Margaret Cavendish.[45] By the late seventeenth century, however, almost no one had heard of her, and except for a few separate attempts to publish her writings, her work wasn't revived until the late twentieth century by a few feminist scholars.[46]

Starting with the birth of her first child in 1394 and continuing after the births of her thirteen other children, Margery Kempe of England had visions of Christ. It was an awkward development, because she wasn't the typical vessel for God's revelations: she was not a man or a nun, and she enjoyed sex. Still, she was determined to explore this religious side germinating in herself. In an effort to become holier— that is, virgin-like—she wore bridal-white clothing and stopped having sex with her husband. This decision wasn't difficult to carry out, because she left him behind when she went on her long pilgrimages to holy sites in Europe and Asia.

On one of her journeys, she met with Julian of Norwich, who told her to trust herself and the voices. But some churchmen questioned whether Kempe's visions were holy and charged her with heresy. To defend herself, she dictated a book in 1436 titled *The Book of Margery Kempe*, the first autobiography written in English and a work infused with philosophical and theological ideas. It included maternal insights, too, which she believed people should adopt whether or not they were mothers: "Make every Christian man and woman your child in your soul."[47]

Around 1584, by age eighteen or nineteen, Marie le Jars de Gournay had taught herself Latin and Greek and become an expert on French literature. She was especially drawn to the work of Montaigne, whose *Essays* moved her. His work "revealed me to myself," she explained.[48] She wrote him a letter of admiration and they soon became friends. She went on to write fiction and translations of Cicero, Tacitus, and Virgil. She also wrote the treatise *The Equality of Men and Women*, in which she identifies the cause of women's relative underperformance in intellectual spheres: "If the ladies arrive less frequently to the heights of excellence than do the gentlemen, it is because of this lack of good education. It is sometimes due to the negative attitude of the teacher and nothing more. Women should not permit this to weaken their belief that they can achieve anything."[49]

In Holland in the early seventeenth century, at a time when doctors believed women's wombs roamed their bodies like vagabonds, Anna Maria van Schurman learned fourteen languages and wrote a book in Latin on Amharic grammar.[50] One night she had a strange dream in which a woman named Lady Philosophy told her she would be a famous writer. Emboldened, van Schurman applied to the local university, which admitted only men. She was accepted on the condition that during class she would sit behind a curtain.[51] She said yes, though I imagine during those lectures she must have boiled with anger in her seat. For after van Schurman finished her studies, she wrote a book arguing that her genius was not exceptional and that women ought to have a full education. When the rector of the University of Utrecht asked her to write a poem to commemorate its opening, she included these bold lines: "But, you may ask, what is bothering you? / Well, these sacred halls are inaccessible to women! / The sowing and reaping that will be done here, should be for each and everyone."[52]

Despite Elisabeth's royal ties (she was also known as Princess of Bohemia), no institute of learning would admit her. So she exchanged letters with brilliant people instead. In 1639, she wrote to van Schurman, kicking off a lifelong friendship.[53] Their heroes—for van Schurman, the Aristotelian philosopher Voetius, and for Elisabeth, the groundbreaking Descartes—despised one another. But van Schurman and Elisabeth corresponded about their own intellectual differences, and each took pleasure encountering the mind of another thinking woman.

Elisabeth also exchanged letters about philosophical matters with Descartes for nine years and was the first to identify a central problem in his epistemology.[54] She argued that his conception of the mind and body—two substances that are totally unlike one another yet somehow interact—was problematic. "I beseech you," she wrote to him, "tell me how the soul of man (since it is but a thinking substance) can determine the spirits of the body to produce voluntary actions."[55] He was impressed and dedicated his 1644 treatise *Principles of Philosophy* to her, saying she was "the only person I have so far found who has completely understood all my previously published works."[56]

Descartes corresponded with other philosophers, including Hobbes and Pierre Gassendi, who appear in a famous edition of Descartes's texts that students and professors study today.[57] Elisabeth is not included—though I've heard that sometimes her letters are photocopied and passed around in class.

In 1654, Margaret Lucas married William Cavendish, First Duke of Newcastle upon Tyne, who was thirty years older than her and well connected. He introduced her to a group of intellectuals he sponsored called the "Cavendish Circle," which included Hobbes and Gassendi. Margaret had no formal education beyond dance, music, reading, and writing, but she loved this salon.

She wrote to Hobbes on numerous occasions, and he ignored every single letter she sent. Still, her thinking and writing knew few bounds, and she composed poems, plays, fiction, and scientific and philosophical treatises. Her writerly voice could be thrillingly puckish. In the preface to *The Blazing World*, a work of science fiction, she said she was "as Ambitious as ever any of my Sex was, is or can be." Since she would never rule the world, like Alexander the Great or Henry V, she turned to fiction and "made One of my own." In this world, her female protagonist, Duchess Margaret, meets the male species—"Fly-men," "Worm-men," and "Fish-men"—who, unlike Earthmen, willingly engage with her about mathematics and philosophy.[58] Here, souls are able to leave bodies and inhabit others. When she is asked whose soul she would like, the duchess replies, "I'le have the Soul of one of the most famous modern Writers, as either of Galileo, Gassendus, Des Cartes, Helmont, Hobbes, H. More, &c." She is told none of these souls would agree to live in her body, because they were "so self-conceited, that they would scorn to be Scribes to a Woman."[59]

Cavendish was the first woman allowed into a meeting of the Royal Society in London. An eccentric, she attended the meeting in a stunning outfit that left bystanders gasping. Some sources say she was bare breasted and her nipples painted red.[60] This purported sartorial decision, which I, too, have a hard time not seeing, is often what history remembers of her—when it remembers her at all.

In 1659, in a village in the shadow of Popocatépetl, a volcano in what is now central Mexico, a precocious girl of eight who taught herself to read and write declared her wish to dress as a boy so she could enroll at the male-only university.[61] She did not get her wish, but a few years later she earned a spot in the royal court of New Spain as a lady-in-waiting, where she was allowed to study. At twenty-one, she didn't want to marry and so entered a convent. She became Sor Juana Inés de la Cruz and lived in her chambers as if it were a literary salon. Here she had a library of over fifteen hundred books, along with various mathematical, scientific, and musical instruments. She also wrote poetry, plays, letters, and treatises, with a commitment to reason inspired by Descartes. She criticized men's double standards in a poem titled "You Stupid Men."

Rich and powerful members of the court funded her work, and by age forty-two she was financially independent. This irked male church superiors. She critiqued a church member, which further enraged them. Then she composed a bold defense of women's right to knowledge and equality with men. For this, church authorities condemned her to silence. She tried ignoring their verbal persecution for a few years and continued with her writing, but over time it wore her down.

When a series of floods caused widespread famine across Mexico, she took it as a sign that God preferred her silence after all.[62] She gave away her entire library, except for three religious texts, and spent her final days helping the sick and the poor. (It was then that she contracted a plague, which some suspect was a death wish, and died.)

*   *   *

In 1721, in the prosperous kingdom of Joseon on the Korean Peninsula, a girl named Im Yunjidang was born to the gentry. She was educated by her five older brothers, who taught her Confucian texts typically forbidden to girls, including *Exemplary Women of Early China*, written around 77 BCE, about the lives of women who studied and wielded power.[63]

Yunjidang married at nineteen but lost both her husband and an infant daughter by age twenty-six. As was customary for widows, she devoted herself to caring for her deceased husband's family. What wasn't customary was what she did at night. Her brother-in-law remarked that "sometimes, when I saw the flickering light of her lamp through my window I knew that the scholar was secretly engaged in the purposeful activity of inquiry and study." She wrote philosophical works, biographies, and poems which were inscribed on objects, including a mirror and a sword. Yunjidang also believed herself a Confucian scholar on the path to sagehood.

Confucius, born in 551 BCE, didn't theorize much about women. His followers in China, Japan, and Korea had more to say on the subject, however, and over two thousand years later, in the time of Yungjidang, most Neo-Confucian thinkers assumed that women were men's inferiors.[64] But Yungjidang wasn't convinced. Her careful study of Confucian texts persuaded her that women were men's spiritual and moral equals: "Though I am a woman, still, the nature I originally received contained no distinction between male and female."

Not that she was immune to seeing the world through the eyes of a woman. In a way, this is one of her philosophy's great strengths. She was sensitive to women's plight, which made her interpretations of Confucian texts more novel and textured. In one of her discourses, for instance, Yunjidang considers the tale of On Gyo, an envoy of the king who chose to leave on a dangerous mission, despite his mother's misgivings: she was so distraught that she grabbed tightly to his lapel as he was trying to leave, ripping the hem as he brusquely turned and departed. Many Confucian writers defend On's decision as noble and loyal. Not Yunjidang. She asked, Why didn't he take a moment to talk to his mother and work it out? He could have sat with her, listened to her thoughts and feelings, and shared his own. Yunjidang says it's possible and even likely that On's mother would have come around, and his moral dilemma between the duty to his parent and the duty to his ruler would have dissolved. The tragedies of men, she suggests, are sometimes grandiose fabrications of their own making.

Decades later in the same kingdom, a woman named Gang Jeonggild-ang read Yunjidang's work.[65] She and her husband were poor, sometimes going days without food. Most of her waking hours were spent supporting her family so that her husband could devote his time to studying. But when her domestic work was done, it was her turn. She wrote, "Although I am just a housewife, shut in the inner room, not hearing or knowing anything, I read the ancient classics between needlework and cleaning, and ponder deeply their meaning so that I may emulate their example and follow those who cultivated themselves in the past."[66]

In 1733, Émilie du Châtelet, a French woman with great mathematical talent, met Voltaire. The two soon became lovers and moved into her country home together with her children—an affair her husband is thought to have tolerated. She hired some of the best mathematicians to tutor her, and soon her skills outstripped Voltaire's.

Voltaire wrote that du Châtelet was "a great man whose only fault was being a woman." (He also said that "all the arts have been invented by man, not by woman.")[67] Yet he admired her mind, as his book on Newton's optics was indebted to du Châtelet's essay on optics. He never explicitly acknowledged her contribution to his ideas, although he did include her essay along with his papers.[68]

Years later as their relationship fell apart, du Châtelet continued her research. Her magnum opus, *Foundations of Physics*, provided the philosophical groundwork for a Newtonian worldview and shaped the future of science in Europe. Her French translations of Newton's works are still widely read.

Less known today are her thoughts about women. She rejected the notion that they were naturally inferior to men, believing the science to be inconclusive. She wrote that if she were king, she would propose an experiment: "I would reform an abuse which cuts off, so to speak, half the human race. I would make women participate in all the rights of humankind, and above all in those of the intellect."[69]

In the mid-eighteenth century, some gloriously titled reformist books by women were published, such as: *Woman Not Inferior to Man* (1739) by the anonymous "Sophia," and *Inquiry into the Causes Preventing the Female Sex from Studying* (1742) by Dorothea Erxleben, the first female medical doctor in Germany. However, these works were hard to find a few decades later when, after the Reign of Terror in France and the execution of women's rights defender Olympe de Gouges, a more conservative movement gained ground across Europe and numerous philosophers, doctors, and anthropologists agreed that women were different from and inferior to men.[70]

Around 1802, Amalia Holst, a German writer and philosopher, tried to get her hands on Erxleben's book only to discover that it was no longer in print.[71] In an effort to revive the case for improving women's education, Holst published her book *On the Purpose of Woman's Advanced Intellectual Development*. She wanted women to have access to all fields of study, believing them capable of greatness on par with Leibniz and Kant. She wrote: "Do our minds function according to other laws of logic, do they grasp things in the outside world differently than those of men? Just who would desire and dare to make such claims?"[72]

During the early decades of the 1800s, in a region that today is part of Nigeria, Nana Asma'u bint Usman 'dan Fodio, a woman fluent in Arabic, Fulfulde, Hausa, and Tamashek, wrote poems and treatises. She was the daughter of a Sufi Islamic preacher and head of the Sokoto Caliphate, a scholastic Sufi sect that held that women were worthy of learning. Her grandmothers were both erudite, and many other women scholars in their caliphate devoted themselves to reading, writing, and theorizing about complex religious concepts.[73] Asma'u strove to bring this practice to illiterate women. She cleverly tucked complex Sufi ideas into her poems, which she encouraged women to memorize and repeat on their own:

> *You may go out to get food or to seek education.*
> *In Islam, it is a religious duty to seek knowledge.*
> *Women may leave their homes freely for this.*[74]

Asma'u and her associates visited the homes of rural women who could not abandon their domestic duties to learn.[75] Women today still recite her poems.

> *If anyone asks who composed this song say*
> *That it is Nana, daughter of the Shehu, who loves*
>   *Muhammad.*[76]

In 1845, the male-female binary was questioned—if for just a moment—by Margaret Fuller, a nineteenth-century American philosopher: "Male and female represent the two sides of the great radical dualism. But, in fact, they are perpetually passing into one another.

Fluid hardens to solid, solid rushes to fluid. There is no wholly masculine man, no purely feminine woman."[77]

When Lou Andreas-Salomé (1861–1937) is remembered, if she is remembered at all, it is usually as a "muse," a "disciple," or an "intellectual consort."[78] It's ironic, as she prided herself on her independence and invented the psychoanalytic concept of positive narcissism. Her place in historians' minds as a follower was sealed with her male friendships. She was close with some of the most formidable thinkers of nineteenth-century Europe, including Friedrich Nietzsche, Rainer Maria Rilke, and Sigmund Freud—men who admired her intellect and, certainly in the cases of Nietzsche and Rilke, fell in love with her. She studied at the University of Zurich, one of a handful of European universities at the time to enroll women, where she deepened her grasp of German philosophy. She wrote works of fiction and nonfiction and was the first female psychoanalyst. Like many philosophers of the avant-garde who criticized organized religion as a false construct, she was captivated by what it meant to be a person in a secular age.[79] She was also interested in *die Frauenfrage*—the woman question.

Salomé described woman as different from man, a being whose psychology is intuitive and, more importantly, who doesn't need a man to feel whole. She was resistant to the women's movement, believing, as did Nietzsche, that it didn't help to confer self-possession and that it was morally and intellectually mediocre.[80] What Salomé didn't seem to appreciate was how her emancipated lifestyle was not just a product of her own will to power but rather of her privilege as a white woman of aristocratic means.

Hedwig Dohm, a contemporary of Salomé and Nietzsche, thought they could both do better. Dohm was the daughter of a factory owner and the third of eighteen children. She married Ernst Dohm, a newspaper reporter, and their household became a prime meeting spot for the intellectual elite of Berlin. Salomé also visited when she was in town.[81] Dohm had five children with Ernst, and it wasn't until she was forty-one, after her children were grown, that she wrote with fervor.[82] With her newfound freedom, she penned feminist polemics, philosophical essays, and fiction.

She was unsettled by the anti-rights rhetoric in the writings of Salomé, whom she ultimately called an anti-feminist, and in those of Nietzsche, whom she declared a disappointment. In her essay "Nietzsche and Women," she wrote, "Oh Nietzsche! you high, priestly mind, profound knower and yet complete ignoramus on simple matters of truth! You can talk with God and gods, with the stars, the sea, with minds and spirits. You just cannot talk with or about women."[83]

Dohm also thought Nietzsche's psychology of woman to be incomplete. For example, Nietzsche had nothing to say about what motivates a woman who is past her childbearing years. Dohm's 1894 novel, *Become Who You Are*, is her attempt to fill this gap. It's the story of a fifty-four-year-old widow with grown children and her dawning awareness that she has been living through others her entire life. She discovers unknown pleasures, including erotic desire for a man much younger than her. But Dohm's overall message transcended age. She stressed that it was hard for a woman to live in the self-assertive way that Nietzsche admired, because prejudice and economic forces work against her.

Meanwhile in the United States, Charlotte Perkins Gilman published works of fiction and nonfiction in defense of women.[84] She was skeptical of political philosophies that relied on what she saw as the egotistical language of individualism and personality, believing, as had many woman philosophers before her, that they undermined the common good.[85] She even proposed that the best society was one run by and composed entirely of women.[86] Her work of nonfiction titled *Women and Economics*, published in 1898, highlights how economies depend upon women's subordination and unpaid labor—an unfair distribution that has kept women from the means necessary to compete with men outside of the home and in intellectual spheres.[87] Gilman was an exception to the rule, divorcing her first husband and providing for herself and her daughter with her writing.

She also suffered from depression, one of the worst bouts arriving after the birth of her daughter. She committed suicide at age seventy-five, just after writing about the right to die by one's own hand.[88] After her death, her work was hardly mentioned, and her papers sat mildewing in her daughter's house. This changed in the 1970s when her papers were transferred to a university library, and her fiction was revived in feminist circles. Today she is most known for her short story "The Yellow Wallpaper" (1892), a critique of society's dismal treatment of women's mental health.

Gilman also harbored xenophobic and racist views. She was an early advocate of eugenics, and in her novel *Herland*, she depicts a utopian, woman-only society that exists on a plateau above a jungle inhabited by Black savages. Gilman's bigotry didn't go unchallenged even in her day.

There were women intellectuals challenging racism from within the feminist movement in the nineteenth century. As early as 1831, Black feminist Maria W. Stewart wondered, "How long shall the fair daughters of Africa be compelled to bury their minds and talents beneath a load of iron pots and kettles?"[89] In 1851 at a women's rights convention in Akron, Ohio, Sojourner Truth posed the question "Ain't I a woman?" to the white women who ignored Black women in their fight for equality.[90] In 1892, philosopher Anna Julia Cooper published her book of essays and speeches titled *A Voice from the South: By a*

Black Woman of the South, in which she asks, "Is not woman's cause broader, and deeper, and grander, than a blue stocking debate or an aristocratic pink tea?"[91]

Cooper asked her readers to appreciate the intersecting ways that race, gender, and class influence one's thinking. She wrote that those in power—including white men, politicians, scientists, and white feminists—fail to take responsibility for how bias infiltrates their theories, and that in the name of "truth" and "equality" they perpetuate cruelties in the world and on Black women in particular. (She had a flair for rhetorical zingers, like the one she used in response to the racist and sexist social Darwinists, whose "survival of the fittest" theories she characterized as "survival of the bullies.")[92]

Cooper was disappointed by how philosophy was just a white man's game, perpetuating the white man's perspective. She held that for a genuine assessment of truth and justice, all perspectives must be accounted for, especially those of Black women, which historically had been muted or ignored. "I feel it essential to a perfect understanding . . . that truth from *each* standpoint be presented."[93] She knew that ideas had real-world influence and, depending on how they were framed and pursued, could be detrimental to the livelihood of others. For this reason, the philosopher must not only be truth seeking but also compassionate. Her message was that philosophy was a powerful tool and a privilege that its practitioners must use wisely: "The philosophic mind sees that its own 'rights' are the rights of humanity."[94]

◆◆

During those initial months in New York, I continued to compose a city of women from materials gathered from my university's library. It was solitary work but not entirely lonely. My life comingled with the lives of my subjects as their words and ideas excited neurons in my brain, sent shivers up my spine, and hovered in my consciousness.

These weren't private resurrections but rather part of a vast conjuring by scholars and enthusiasts. Somehow, independent imaginations scattered across time and space had become connected, lifting me up into a communal consciousness where I wandered around in a different philosophy from the one I'd been taught—one that was less male, white, and European, and more human, complex, and alive.

My Animal Self

S till, my animal self longed for intimacy with real, physical bodies. I decided to start dating. I met a man who told me he wanted to play for a band on a cruise ship. I knew he wasn't my type, but as we headed to another bar, I wondered what it would be like to escape, sailing the seas with a bassist. I caught myself—even in daydreams about men I wasn't particularly interested in, I would sometimes go with their plan, not mine—and corrected my course. Over time, these mental reflexes became weaker and more out of step with my being. Like the vestigial legs of some species of snake, they were evidence only of the creature I used to be.

Then I met Marc. He picked me up outside the door of my building, and I noticed he was slightly taller than me, with a beautifully carved chin and cheekbones and a wonderful smile. On our first date, we went to a brewery that another date and I had attempted to visit a week before but had quickly left, daunted by the crowd. It was busier the night Marc and I arrived, but we confessed to each other our obsession with beer and winnowed our way through the crowd, finding a spot in the middle of a picnic table between two other couples. I appreciated that Marc had majored in philosophy and more than anything that he loved ideas but had no interest in refining my arguments. He had his own successful career and a solid group of friends. He was, as he told me not long after we met, "self-sufficient"—a statement that both concerned and intrigued me. I was compelled by the idea of being in a relationship with someone who was his own person and expected the same of his partner. After all, I had come to New York to be self-sufficient. Not long after we started dating, we were exclusive. I wondered whether it was possible to give myself to someone without experiencing self-loss. Could I be in love and continue to build independence?

This question soon joined a chorus of others, because nearly a year later I was pregnant. Marc and I had already decided we were serious about each other, and we were excited to become parents and bring a baby into the world together. Fast-forward to seven weeks after the birth of our son. One night, I was gently rolling our newborn from side to side on my lap. Marc was watching, hoping what I was doing would get the baby to stop crying and go to sleep. To my mind, there was nothing natural about my actions, but a baby book insisted that these motions simulated life in the womb and would calm an infant and even make them "happy." After what felt like ages, it still wasn't working, and I handed our son to Marc, who successfully bounced him back to sleep on an exercise ball. A few hours later, we woke up baggy-eyed at dawn; Marc went to work, and I nursed the baby and stayed home.

I had taken a semester's leave from my job teaching philosophy in Queens and knew I was fortunate to even have the choice. But I was exhausted and confused by my double consciousness. I felt a profound and protective love for my son, but I was also overcome by the sheer tediousness of caring for a newborn. I harbored resentment and felt guilty for my parental ambivalence. Marc didn't make me feel this way. He wanted me to thrive. I was envious, though, of how he missed our son when he was at work but didn't feel guilty about going. Some mornings I wanted to tear my hair out over my decision to stay at home. I felt monstrous for these thoughts.

A few months later, I returned to teaching in Queens. Jim had offered me the four-year full-time job, and I had happily accepted, though I privately acknowledged to myself that it would likely be my final stint as a professor of philosophy. The few posts in my area of specialization were limited term or located in a place where Marc wouldn't be able to pursue his career. Holding out for an academic job seemed more and more foolish. I wanted a livelihood tied to ideas, but the thought of striking out on my own as an independent researcher and writer felt too risky. I enrolled in a part-time master's program in journalism. After a day of teaching in Queens, I would rush to the Upper West Side for class. I had supportive and inspiring professors and discovered science journalism to be a fascinating area that drew on my combined skills of writing and critical thinking.

After class, I would rush again—home to my son. Although I was lit up by using other parts of my mind, I ached to be with him. I wanted release from this torment—or at least to better understand it—and I realized that this was a path well trodden by modern feminist thinkers but not by the canonical philosophers. They give short shrift to the challenge of how a mother can simultaneously do justice to her children and to her potential outside of motherhood. The only canonical male philosopher I know of who semi-appreciated the problem was Plato. He argues that women can participate in public life as men do but only if they are free of child-rearing duties. For this arrangement to work, Plato suggests abolishing the family and raising children in a commune. His solution is unappealing, and I think intentionally so. He doesn't really want women acting like men, taking up space in their world, philosophizing and ruling as kings. But also, if philosophers started to see women as individuals, to theorize about them as persons with aspirations and ideas, then how could they justify having them spend most of their time caring for children, fetching food and drink, and cleaning the house while the men are free to contemplate?

My recent experience with motherhood brought with it a corollary insight. As it dawned on me how philosophers traditionally ignored maternal ambiguity, a tension unique to women, I saw how

my philosophical training had blinded me not only to my own experience as a woman but also to the problems central to some of the
women philosophers I studied. Between teaching philosophy, studying journalism, and caring for my son—and when I was not utterly
exhausted—I picked up the books of early women philosophers,
curious to see if they had anything to say that might shed light on
my current predicament. I discovered that some of them were indeed
interested in the friction between a woman's self-actualization and
the demands of motherhood. I had almost missed this discussion in
Catharine Trotter Cockburn.

It is not to be doubted, that women are as capable of penetrating into the grounds of things, and reasoning justly, as men are, who certainly have no advantage of us, but in their opportunities of knowledge.

—Catharine Trotter Cockburn

Monsters

As a new mother, it was Cockburn's work I turned to most. She was concerned with one of the unacknowledged crises of her age: how to reconcile the wish (that some thinkers of her time had) to extend to women the freedom to cultivate their intellectual and creative selves with the traditional expectation that they fulfill their duties to others. Maternal guilt was a byproduct of the Enlightenment project, and Cockburn was one of the earliest explorers to roam this territory and comment on it.

I devoured her personal letters. Contained in these missives are instances of Cockburn, a self-directed, rational woman, cultivating her relationships with relatives, friends, and lovers, in ways that are surprisingly modern. In the background of this correspondence lies her philosophical belief that our ideas about freedom and society should be rooted in benevolence and not just selfishness—a belief that put her in the company of other vanguard Enlightenment thinkers. But unlike her male peers, she goes a step further and applies these insights to gender. Women have duties to others but, she believes, men do too; traditionally, men behave more selfishly and women more altruistically—the effects of systemic oppression. Cockburn's solution, as expressed in her letters, is for men to care more for others and for women, who are conditioned to give themselves up to the role of mothers and wives and friends, to be a bit more selfish.

There is an engraving of Cockburn printed on yellowing paper about the size of a book cover. The artist is unknown, as is the reason for the portrait, but the National Portrait Gallery of London dates it to the middle of the eighteenth century, placing Cockburn in her seventies.[1] Yet she looks much younger. Her face and neck are unlined, her hair falls long and wavy down her back. She gazes calmly, if not sympathetically, into the eyes of the viewer. Her nose is strikingly long and large. All in all, she bears an uncanny resemblance to John Locke—especially because of the aquiline nose—and possibly she did look like him. Or perhaps the artist could not separate in his mind the physical form of Cockburn as a woman from that of the philosopher whose ideas she famously defended—an artistic decision that must have both flattered and bothered her.

In an age when the image of the philosopher in the social imagination was of a man, being represented like one of the most significant male thinkers of the time could be construed as a compliment. Cockburn believed Locke to be a genius, and she was respected in the English philosophical community for her analysis of his ideas. However, it irritated her when people assumed that a woman's best ideas came from a man, which happened to her when readers sometimes attributed her work to Locke. When a male friend wrote to Cockburn that he suspected Locke was the true author of Damaris Masham's philosophical writings, she flew into a rage: "I pray be more equitable to her sex, than the generality of yours are; who, when any thing is written by a woman, that they cannot deny their approbation to, are sure to rob us of the glory of it, by concluding 'tis not her own; or at least, that she had some assistance."[2]

In her portrait, Cockburn looks thoughtful and alert, and that she would have liked. She described herself as serious, and a friend wrote that she was so knowledgeable that she "delighteth."[3] She was also passionate and rejected the view that "the affections of love, hatred, &c. must disorder the mind."[4] Many early modern thinkers understood the passions to be a cause of suffering and so evidence of human imperfection, something to overcome. Although she believed that a soul needed reason to organize the emotions,

Cockburn did not want it to quash them. She pictured God as a rational and emotional being, feeling all that humans feel in some unknowable but perfect way.[5]

In her own life, she allowed her frustration to fuel her imagination and inspire her work. She had a restless intellect and a rich emotional life, and when she wasn't writing plays or philosophical tracts, she wrote dedications to other women's plays and kept up a fierce correspondence. She addressed women's oppression from these different angles, always with a hope of improving her reader, whether male or female, and raising their esteem for women as intellectual creatures. What's remarkable is how early this creative impulse began for her and how it persisted from girlhood to old age.

We know that Cockburn was born Catharine Trotter, but many other details of her childhood are obscure. Even her birth year is uncertain. Her first biographer places it in 1679, but a few scholars think it may actually have been in 1674. Her father died in 1684 of the plague while on a tour for the British navy in Turkey.[6] Although her family had ties to royalty, she, her older sister, and her mother had little money left after his death. Her mother was unable to recoup her husband's investments, and a few years later she secured a modest, if unreliable, annual compensation from Queen Anne.[7] During this time, young Cockburn got lost in books.

She was a sponge for knowledge. She taught herself logic and French. Once, when relatives were visiting, she surprised them with extemporaneous poetry recitations. Her uncle remarked that her father would have been proud of her.[8] That Cockburn had the time and liberty to fill her mind with ideas, language, and literature suggests that her mother must have tolerated her appetite for knowledge, if not indulged it. It was clear from girlhood on that Cockburn was interested in how to live well. As a teenager she grappled with her faith, and after multiple conversations with others, she broke from her family's affiliation with the Church of England to become a Catholic. (She would reconvert years later after a period of rigorous deliberation.)

As a girl, Cockburn believed that her conscience mattered and that living a good life required her to exercise self-determination—a confidence that strikes me as preternatural. And along with this conviction sprouted another uncommon psychological motivation: she believed her calling was to share her thoughts with the world. She would not be silent, despite the majority of opinions that said women should be.

Cockburn emerged into history through her writing. From a young age—either fourteen or nineteen, depending which birthdate is authentic—she made her debut with a poem, unpublished but shared with others, to Bevil Higgons, an acquaintance of the family, written after his recovery from smallpox.[9] "Cruel disease!" she opens her poem, but then soon roams across unexpected and self-revealing terrain. She says that of all Higgons's friends, she is the "least recorded in the leaves of fame" but "the first to show" the world how lucky they are that he survived. Cockburn was aware of fame and her relationship to it. In composing these lines, she was tactical: Higgons had ties to the world of theater, and Cockburn had ambitions to write plays.

That same year she published her novella *The Adventures of a Young Lady*. This short work is a testament to the value of the education of a young girl. It's organized as a series of letters between the protagonist, Olinda, and a few men in her life. Some of it is autobiographical: Olinda's father is dead, and her mother barely has enough money to keep up their middle-class lifestyle, though she does invest in her daughter's education. Olinda's mental acuity helps her navigate potentially life-changing decisions, such as, for example, when older, worldly men want to marry or have an affair with her. And although Olinda asks her mother for advice, she is always the one who makes the final decisions. Olinda is young—thirteen years old—while a sixty-year-old is trying to court her.[10] Cockburn thinks

Olinda is underage, and her heroine says as much about herself: "I was too young to think of Love, or Marriage."[11] Yet this was the world she lived in, which makes Cockburn's case for girls to cultivate discernment and autonomous judgment all the more important. When a suitor asks her mother for Olinda's hand, Olinda tells him: "I hate a Man that will depend upon any other for my Favour than my self."[12]

Her novella was a success in England and went through multiple reprintings.[13] As Cockburn approached her twenties, she had to think more seriously about her financial future. She could seek a husband, she could become a kept woman, or she could continue in the arts, risking failure while exposing herself to the public gaze. She chose the latter.

She fell into the company of literate, ambitious women in London and earned an early patron and close friend in Lady Sarah Piers, a wealthy aristocrat who also aspired to do creative work. She befriended two women playwrights: Mary Pix and Delarivier Manley.[14] The membrane between novel writing and playwriting was highly permeable, because the audiences and publishers overlapped, and a number of writers in one camp had success in the other.[15] Cockburn broke into playwriting and had a wonderful support network in these women. They wrote prologues for one another's plays, sometimes pitting themselves against men who they believed had grasped too much from women. Cockburn prefaced a play by Manley:

> Well you've maintain'd our equal right in Fame,
> To which vain Man had quite engrost the claim.

And Manley prefaced one of Cockburn's plays:

> Fired by the bold Example, I would try
> To turn our Sexes weaker Destiny.
> . . . For thus Encourag'd, and thus led by you,
> Methinks we might more Crowns than theirs Subdue.[16]

Cockburn, Piers, Manley, Pix, and a few others contributed poetry to a collection, each assuming the role of one of the nine Greek muses. Cockburn was Calliope, the muse of philosophy.

The year 1695 was an auspicious moment for Cockburn to make her theatrical debut in England.[17] The audiences were large, totaling some fifty thousand, and receptive to new ways of thinking about women and their place in society. The Drury Lane Theatre was desperate for fresh plays after a competing theater opened.[18] A few women, including Cockburn, stepped in to fill the void.[19] Seasoned actors were cast in the leading roles, including the tall, handsome, and slightly knock-kneed Jack Verbruggen and the actor-manager and writer Colley Cibber.[20] The space itself was amphitheater-like: open to the sky, with three walls, and benches covered in green cloth. Audience members talked to one another throughout performances, making it difficult to hear what was being said onstage unless you were seated near the pit, and sometimes even then it was difficult.[21] But the audience members who could make out what was happening onstage the night of Cockburn's play would have experienced a groundbreaking production.

The play was an adaptation of Aphra Behn's 1688 novel *Agnes de Castro*. Behn was a dramatist, novelist, and poet, a contemporary of Dryden and Milton, and the first woman in England to make a living as a professional writer. Cockburn wrote the adaptation in part as a way to align herself in the public imagination with the wildly popular Behn, who had died a few years before. *Agnes* is a complex play that tells the story of a princess who decides not to marry a prince and have "Golden Chains, / A Shining Prison" but instead to live alone with a "quiet, though Poor, freedom."[22]

Cockburn drew in viewers not with sex—like Manley, who used female sexuality to subvert gender paradigms and titillate— but rather by subverting notions about women in other ways. The character of Agnes is more deliberate and rational than the men in her life. Cockburn wanted to show that women not only could but *should* think for themselves. She had Agnes work through moral dilemmas—"these Wars, the Combats of the Mind"—and with great skill, making the case to her audience to defend women's freedom of conscience.[23]

I realized when reading *Agnes* and Cockburn's other plays that she wasn't merely exploring women's oppression. She wanted to undo it. Aristotle argued that the best drama is cathartic, transforming the emotional state of audience members so they are inclined to virtue.[24] Cockburn had such ambitions, which she believed set her apart from most other English playwrights. Her plays' "chief design is to instruct whilst they delight."[25]

She knew that keeping her audience on their toes instead of delivering what they expected was a clever ploy to teach lessons: "Those turns, which surprise and keep the mind in agitation, have a great beauty in such pieces . . . I am no friend to those plays, where the heroes distress is only as they are lovers."[26]

She wanted her audience to fall for her brilliant female characters, whose powers of reason were at least equal to those of the male characters. In her play *The Revolution of Sweden*, a female character asks:

> . . . Are our Souls too
> . . . of weaker frame than Mans?
> Or can the force of Custom and Opinion
> Effect this difference? 'Tis so, the Hero
> Who undaunted, faces death midst Cannons,
> Swords and Javelins, sinks under the less
> Honourable Dangers of Pain, Disease,
> Or Poverty, below a Womans weakness:
> And we whom Custom bars this active Valour,
> Branding it with Reproach, shrink at th'Alarm
> Of War, but where our Honour's plac'd, we oft
> Have shewn in its Defence a no less Manly daring.[27]

I was won over by Cockburn's tone, which is snappy and embold-ening. In the prologue to *The Revolution of Sweden*, she wrote, "If by a Woman you to night are taught, / Think on that Source from whence th'Instruction's brought."[28]

Cockburn did well and had a run of five plays. But I think her best play was her one comedy, *Love at a Loss: Or, Most Votes Carry It*. In the dedication, she described the current condition of women: "Wives are scarce look'd on but as the impediments of a Man's Plea-sure, or at best a Convenience in the setling his Affairs, without aim-ing at a Satisfaction in her self."[29] Cockburn would aim higher. In the prologue she made clear that women were capable of autonomy: "We think she's safe by forces of her own, / And like her Native Isle depends on none."[30]

There are three plots, but the story of Lesbia is the most auda-cious. Lesbia must choose between two suitors, one admirable and the other not. But rather than decide for herself, she has her friends vote instead.[31] By having friends decide for Lesbia, Cockburn was making a political statement: women were still not free. Cockburn's play represents the creep of external forces keeping women's freedom from them.

These forces, which take the form of opinions and norms, are not neutral but driven by male prerogative. At one point in the play, one male character feels remorse and reflects: "For treating them [wives] with rudeness, or neglect, / Does most dishonour, on our selves reflect."[32] By ending the play with the story of how Lesbia internalizes patriarchal norms and opinions, Cockburn was implicitly telling men: I see you. I am aware of what you are doing. Cockburn defined free-dom as the "power we have to act or not act, as conscience directs."[33] A woman may not have the freedom to will what she wants to see in the world, but she can observe. She can judge. She can comment.

Cockburn discovered that some men found her intelligence attractive. They wrote her letters, some anonymously, praising her wit.[34] Other men, however, were threatened by her powers. Cockburn, along with fellow women playwrights, stretched in new directions the narrative of a woman's way of being. How far they could go was not ultimately up to them, and the will and tolerance of men were bound to snap back and sting.[35]

Cockburn must have been prepared for some verbal battering, and it was common for members of the theater community to mock one another. She did attract criticism—something she was proud of: "It is the fate of all men of great merit to have many enemies."[36] But the most personal attack came when she was mocked in the play *The Female Wits*.

The Female Wits, which was written anonymously and performed at Drury Lane Theatre in 1697, ridiculed women playwrights: Cockburn for being an obnoxious faux intellectual, "a lady who pretends to the learned, Languages, and assumes to her self the name of a Critick"; Manley for being a slut; and Pix for being fat. The play cast them as backbiting and incompetent. It also accused them of bad writing and plagiarism—offenses taken seriously in the seventeenth-century literary community.[37] The play ran for six nights. The three women's work and personalities were parodied before thousands of people. It affected them all. Manley didn't produce another play for almost a decade. Pix and Cockburn couldn't imagine staying at Drury Lane Theatre, where *The Female Wits* was performed, and so staged their next plays at Lincoln's Inn Fields Theatre.

In 1701, after staging three more plays, Cockburn decided to take a break. She hadn't been feeling well. She was fatigued and had "colic," an illness eighteenth-century medical doctors categorized as one of the "Diseases of the Head, Nerves or Spirits."[38] She confessed to a friend that she was retiring from literary endeavors and left London for Salisbury, a town eighty miles to the southwest, to live with her sister and her family. Once she was far from the theater scene, she didn't miss it.[39]

For years, Cockburn had tirelessly sketched the character of the free woman, a woman who finds a way to maneuver through the world as a rational, virtuous being. A woman not unlike herself, leading a life guided by her creative intellect. Cockburn's sojourn in Salisbury gave her the space to step back from this project and consider the wider picture. She wasn't satisfied simply asserting woman's freedom; she wanted to formulate the principles that guaranteed it. When some theater critics declared her a fake intellectual, a pretender who puffed up women's rights without solid reasoning, Cockburn turned to philosophy.

In Salisbury, she befriended the philosopher and historian Gilbert Burnet and his wife, Elizabeth Burnet, who was also interested in philosophical and theological debates.[40] Cockburn especially admired Elizabeth's "extraordinary clear and solid judgment" and was touched by her confession that she had read and enjoyed her plays, especially *Love at a Loss*. Elizabeth didn't share with Cockburn the fact that she was hesitant at first to befriend her because of her involvement in theater. Besides Cockburn's reputation as a poser, she also had to deal with the stereotype that some women in theater would prostitute themselves when they struggled to sell their plays.[41] Elizabeth even warned her friend John Locke about Cockburn because of the "great blemishes on her reputation."[42] Elizabeth did eventually warm to Cockburn, once she realized she was religiously sincere and committed to a life of the mind.[43]

The Burnets introduced Cockburn to John Locke's ideas, which changed her life.[44] By the turn of the eighteenth century, most thinkers had accepted Locke's work as the standard model for human understanding, and Cockburn now counted herself among them. She agreed with Locke that human reason was limited by what we sense and by our reflections on those sensations, and she wrote that such "weakness and scantiness of our knowledge" makes it impossible for us to know grand metaphysical principles.[45] She shared his skepticism of university learning, a somewhat self-serving view, as she had no formal education.[46]

Not everyone was comfortable with the dominance of Locke's theory of knowledge, because it left questions about the status of morality and religion open-ended, allowing atheism to take root. Locke's groundbreaking empirical theories, which helped form the backbone of the scientific revolution, were not clearly in step with Christianity, the moral spirit of Europe.

That first year in Salisbury, Cockburn read the critiques of Locke's theories by philosopher Thomas Burnet (who had no relation to her friends the Burnets) and wasn't impressed.[47] Uniting Locke's epistemology with Christian morality—which seemed to Burnet and other critics like squaring the circle—was for Cockburn a delicious challenge. No matter that Locke's philosophy was vague about the foundation of morality and religion. She saw a path forward, a way to join Locke's empirical account of human understanding with the eternal soul. In the back of her mind, she knew this path would also lead in the direction of placing the freedom of women on more certain ground.

She wrote a work entitled *A Defence of Mr. Locke's Essay of Human Understanding*, in which she took Locke's "hints" at a foundation for morality and built them out into a moral vision compatible with Christianity.[48] As for the criticism that Locke entertains the possibility of heretical ideas such as thinking matter (if matter can think, then there is no need to posit a soul in order to explain thought), Cockburn was nonchalant. She viewed this question—whether thought requires a soul—as an example of the many things that the human intellect cannot reach. She argued that what does concern us, how to earn salvation, is knowable.

In early 1702, Cockburn published her *Defence* anonymously, explaining to a friend: "A woman's name would give a prejudice against a work of this nature; and truth and reason have less force, when the person, who defends them, is prejudged against."[49] Her friends the Burnets praised it and with her permission shared it with Locke, along with her name. Locke read her defense and was impressed. He sent her books and money along with a letter, writing "that as the rest of the world take notice of the strength and clearness of your reasoning, so I cannot but be extremely sensible, that it was employed in my defence."[50]

Over the next few years, as word got out about the true identity of the author of the well-received *Defence*, Cockburn's intellectual circle expanded. Her connection to Locke brought her into the orbit of Damaris Masham, and they exchanged their works.[51]

Cockburn's health, while still fragile, was improving, and the success of her *Defence* inspired her to pursue more projects. She realized that living with her sister and her family was too disruptive: "I have so little time to myself, when I am in the family, that I found my writing go on very slowly."[52] So she moved back to London to her own place: "[I'm] so resolved to stay [in London], till I have finished what I am about, in a place, where I am as solitary as I can wish."[53]

She wrote about her reconversion to the Church of England in *A Discourse Concerning a Guide in Controversies*, published in 1707.[54] She also wrote and staged her last play, *The Revolution of Sweden*, in which she addressed, among many topics, the cause of women's ignorance: social bias. "There are so great Difficulties, and such general Discouragements, to those of our Sex who wou'd improve their Minds, and employ their Time in any Science, or useful Art," she wrote in its dedication.

While living on her own in London, Cockburn, in spite of her critical views of the institution, began to think about the possibility of marriage for herself. She didn't like how young girls were taught to prioritize it—usually at the expense of their intellectual development. But she was older now and already had established her intellectual life. She shared with a friend that the hard part was finding someone to trust. "I believe I shall end my days as I am. Indeed, I have been always very fearful of putting my happiness entirely in the power of any one."[55]

Cockburn's letters to her suitors offer an entertaining glimpse into eighteenth-century dating. She included them in her published works years later so women could learn from them; they revealed how Cockburn expressed her wants to her suitors without apology or reservation, and how she was honest when uncertain about her feelings. Most importantly, she knew who she was before she started dating. She was picky: "I had never before known any man, that I liked, or liked not, in whose manners, or temper, I did not find something, that would have made me unhappy; and therefore I had long thought it would be best for me to continue as I am."[56] That is, alone. But she was attractive and internationally renowned, and many men were after her, so she decided to play the field.

Her friend Thomas Burnet (yet another Burnet, not to be confused with the Locke critic or her friends the Burnets) was a contender for Cockburn's affections. He was a brilliant man and traveled throughout Europe, sending Cockburn missives from Paris, Leipzig, and Luxembourg. He was on personal terms with leading continental philosophers, including Leibniz and Malebranche, and spoke to them about her work.[57] He took pride in Cockburn's intellectual accomplishments, encouraged her to have her works translated, and seemed a good match for her ambition.

Yet he was a boaster. He visited Queen Caroline in Germany, and he said that she could not get enough of his presence, drawing him from his bed to spend time with her in the evenings. He was also shifty, injecting qualifications into his proclamations of love: "Yet I cannot conceal, that I have the most passionate ardour of mind and soul to cultivate a perpetual friendship with you, and in your personal society and presence, one way or another, so far as may be practicable."[58] It certainly didn't help his case that he suspected that Masham didn't pen her own works, an opinion he expressed to Cockburn. She told him that it was not going to work out between them. But this didn't end their friendship. They continued to share thoughts about religion and philosophy, a testament to Cockburn's willingness to accept other people's imperfections, a desire to find ways to work through disagreements together. "You was not, you see, mistaken in apprehending, that our intimacy would turn to love," not a romantic love as Burnet had once hoped but rather a friendly love.[59]

Another suitor was Reverend Fenn. He was head over heels for Cockburn, and she liked that he was kind, virtuous, and respectable. The problem was that she wasn't in love with him. The spark was missing.[60]

Patrick Cockburn was a different story. Here was a reverend, virtuous and "esteemed," to whom she was wildly attracted. His only problem was his reticence. He wasn't convinced that bodily pleasures were holy. Cockburn, on the other hand, who had read her Masham, had "no aversion for pleasure" between humans, especially a husband and wife.[61] In a passage directly inspired by Masham's philosophy of love, she wrote:

> *To say the truth, if it was the duty of Christians to love nothing but God, and that (as Mallebranche constantly asserts) all affection to the creatures were sinful, I think solitude would not only be necessary for you, but for all mankind: we should no longer be called social creatures, but all become unsociable hermits. But God, who designed us to be useful, has thought fit to make us agreeable too to one another, to sweeten our cares and services; and had not imposed such hard laws on us, as some maintain.*[62]

Love me, Catherine was saying to Patrick, open yourself to care for another; it feels good and it's granted by God. She persuaded him, and in 1708 they married and she took his last name. The following year she gave birth to the first of their three children.

After becoming a mother, Cockburn didn't publish anything for almost seventeen years—until her youngest child was almost grown and gone. Why had the irrepressible writer, who had been a fount of ideas since she was a teenager, suddenly gone mute?

Years later, she explained this period in a letter to Alexander Pope (which she never sent to him, though she was a huge fan): "Being married in 1708, I bid adieu to the muses, and so wholly gave myself up to the cares of a family, and the education of my children, that I scarce knew, whether there was any such thing as books, plays, or poems stirring in *Great Britain*."[63] Things were also difficult at home. In 1714, Patrick lost his job because he refused to take the Oath of Abjuration against James Stuart.[64] To get by, he tutored boys in Latin. In 1726, after years of financial struggle, he finally caved and took his oath. He subsequently was hired as a cleric in Aberdeen. There was also a disruption from her past life. In 1709, the year Cockburn's first child was born, Delarivier Manley published a tell-all filled with gossip about people she'd known in theater. She took jabs at Cockburn, whom she described as hypocritical and lascivious, and said she'd slept with men outside of wedlock.[65] Making matters worse, it was a popular work that was "sold at every shop."[66] This may have been reason enough for Cockburn to hide out for a while and let it blow over.

I accepted this story as fact for years, and as a young mother I believed that Cockburn had simply set aside her books and abstract thoughts while she cared for her children. But it didn't sit comfortably with me; I wanted her to be more, to push back more, to be for me the brassy woman of her plays who insisted that women's interior lives mattered. I didn't want her to disappear into oblivion, as I feared I was doing with the change of each diaper. How could she give up the muses? Didn't that terrify her?

So I was pleased to discover Cockburn had actually continued reading and writing while being a mother. Between her maternal and wifely duties—or who knows, perhaps sometimes even in lieu of them—she was off on her own, composing a series of fictional letters. She never published them, and a scholar only recently found them in her biographer Thomas Birch's collected letters, which are archived at the British Library. The fictional correspondents are mostly women, and the themes they address are fascinating. They are working out their friendships while dealing with the challenges of home life. They are united in their shared oppression and seek one another's company for support. Cockburn had one woman say to another: "The perusal of yours gave me Pleasure & Pain Alternately Pleasure on Consideration of my being Blessed wth a generous F,nd to whom I can unbosom my self wthout fear of Pervertion, Pain w^n I reflect y^t F,nd is not happy as [I] cou'd Wish & you Merit."[67] Cockburn was tinkering again with her vision of women's freedom, imagining female friendship as a form of earthly salvation.

But to indulge in her own work was to risk her reputation as a good wife and mother. She would have recognized the sentiments expressed in this contemporary text: "It is laudable, commendable, a note of a virtuous woman, a dutiful wife, when she submits herself with quietness, cheerfully, even as a well broken horse turns at the least turning, stands at the least check of the rider's bridle."[68] A mother who stepped away from her duties to write wouldn't be judged a mother but rather a wild animal for orienting herself outside custom and civility. Other sources would judge such a mother more harshly. She would be a perversion. A monster.

In the mid- to late- eighteenth century, England took a conservative turn culturally, and the role of the mother became more exacting than it had been decades before. There was a greater expectation for mothers to devote themselves to nurturing and educating their children and to stay out of the public sphere. (It was also the days of early capitalism and banking, and keeping women in the home was another way to prevent them from acquiring wealth.[69]) Women received the message from multiple channels that a mother who steps out of line is a danger to her child and her community. Malebranche had already warned that a pregnant woman enjoying a work of art risks giving her unborn child birth defects. Jonathan Swift and Alexander Pope depicted mothers who were writers as monstrous: they were destroyers of literature and threats to social stability.[70] There was also a racist current running through these popular images. Some thinkers argued that the more civilized nations had the greatest sex differences between men and women and that those nations or groups with a higher rate of hermaphroditism were less civilized. It was a sexist and racist logic that presupposed women were nurturers designed to stay in the home and raise good citizens and that "uncivilized" nations or groups lacked committed mothers.

Perhaps Cockburn said she wasn't reading or writing during that period because she feared the criticism that would follow if she admitted the truth. Although Cockburn claimed that she gave up her scholarly pursuits out of maternal duty—informing Pope in her letter that she spent her time nurturing and educating her children—I don't think she was persuaded that her role was to be silent. One of her poems contains this ambiguity: she wrote that a good education would help women fulfill "the duties of the mother, friend, and wife."[71] But in that same poem she also imagined a day when women would generate original insights in the fields of science and philosophy. Cockburn had her fictional letters preserved by Birch, perhaps as an act of defiance of her own embrace of the silent mother.[72]

Toward the end of these years, or just after them, Cockburn wrote an undated missive to her son, the youngest of her three children and the only boy. He was most likely in his early teens—too young to know what profession to take up but old enough to benefit from his mother's words about how to avoid the sort of trouble men get into. She included this letter in her collected works and titled it a "Letter of Advice." As such, it's educative and could technically be described as an example of a mother doing her job well. But it has her philosophical fingerprints all over it and includes many ideas that she would publish later—evidence that she was working on her philosophy while raising a child still at home. Additionally, it's a wonderful letter; though quite formal in tone, its emotional force ripples just under the surface.

Cockburn tells her son, who is fast approaching the age of independence, that she is proud of him, and she writes with the seriousness of a mother who knows this is one of her last chances to have her say. She counsels him about religion, employment, and then the one topic that worries her the most: women.[73] She is terrified for her son, for what he will become once he "enters on the stage of the world."[74] Most men treated women as creatures different from themselves, not as rational or worthy of ethical consideration but instead more like objects.[75] She tells him that treating women as instruments of pleasure has devastating effects on their lives, bodies, and minds. "And yet this very practice towards women passes for a trifle, the amusement of a man of gallantry."[76]

Her recommendation is for her son to do the opposite of what was commonly done: that is, to summon his natural goodwill and treat women as his equals.

Her advice rests on her understanding of human nature. For Cockburn, everything, including humans, has a God-given purpose, and the existence of human reason is evidence that God intends humans to use it.[77] If we reflect on our natures, we see that we're rational, and this obligates us to treat each other as equals because we are "equal by nature."[78] She says it's something we can know just by feeling. Cockburn says that, as emotional creatures, we're motivated to care for one another.[79] In other works, she writes that our benevolent affections are evident "in that admiration and delight, which we are apt to feel, on hearing or reading of heroic disinterested actions, tho' done many ages ago, in distant countries, where our interest can have nothing to do" or in parents' care for their children.[80] If God didn't intend for humans to be social and kind, he could have made us more selfish than he did: he could "certainly have created us more self-sufficient, less dependent upon one another, and less disposed for the offices of social life, if these duties, however distinct in idea, were not designed to be united in practice, and mutually to promote each other."[81] Her appeal to care and interdependence is an echo of the letter she wrote to the boy's father years before.

Cockburn rejected Hobbes's well-known claim that self-preservation was the most consistent of human motives and should therefore form the basis of any theory of government that sought stability. She found it disturbing. Because it didn't invoke benevolence as essential to our political bonds to one another but rather emphasized selfishness, she saw it as eroding a sense of obligation to others. More than anything, she believed Hobbes's account threatened freedom—the essence of what it is to be human.

Cockburn argued that a life based on selfish passions was not a free life. True freedom was not a license to do as one pleased but rather, as we have seen, the liberty to use one's reason and follow one's conscience. Since our conscience tells us the right thing to do, a free person is someone who knows and does what is good. (It's a notion that might sound odd to secular ears.) Therefore, a free man treats women as his equals.

This message also shows up in the prologue to one of her plays, in which Cockburn asks her audience to praise those who stand up to the oppression of women: "There cannot be a more distinguishing Mark of a Free, and Beneficent Spirit, than openly to condemn that ill-grounded Custom, by giving Countenance and Protection to those, who have attempted against it."[82]

There is an irony here. To prevent her son from becoming captive to his base pleasures and behaving beastly toward women, Cockburn needed to take time away from her children to read, think, and write and therefore be, at moments, what others in society might call monstrous. I don't think Cockburn saw herself as a terrible mother when she was cultivating her mind and entertaining philosophical ideas. This is the same woman who, in 1732, told the queen to make a statue in her likeness for the royal library. Cockburn wrote in a poem to the queen, "occasioned by the busts set up in the Queen's Hermitage," of her great disappointment that there was not one woman in the collection. She asked, "Would royal *Caroline* our wrongs redress"? She refused to be silent and passive, rejecting those female virtues at the risk of appearing impudent. In fact, she seemed to relish it, ultimately publishing the poem in a men's magazine. There was a self-interestedness coursing through Cockburn, a robust sense of dignity and self-worth that didn't derive from her domestic roles but rather from her intellect. She wanted to be an example to inspire women to love themselves, to be a bit more self-assertive and guilt-free about it.

In 1726, when her children were older and more independent, Cockburn started publishing philosophical works again. A few years later, in 1732, she began a correspondence lasting over ten years with her niece, Ann Arbuthnot, who had just married and wanted intellectual instruction. Cockburn was thrilled and loaded her niece with books by Locke and Samuel Clarke, along with this note: "I should be loth to have any thing I send you for the entertainment of your leisure hours, prove a hindrance to your good housewifry, which is certainly a very commendable quality (though not the only virtue) in our sex."[83]

Cockburn was an unreliable correspondent. She took weeks to respond, always with an excuse about her health. She could be insensitive. When her niece's husband died suddenly, and she was alone with her infant, Cockburn didn't get back to her for over half a year and then encouraged her to put her pain in perspective. She told her niece it could be worse.[84]

One of her quickest replies was sent when her niece criticized Alexander Pope, Cockburn's literary hero, and she wouldn't have it.[85] Yet she was most passionate in defense of her own work. Over the years, her niece's critical judgment became sharper, and Cockburn asked her to read her latest philosophical work. When her niece compared her to Anthony Ashley Cooper Shaftesbury, a philosopher from whose ideas Cockburn wanted to distance her own, she shot back: "If you would read my *Remarks* with a proper attention, I doubt not you would be better acquainted with my opinions." Is she being rude to her niece or simply defending herself? Envious and resentful of her niece or proud and protective of her work and reputation? Is she being monstrous or moral? Probably all of these. The only hint she gives us is this: "You may observe, that when I speak of desiring the happiness of others, it is upon a supposition, that this does not interfere with our own."[86]

In a world where women were expected to put the happiness of others before their own, Cockburn refused. She wanted her niece's mind to improve, but she also had a mind of her own that mattered. She didn't have a perfect ethical solution to the dilemma of how to balance duty to self and duty to others. I don't believe she saw this as an ethical issue an individual could resolve on her own but rather a systemic problem that would require a general shift in social attitudes. What we see through her letters and poems and longer works is the model of a woman who, in the details, lived an equivocal life as a mother and an intellectual.

I had wanted Cockburn to answer my question for me: Am I being monstrous? And how and when am I being monstrous? I looked to her behavior for an answer, trying to wedge her into a familiar slot: the philosopher who sacrificed moments of motherhood or the mother who couldn't manage being a philosopher. Neither of those interpretations is correct, but I learned as much about myself as I did about her when I looked through her works and revisited them years later. Part of thinking like a woman, I learned, is to be satisfied with ambiguity.

The years after her children left home were Cockburn's most prolific, and in addition to her letters she wrote philosophical works exploring the foundation of morality. She died in 1749 at age seventy-five (or possibly seventy-one). By then the world had nearly forgotten her. In 1751, Catherine Talbot, an author and Bluestocking, wrote, "She was a remarkable Genius, & Yet how Obscure her Lot in Life!" And in 1789, James Beattie, a poet and philosopher, wrote that "she lived many years (between 1726 and 1737) in Aberdeen; and yet I have never heard any person there speak of her, though I have often heard her husband spoken of by those who must have known both."[87]

Not long before she died, she and a friend, Henry Etough, decided to sift through her works and compile two volumes for publication. Etough wrote of her that "M.[rs] Cockburn deserveth the first Rank among the best Moral Writers. In Strength & Clearness of Reasoning in force & propriety of Language few have been her Equals. Her Manner & Matter are greatly superior to all the Performances of the Whole Sex in all Ages and Places of the Whole World. Some memorial should be preserved of so extraordinary a Person."[88] Etough hired an editor who was pulling together a collection of Alexander Pope's works. But this editor was distracted and allowed Cockburn's project to languish for almost a decade. This is when Thomas Birch took over and finished the job.[89] Although Cockburn died two years before the volumes were published, she had a hand in curating the pieces that would be included. She left out her novella and four of her five plays, but she did include the letters to her son and niece. If we are not distracted by the voice of a philosopher but attend to the portrait of her that emerges from her pages, we see that it's rich and surprisingly complex. She's not the perfect mother or aunt. She allowed us to see her as a thinking woman who cares for her community but also her own mind.

When I look at her portrait now, in the context of her opus, I see something more than a passing resemblance to Locke. There are no outward signs of agitation, although frustration was her first response to patriarchy. Her second response was a calm rejection of it: to live with personal integrity—while feeling the full complexity of human emotions ruled by reason—is key to facing an unfair world. As is the effort to change it. But there are her eyes, outsize and intelligent, the knowing look of the female gaze, constant, unmovable. Not letting up.

Muses

Those same eyes were staring out at me from a book on my office desk one spring day. I was packing up my belongings after resigning from my four-year contract teaching job in Queens. My departure had come a year earlier than I'd planned, but I'd just earned my master's degree in journalism, and it seemed the best moment to look for a new job. I wondered, as I placed my books into a box, whether my new job, whatever it might be, would be so consuming that I wouldn't have time to return to Cockburn and the other women philosophers.

My son, who was three, was also with me. Together we loaded up my books and papers. He shook Jim's hand, and the secretary let him choose a candy from the glass bowl on her desk. I taught my final feminist philosophy class, while my son sat next to me, drawing and eating candy. I wanted him to see this world that I had a role in, with the hope that maybe one day in the future he would remember his mother was once a university professor. I held his hand as we walked across campus for the last time, over the green lawn and past the library to our car in the parking lot.

Soon after, I was hired at an ambitious science magazine startup in Manhattan. The work was intellectually demanding and collaborative; it was exhilarating to be part of a team producing pieces of a high literary and intellectual caliber. I threw myself fully into it— fact-checking, writing, and editing; I relished speaking to researchers over the phone to make sure we were getting stories right. I coedited

a special edition on the cosmos and commissioned pieces by leading scientists and philosophers about the limits of the universe, the
nature of dark matter, and how prepared world religions are for an
alien visitation (turns out, more than I'd expected). I pushed for more
pieces by women, people of color, and LGBTQI community members
and for the stories of their achievements and suppression in science.

When I wasn't working, I was home with my family, which in
the previous year had expanded with the birth of my daughter. Every
now and then I would spot one of Astell's books on my shelf, or
my pile of research papers stored in a plastic bin in the back of my
closet, obscured by shoes and dresses, and I would feel a dull ache in
my chest. Otherwise, I didn't think of academia or my four women
philosophers much, until two years later.

I had volunteered to participate in Women of Letters, a monthly
literary salon featuring women in media and entertainment. At the
time when I took part, participants were asked to write an original
letter inspired by a prompt and then read the letter aloud to a crowd at
Joe's Pub in Astor Place. The prompt for the month was "my muse."
I was surprised by how quickly my letter came together.

That evening finally came around. Backstage, I waited with the
other women—two comedians, a singer, and two actresses—to make
our entrance. Then it was time, and we walked out into near darkness
through tunnels of velvet curtains, over electric cords, and onto the
bright stage. When it was my turn, I stood up to read. I hesitated.
Among the silhouettes of strangers, I could just make out Marc, my
friends, and some work colleagues. There was a hushed, anticipa-
tory silence. And then I spoke. My voice filled the space. I told the
story of Damaris Cudworth Masham's life in philosophy—and my
own. I spoke about my shameful silence in graduate school. About
Alex and my embarrassment for depending as much as I did on a
man for validation. About my confusion of being inspired by the
philosophies of thinkers who thought so little of women. And about

how Masham and other women philosophers helped me make sense of this confusion.

Toward the end of the letter, I said, "It's funny how improbable our connection is, muse: separated by centuries and customs. But that we've been brought together points to something deep about the culture of this discipline . . . Muse, did you find it hard to theorize about the universe without reflecting on your gender? Why does that happen to us?"

I finished my letter and sat down. Afterward I joined some of the participants and my friends for drinks in the lounge, celebrating the night. Yet a part of me was agitated, as if I'd released something in myself that I could no longer repress without great discomfort. Later, in my apartment, I took the plastic bin out of the closet, pulled down their books from the shelves, and began work on this story.

More recently, I was at my local bookstore, perusing what was new in nonfiction. There on the shelf with a bright white cover was a book with a simple, boldface title: *The History of Philosophy.* The author was a well-known academic. I approached it, skeptical but with a dash of hope. I picked it up and leafed through the table of contents. It was a survey promising to introduce the reader to "philosophy's main figures and ideas." Except for one chapter on feminist philosophy (focusing on the twentieth century and occupying a total of five pages, whereas Gottlob Frege, a late nineteenth- and early twentieth-century philosopher, got eight pages) and a final section devoted to non-European and non-American thought, most of the contents were not much different from histories of philosophy written a hundred years ago. Across 584 pages divided into short chapters devoted to individual thinkers, not one of those thinkers was a woman.

I squinted at the cover then glanced outside. How could this still be?

This delivered me back to that day in Berg's class, and I remembered how being a woman in that room full of self-important men had felt isolating and wrong, how I'd wanted to just disappear. Now, as I stood in the sunlit bookstore, the uncertainty and shame that typically accompanied these associations dropped away, and something else took over: angry defiance.

I imagined standing up and facing Berg in that classroom, declaring: "You must be kidding!" I would tell him that statements like the ones he'd made are reckless and counterproductive. I would recruit other members of the department to join together and talk about the lack of diversity in our field and our mutual responsibility for improving its exclusionary culture. I would seek out philosophy lectures by women to learn from them. I would practice sharing my ideas with many people, identifying those professors who were kind and eager to help cultivate the flowering of my mind. I would begin making a list of allies for my professional network. I would make a list of successful women intellectuals to inspire me when I felt downtrodden. I would mail thank-you letters to scholars whose articles and books I admired. I might even apply to another philosophy department, one where I could study under a philosopher as lit up as I was about gender theory in the history of ideas. I fantasized about all of this while standing there in the bookstore, feeling a twinge knowing it hadn't gone like that but also appreciating how easily I'd conjured myself, confident and powerful, as if it had. Then I noticed that the torment I'd once experienced in association with that memory of Berg, which had profoundly shaped the trajectory of my young adult life, was greatly diminished. I felt suddenly free—not released from the net that I had become tangled in years before but now exquisitely aware of myself and my relationship to that net. I laughed aloud.

When I'd set out nearly twenty years ago to embark on a graduate career in philosophy, I'd dreamed of becoming a philosopher like the one Aristotle described in his metaphysics, a person who spent her days contemplating eternal truths—an edifying experience and the closest a human could come to immortality. That's not the sort of thinker I became. My intellect wasn't shaped in the glory of transcendent questions but rather in response to the insidious systems of oppression. In this sense, I am a woman thinker.

For centuries, men have told us how women think or how they ought to think. And it's typically in a way that is inferior to their way of thinking and serves their purposes. I don't believe that there is one way to think like a woman, just as I don't believe there is a single way to be a woman. A few things are common to all of us: patriarchy makes it hard for a woman to think for herself, to voice her own thoughts, and for the most part, philosophy hasn't done us any favors. Astell, Masham, Cockburn, and Wollstonecraft gave me an intellectual community when I was struggling without one. I marvel at how our lives are so different, and yet we are united by the same recognition of the fucked-up-ness of patriarchy. They also taught me something else. Because of them, I have a better idea of what it might mean to be a woman and to be free.

Physics tells us the universe is unintelligent, ignorant of our plight. We're on an orb spinning through an indifferent immensity toward an end billions of years in the future that will be cold and lifeless. Our individual moments here stand no chance of leaving permanent traces within this vast flux of matter and forces; the writings and ideas of Plato and Einstein could never leave a deep enough impression for this universe to remember them, and they will go the way of ancient soft-bodied creatures whose vestiges sit on the cusp of oblivion.

Art, philosophy, and literature tell us a different story. That the brief time we are here matters, that it is meaningful and contains beauty. We've learned to talk to ourselves in this expansive and dark vacuum to keep ourselves company, so that we can transcend our finite, perplexing condition—if not in fact, then in our imaginations. We've learned to free ourselves—if only for the duration of a poem, an equation, a book, a prayer—from our despair.

In sharing this condition, we share in a riddle. If we don't belong to a God, then at the very least, we belong to each other. I'm starting to think this insight is somehow relevant to the good life that the ancients were after; it's something that Astell, Masham, Cockburn, and Wollstonecraft well understood—that to be a self is to be profoundly connected to others, and to be free is to aid in the freedom of others. Perhaps this is all there is to rapture—to free each other to hear our own voices.

The Oxford philosopher Amia Srinivasan says that in our pursuit of knowledge, we should ask not only whether our ideas are true "but what do our representations do? What practices and forms of life do they help sustain, what sort of person do they help construct, and whose power do they help entrench?"[1] I have a hope for the world of ideas, that its stewards will continue to be more open to the ways ideas function and the profound impact they can have on the lives and minds of others.

Such openness is admittedly scary. It's unpleasant to face the ugliness of your own ignorance and error and to be open and charitable to unfamiliar logics that challenge the foundations of your own. What if what you learn breaks you—and then could you survive it? This may be another reason why the canon is still so white and male, as are the majority of philosophy faculty and students. In myself, I have observed that there is a terror in learning to speak, but there is also a terror in learning to listen.

When I started to work on these women philosophers, I wanted to place them alongside the more famous white male European thinkers by expanding the canon itself. But the more I learn from other scholars about philosophers from different historical periods and different cultural and ethnic backgrounds, the less this feels right. We need to rethink the concept of a canon itself. I wish for a history of thought that accurately represents the *human* intellectual endeavor: one that is self-consciously inconclusive and constantly renewing, one that includes the undisciplined parts of intellectual history, and one that isn't monolithic but dynamic and feral like a great cat.

I think this back in the bookstore as I stare at the copy of *The History of Philosophy* in my hands. What a pitifully narrow read. As I set the book carefully back on the shelf, I notice its soft cover and small size in relation to the thousands of other books in the shop. Outside the window, the sun is bright and the bare winter trees in their cramped sidewalk plots have branches like wild fingers. I step from the bookstore and head home to write.

Acknowledgments

This book would not exist without the resources and support of the New York Public Library and the Manhattan Research Library Initiative. To the scholars whose meticulous research helped me tell this story: I'm honored I had the opportunity to spend time with your invaluable work. Special thanks to scholars who provided me with feedback on specific sections of this book (any mistakes are my own): Leyla Amzi-Erdogdular, Melanie Bigold, Brian Black, Jacqueline Broad, David Buchta, Andrew Elfenbein, Philip Ivanhoe, Jo Ellen Jacobs, Andrew Janiak, Anne Kelley, Anne R. Larsen, Marcy P. Lascano, Johanna Luthman, Helen McCabe, Beverly Mack, Heidi Marx, Laura Saetveit Miles, Dale E. Miller, Lydia Moland, Katharine O'Reilly, Caterina Pelló, Ruth Perry, Eric Schwitzgebel, Patricia Sheridan, Walter P. Simons, Janet Todd, Christina Van Dyke, Hwa Yeong Wang, and Sandra Wawrytko.

Thanks to my incredible editor, Katie Raissian, for inspiring edits, conversation, and overall esteem for the creative process; I'm indebted to the impressive team at Grove Atlantic. Thank you to Peter Blackstock and Clare Drysdale of Grove UK for your enthusiasm. Thanks especially to my agent Tisse Takagi for your brilliance and belief in my work.

Thanks to Carrie Frye for your sharp eye. To Janet Byrne for all of the catches. I'm also grateful to Sophie Amieva, Susu Bagert, Ariel Bleicher, Hillary Brenhouse, Skye Cleary, Sarah Gerard, Liz Greene,

Alex Ivey, Anik Levy, Rachel Papo, Brooke Penaluna, Lisa Sardinas, Stephanie Shore, Chelsea Wald, and many others.

To my mentors at Columbia University Graduate School of Journalism: Kevin Coyne, Paula Span, Jonathan Weiner, and, especially, Sam Freedman who championed this project in its earliest form. To my former colleagues at *Nautilus* and *Guernica* magazines for giving me a home after academia: you continue to inspire me.

To my partner, Mark, for your love, support, and enthusiasm for my work, not to mention your wisdom and overall radiance—*j'aime le way qu'à hang*; and to Loïc and Clio, my two sweet loves. Finally, to my parents and my sisters. This book is for you.

Notes

Author's Note

1. The contemporary philosopher Kate Manne writes that misogyny isn't restricted to the hatred of women but that it also includes behaving in a way that keeps women down, which can take many forms. It can be overt, such as harassing or assaulting women, or it can be subtle, such as contributing to a "chilly" environment where women are ignored and their concerns and ambitions are not taken as seriously as men's. Kate Manne, *Down Girl: The Logic of Misogyny* (New York: Oxford University Press, 2017).

2. Sarah-Jane Leslie, Andrei Cimpian, Meredith Meyer, and Edward Freeland, "Expectations of Brilliance Underlie Gender Distributions across Academic Disciplines," *Science* 347, no. 6219 (January 16, 2015): 262–65, https://doi.org/10.1126/science.1261375.

3. Morgan Thompson, Toni Adleberg, Sam Sims, and Eddy Nahmias, "Why Do Women Leave Philosophy? Surveying Students at the Introductory Level," *Philosopher's Imprint* 16, no. 6 (March 2016): 16, http://hdl.handle.net/2027/spo.3521354.0016.006.

4. See: Jerry Bamburg, *Raising Expectations to Improve Student Learning* (Oak Brook, IL: North Central Regional Educational Laboratory, 1994); and Jean Stockard and Maralee Mayberry, *Effective Educational Environments* (Newbury Park, CA: Corwin Press, 1992).

5. Only 17 percent of full-time academic philosophers are women, matching the number in astronomy and just beating the number in physics (12 percent). See: Andrew Janiak and Christia Mercer, "Philosophy's Gender Bias: For Too Long, Scholars Say, Women Have Been Ignored," *Washington Post*, April 28, 2015, https://www.washingtonpost.com/news/grade-point/wp/2015/04/28/philosophys-gender-bias-for-too-long-scholars-say-women-have-been-ignored/. And these paltry numbers matter, because there is evidence that the percentage of women faculty in a field directly correlates to the number of women who graduate with PhDs. See: Eric Schwitzgebel, "In Philosophy, Departments with More Women Faculty Award More PhDs to Women (Plus Some Other Interesting Facts)," Splintered Mind, March 1, 2019, http://schwitzsplinters.blogspot.com/2019/03/in-philosophy-departments-with-more.html.

6. Eric Schwitzgebel, "Citation of Women and Ethnic Minorities in the *Stanford Encyclopedia of Philosophy*," Splintered Mind, August 7, 2014, http://schwitzsplinters.blogspot.com/2014/08/citation-of-women-and-ethnic-minorities.html.

7. Eric Schwitzgebel and Carolyn Dicey Jennings, "Women in Philosophy: Quantitative Analyses of Specialization, Prevalence, Visibility, and Generational Change," *Public Affairs Quarterly* 31 (2017): 83–105; also see: "Data on Women in Philosophy," American Philosophical Association, accessed November 21, 2021, http://www.apaonlinecsw.org/data-on-women-in-philosophy/.

8. Schwitzgebel, "Citation of Women and Ethnic Minorities in the *Stanford Encyclopedia of Philosophy*"; Liam Kofi Bright, "Publications by Black Authors in Leiter Top 15 Journals 2003–2012," *Splintered Mind*, January 18, 2016, http://schwitzsplinters.blogspot.com/2016/01/publications-by-black-authors-in-leiter.html.

9. For instance, ethnic minorities make up a tiny fraction of total philosophy PhDs: Latinx (6.3 percent), Asians or other Pacific Islanders (3.2 percent), Blacks (3 percent), and American Indians or Alaska Natives (.1 percent). For recent data on Black PhD recipients in philosophy see: Eric Schwitzgebel, "Diversity in Philosophy Departments: Introduction," American Philosophical Association Blog, June 11, 2020, https://blog.apaonline.org/2020/06/11/diversity-in-philosophy-departments-introduction/; for data on other ethnic minorities, see: Eric Schwitzgebel, "Percentages of U.S. Doctorates in Philosophy Given to Women and to Minorities, 1973–2014," Daily Nous, January 13, 2016, https://dailynous.com/2016/01/13/percentages-of-u-s-doctorates-in-philosophy-given-to-women-and-to-minorities-1973-2014-guest-post-by-eric-schwitzgebel/.

10. See, for instance: Michelle Bastion, "Philosophy Disturbed: Reflections on Moving Between Field and Philosophy," *Parallax* 24, no. 4 (2018): 449–65, https://doi.org/10.1080/13534645.2018.1546723; Kristie Dotson, "How Is This Paper Philosophy?," *Comparative Philosophy* 3, no. 1 (2012): 3–29; Gayle Salamon, "Justification and Queer Method, or Leaving Philosophy," *Hypatia* 24, no. 1 (2009): 225–30, https://doi.org/10.1111/j.1527-2001.2009.00015.x.

11. Shelley Tremain, "Disabling Philosophy," *Philosophers' Magazine*, no. 65 (2014): 15–17. A survey of disabled philosophers in the field suggests they represent less than 4 percent of full-time faculty in the United States—well below the 20 to 25 percent of disabled people in the overall population.

12. Salamon, "Justification," 230.

A Woman Thinker

1. A little note on usage: In this book, I often use the terms sex and gender to signify two different things: Sex is biological, whereas gender is psychological and social. But sometimes I collapse them—intentionally.

   This is because I do not see these terms as representative of absolute categories, but helpful tools with significant shortcomings. The sex/gender distinction is helpful because it creates a space to say that the physical hardware a person is born with is not the same thing as and so not necessarily indicative (or predictive) of how they (will) think, feel, or behave in society. That said, there are also good reasons to see sex, and not just gender, as culturally contingent. For example, the history of science reveals how things we often take to be biological facts are instead laden with theory (and bias). In addition, holding fast to sex as an essential category serves to exclude individuals who in other ways identify as women.

In the time of the four main philosophers I write about in this book, the sex/gender terminological distinction did not exist. This is probably because most people took for granted that a person's reproductive organs were determinative of a person's behavior and roles in society. But this doesn't mean no one was making a distinction between sex and gender that would be familiar to us today. The women philosophers I write about took for granted that women had female sex organs but questioned what this implied about their social roles and identity.

On the Prejudices of Philosophers

1. For this bird's-eye view of patriarchy throughout intellectual history, I'm grateful to many scholars, including Prudence Allen, *The Concept of Woman*, 2 vols. (Grand Rapids, MI: Eerdmans, 1996–2007); Londa Schiebinger, *The Mind Has No Sex?: Women in the Origins of Modern Science* (Cambridge, MA: Harvard University Press, 1991); Gerda Lerner, *The Creation of Feminist Consciousness: From the Middle Ages to Eighteen-Seventy* (New York: Oxford University Press, 1994) and *The Creation of Patriarchy* (New York: Oxford University Press, 1987); Beverley Clack, ed., *Misogyny in the Western Philosophical Tradition: A Reader* (New York: Routledge, 1999).

2. Quoted in Aristotle, *The Athenian Constitution, the Eudemian Ethics, on Virtues and Vices* (Cambridge, MA: Loeb Classical Library, 1935), vol. 7, 1.

3. For more on the lives of women in ancient Greece, see: Sue Blundell, *Women in Ancient Greece* (Cambridge, MA: Harvard University Press, 1995); Pierre Brule, *Women of Ancient Greece* (Edinburgh: Edinburgh University Press, 2003).

4. Aristotle in bk. 10 of the *Nicomachean Ethics* argues that being born in the right place at the right time is necessary to do philosophy; Plato is believed to have said he was thankful he was not born a woman: "'I thank God,' he used to say, 'that I was born Greek and not barbarian, freeman and not slave, man and not woman; but above all, that I was born in the age of Socrates.'" From Will Durant, *The Story of Philosophy: The Lives and Opinions of the World's Greatest Philosophers* (New York: Pocket Books, 1991), 13.

5. Slavery was another source of labor these early questioners made use of without question. Moses I. Finley and Brent D. Shaw, *Ancient Slavery and Modern Ideology* (Princeton, NJ: Markus Weiner Publishers, 2017), 80; Bertrand Russell, *The History of Western Philosophy* (New York: Simon and Schuster, 1945), 34. Russell says ancient philosophers relied "upon the labor of men whose inferiority is unquestioned."

6. For an overview of Pythagoras and his school, see: John Burnet, *Early Greek Philosophy* (London: A. and C. Black, 1908), 319–56; for the Pythagoreans on women, see: Allen, *The Concept of Woman*, vol. 1, 19–24.

7. Cornelia J. de Vogel, *Pythagoras and Early Pythagoreanism: An Interpretation of Neglected Evidence on the Philosopher Pythagoras* (Assen, Netherlands: Van Gorcum, 1996), 90.

8. "Democritus," *Internet Encyclopedia of Philosophy*, accessed November 21, 2021, https://iep.utm.edu/democrit/.

9. Sylvia Berryman, "Democritus," *Stanford Encyclopedia of Philosophy*, Winter 2016, https://plato.stanford.edu/archives/win2016/entries/democritus/.

10. Quoted in Kathleen Freeman, *Ancilla to the Presocratic Philosophers: A Complete Translation of the Fragments in Diels* (Cambridge, MA: Harvard University Press, 1996), 103.

11. See Monte Johnson and Catherine Wilson, "Lucretius and the History of Science," *The Cambridge Companion to Lucretius* (Cambridge: Cambridge University Press, 2007), 131; Stephen Greenblatt, *The Swerve: How the World Became Modern* (New York: W. W. Norton and Company, 2012), 5–6 and chap. 3; Sylvia Berryman, "Ancient Atomism," *Stanford Encyclopedia of Philosophy*, Winter 2016, https://plato.stanford.edu/entries/atomism-ancient/.

12. "Lucretius," *Internet Encyclopedia of Philosophy*, accessed March 2, 2019, https://www.iep.utm.edu/lucretiu/.

13. Lucretius, *On the Nature of Things*, trans. Cyril Bailey (Oxford: Clarendon Press, 1910), 220 (for "pity on the weak"), 231 (for "race of men"), and 182 (for "assign to women excellencies which are not theirs").

14. Diogenes Laërtius, *Lives of Eminent Philosophers*, trans. R. D. Hicks (Cambridge, MA: Harvard University Press, 1925), bk. 3.

15. Allen, *The Concept of Woman*, vol. 1, 129–30; Richard C. Lewontin and reply by R. J. Nelson, "Plato's Women," *The New York Review of Books*, October 25, 1984, https://www.nybooks.com/articles/1984/10/25/platos-women/.

16. Plato, *The Republic*, trans. Benjamin Jowett (Oxford: Clarendon Press, 1888), bk. 5.

17. Lewontin, "Plato's Women."

18. Laërtius, *Lives of Eminent Philosophers*, bk. 5.

19. Terence Irwin and Gail Fine, introduction to Aristotle, *Selections* (Indianapolis, IN: Hackett, 1995), xiii–xiv; Jonathan Barnes, *Aristotle: A Very Short Introduction* (New York: Oxford University Press, 2000), 1–6; Gerard J. Hughes, *The Routledge Guidebook to Aristotle's Ethics* (New York: Routledge, 2013), 1–7; Anton-Hermann Chroust, *Aristotle: New Light on His Life and on Some of His Lost Works, Volume 1: Some Novel Interpretations of the Man and His Life* (London: Routledge, 2017), 199–209.

20. Laërtius, *Lives of Eminent Philosophers*, bk. 5.

21. Donald Ernest Wilson Wormell, "Hermias," in *The Oxford Classical Dictionary* (Oxford: Oxford University Press, 2005), http://www.oxfordreference.com/view/10.1093/acref/9780198606413.001.0001/acref-9780198606413-e-3042.

22. For a discussion of the relationship between biology and behavior in Aristotle's teleology, see: Hughes, *Guidebook to Aristotle's Ethics*, 5–7, 36–44, 48, and 148–49.

23. Kate Campbell Hurde-Mead, "Pythias," in *A History of Women in Medicine: From the Earliest of Times to the Beginning of the Nineteenth Century* (Haddam, CT: Haddam Press, 1938); Marilyn Ogilvie, Joy Harvey, and Margaret Rossiter, "Pythias of Assos," in *The Biographical Dictionary of Women in Science: Pioneering Lives from Ancient Times to the Mid-20th Century* (London: Routledge, 2000), 1062.

24. Aristotle, *Aristotle's Generation of Animals: A Critical Guide*, ed. Andrea Falcon and David Lefebvre (Cambridge: Cambridge University Press, 2018), 173.

25. Aristotle, *Aristotle's Politics: A Critical Guide*, ed. Thornton Lockwood and Thanassis Samaras (Cambridge: Cambridge University Press, 2015), 58.

26. Michael Nolan, "Passive and Deformed? Did Aristotle Really Say This?" *New Blackfriars* 76, no. 893 (1995): 237–57. For more on the implications of Aristotle's philosophy of biology for females, see: Robert Mayhew, *The Female in Aristotle's Biology: Reason or Rationalization* (Chicago: University of Chicago Press, 2004).

27. C. D. C. Reeve, introduction to Aristotle, *Politics*, trans. C. D. C. Reeve (Indianapolis, IN: Hackett, 1988), xvii–xviii.

28. The historical sources are not in agreement on when Pythias died. Aristotle's will as recounted by Diogenes Laërtius in *Lives of Eminent Philosophers*, vol. 1, bk. 5; the Arabic version of the philosopher's will is slightly different and refers to Herpyllis as a "maid-servant" and "concubine": Chroust, *Aristotle*, 198.

29. Allen, *The Concept of Woman*, vol. 1, 131.

30. Aristotle, *Politics*, trans. C. D. C. Reeve, 24.

31. Chroust, *Aristotle*, 198.

32. Barnes, *Aristotle*, 16. Barnes reports that Pythias bore both of Aristotle's children.

33. Galen, *On the Usefulness of the Parts of the Body*, trans. Margaret Tallmadge (Ithaca, NY: Cornell University Press, 1968), B14.

34. Galen, *On the Usefulness of the Parts of the Body*, B14.

35. Susan P. Mattern, *The Prince of Medicine: Galen in the Roman Empire* (New York: Oxford University Press, 2013), 31, 281–85.

36. Allen, *The Concept of Woman*, vol. 1, 234.

37. Augustine, *De Beata Vita (Happiness—A Study)*, trans. Francis E. Tourscher (Philadelphia: The Peter Reilly Company, 1937), 27.

38. Stephen Greenblatt, *The Rise and Fall of Adam and Eve: The Story That Created Us* (New York: W. W. Norton, 2018), 111.

39. Quoted in Allen, *The Concept of Woman*, vol. 1, 231.

40. Augustine, *Confessions*, trans. F. J. Sheed, (Indianapolis, IN: Hackett, 2007), 152.

41. Ibn Rushd (Averroes), *Aristotelis Opera cum Averrois Commentariis* (Frankfurt: Minerva Verlag, 1962) vol. 3, 234. For more on Ibn Rushd, see: Peter Adamson and Matteo Di Giovanni, eds., *Interpreting Averroes: Critical Essays* (New York: Cambridge

University Press, 2019) and Josép Puig, "Ibn Rushd's Natural Philosophy," *Stanford Encyclopedia of Philosophy*, Fall 2018, https://plato.stanford.edu/archives/fall2018/entries/ibn-rushd-natural/.

42. Ibn Rushd (Averroes), *On Plato's Republic*, trans. Ralph Lerner (Ithaca, NY: Cornell University Press, 1974), 58.

43. Quoted in Allen, *The Concept of Woman*, vol. 1, 400.

44. James Axtell, *Wisdom's Workshop: The Rise of the Modern University* (Princeton, NJ: Princeton University Press, 2016), 25–26.

45. In the fourteenth century, a few women were allowed to study and teach medicine at the University of Bologna, though enrollment was not officially open to women. See: Leigh Whaley, "Networks, Patronage and Women of Science during the Italian Enlightenment," *Early Modern Women* 11, no. 1 (2016): 187–96.

46. Quoted in Allen, *The Concept of Woman*, vol. 1, 399.

47. Jill Kraye, "The Printing History of Aristotle in the Fifteenth Century: A Bibliographical Approach to Renaissance Philosophy," *Renaissance Studies* 9, no. 2 (1995): 189–211, http://www.jstor.org/stable/24412321.

48. Sarah Schuetze, "Early America's Guide to Sex: Aristotle's Masterpiece," *Common-Place* 17, no. 3 (2017), http://commonplace.online/article/early-americas-guide-to-sex/.

49. Martine van Elk, *Early Modern Women's Writing: Domesticity, Privacy, and the Public Sphere in England and the Dutch Republic* (New York: Palgrave Macmillan, 2017), 47.

50. Quoted in Elk, *Early Modern Women's Writing*, 34.

51. Phyllis Stock, *Better Than Rubies: A History of Women's Education* (New York: Putnam, 1978), 50–54; and Elk, *Early Modern Women's Writing*, 29–31.

52. G. W. Bernard, "The Dissolution of the Monasteries," *History* 96, no. 324 (2011): 390–409, https://doi.org/10.1111/j.1468-229X.2011.00526.x.

53. Allen, *The Concept of Woman*, vol. 2, 72–3.

54. Merry E. Wiesner-Hanks, *Women and Gender in Early Modern Europe* (Cambridge: Cambridge University Press, 2019), 15.

55. Jean de La Bruyère, *The Characters*, trans. Henri Van Laun (New York: Scribner and Welford, 1885), 74.

56. Jennifer Rampling, "History of Science: Trial by Gender," *Nature* 527, no. 7577 (November 2015): 164–64, https://doi.org/10.1038/527164a.

57. James Sprenger and Henry Kramer, *Malleus Maleficarum (1486)*, trans. Montague Summers (New York: Dover, 1971), 41.

58. Ritta Jo Horsley and Richard A. Horsley, "On the Trail of the 'Witches': Wise Women, Midwives and the European Witch Hunts," *Women in German Yearbook: Feminist Studies in German Literature and Culture* 3 (1986): 1–28, doi: 10.1353/wgy.2012.0014.

59. Wiesner-Hanks, *Women and Gender*, 253.

60. Ulinka Rublack, *The Astronomer and the Witch: Johannes Kepler's Fight for His Mother* (Oxford: Oxford University Press, 2017), 198.

61. Laura Snyder, "Science, Sorcery and Sons," *Wall Street Journal*, January 27, 2016, https://www.wsj.com/articles/science-sorcery-and-sons-1453854270.

62. R. E. R. Bunce, *Thomas Hobbes* (New York: Continuum, 2009), 15.

63. Sharon A. Lloyd and Susanne Sreedhar, "Hobbes's Moral and Political Philosophy," *Stanford Encyclopedia of Philosophy*, Fall 2020, https://plato.stanford.edu/archives/spr2019/entries/hobbes-moral/.

64. Benedict de Spinoza, *The Chief Works of Benedict Spinoza*, trans. R. H. M. Elwes (London: George Bell and Sons, 1887), 387.

65. Quoted in Schiebinger, *The Mind Has No Sex?*, 39–41.

66. Annette Baier, "Good Men's Women: Hume on Chastity and Trust," *Hume Studies* 5, no. 1 (1979): 1–19, https://muse.jhu.edu/article/389405; David Hume, *A Treatise of Human Nature* (New York: Oxford University Press, 2000), 364.

67. Aaron Garrett and Silvia Sebastiani, "David Hume on Race," ed. Naomi Zak, *The Oxford Handbook of Philosophy and Race* (New York: Oxford University Press, 2017), 31–43.

68. Justin E. H. Smith, "The Enlightenment's 'Race' Problem, and Ours," *New York Times*, February 10, 2013, https://opinionator.blogs.nytimes.com/2013/02/10/why-has-race-survived/.

69. Barbara Taylor, "Feminism and the Enlightenment, 1650–1850," *History Workshop Journal* 47 (Spring 1999): 264–65. Taylor writes that "the Enlightenment world resisted feminist ideas as much as it encouraged their emergence."

70. Immanuel Kant, *Observations on the Feeling of the Beautiful and Sublime and Other Writings*, ed. and trans. Patrick Frierson and Paul Guyer (Cambridge: Cambridge University Press, 2011), 61.

71. Lord Chesterfield, *Letters* (Oxford: Oxford University Press, 1998), 91.

72. Barbara Whitehead, introduction to *Women's Education in Early Modern Europe: A History, 1500 to 1800* (New York: Routledge, 1999), xi.

73. Georg Wilhelm Fredrich Hegel, *The Philosophy of Right*, trans. H. B. Nisbet (Cambridge: Cambridge University Press, 1991), 207.

74. Vincent Philippe Emmanuel Guillin, "Auguste Comte and John Stuart Mill on Sexual Equality: Historical, Methodological and Philosophical Issues" (PhD diss., London School of Economics and Political Science, 2005), 49. In the 1830s, coeducational schools were new and controversial. See Claudia Goldin and Lawrence F. Katz: "Putting the 'Co' in Education: Timing, Reasons, and Consequences of College Coeducation from 1835 to the Present," *Journal of Human Capital* 5, no. 4 (December 2011): 377–417.

75. Quoted in Guillin, "Auguste Comte," 16.

76. Quoted in Guillin, "Auguste Comte," 15.

77. Charles Darwin, *Descent of Man, and Selection in Relation to Sex*, vol. 2 (London, 1871), 327.

78. "Darwin's Women," University of Cambridge, accessed November 3, 2020, https://www.cam.ac.uk/research/news/darwins-women.

79. Edward H. Clarke, *Sex in Education; or, A Fair Chance for Girls* (Boston: James R. Osgood, 1873), https://www.gutenberg.org/ebooks/18504; Rosalind Rosenberg, *Beyond Separate Spheres: Intellectual Roots of Modern Feminism* (New Haven, CT: Yale University Press, 1982), 8, 38.

80. Friedrich Nietzsche, *Beyond Good and Evil: Prelude to a Philosophy of the Future*, trans. Walter Kaufmann (New York: Vintage, 1989), 13.

81. Jane Kneller, "Feminism," in *The Oxford Handbook of German Philosophy in the Nineteenth Century*, ed. Michael N. Forster and Kristin Gjesdal (Oxford: Oxford University Press, 2015), https://doi.org/10.1093/oxfordhb/9780199696543.013.0027.

82. Sue Prideaux, "Far Right, Misogynist, Humourless? Why Nietzsche Is Misunderstood," *Guardian*, October 6, 2018, https://www.theguardian.com/books/2018/oct/06/exploding-nietzsche-myths-need-dynamiting.

83. Ray Monk, *Ludwig Wittgenstein: The Duty of Genius* (New York: Penguin Books, 1991), 498.

84. Stock, *Better Than Rubies*, 225.

85. J. R. Lucas, "Because You Are a Woman," *Philosophy* vol. 448, No. 184 (1973): 165.

86. Richard Swinburne, "The Problem of Evil," *Reason and Religion*, ed. S. C. Brown (Ithaca, NY: Cornell University Press, 1977), 88. See also: Clack, *Misogyny in the Western Philosophical Tradition*, 5–6.

87. Luce Irigaray, *This Sex Which Is Not One*, trans. Catherine Porter, (Ithaca, NY: Cornell University Press, 1977) 76.

88. Quoted in Nathan Heller, "The Philosopher Redefining Equality," *New Yorker*, December 31, 2018, https://www.newyorker.com/magazine/2019/01/07/the-philosopher-redefining-equality.

Discovery in the Margins

1. J. A. Passmore, *Ralph Cudworth: An Interpretation* (Bristol, UK: Thoemmes, 1990), 79.

2. Tjitske Akkerman and Siep Stuurman, "Introduction: Feminism in European History," in *Perspectives on Feminist Political Thought in European History: From the Middle Ages to the Present*, ed. Tjitske Akkerman and Siep Stuurman (New York: Routledge, 1998), 13; Valerie Bryson, *Feminist Political Theory* (New York: Palgrave Macmillan, 2003), 12–13 and *Feminist Debates* (New York: New York University Press, 1999), chap. 2; Arvonne S. Fraser, "Becoming Human: The Origins and Development of Women's Human Rights," *Human Rights Quarterly* 21, no. 4 (1999): 853–54; Carol Gilligan, *In a Different Voice: Psychological Theory and Women's Development* (Cambridge, MA: Harvard

University Press, 1996), 129; Lena Halldenius, "The Primacy of Right: On the Triad of Liberty, Equality and Virtue in Wollstonecraft's Political Thought," *British Journal of the History of Philosophy* 15, no. 1 (2007): 75–99; Gerda Lerner, *The Creation of Feminist Consciousness: From the Middle Ages to Eighteen-Seventy* (New York: Oxford University Press, 1993), 19, 209; Karen Offen, "Reclaiming the European Enlightenment for Feminism: Or Prolegomena to Any Future History of Eighteenth-Century Europe," in *Perspectives on Feminist Political Thought*, 86; Susan Moller Okin, "Justice and Gender," *Philosophy and Public Affairs* 16, no. 1 (1987): 43; Hilda Smith, "Intellectual Bases for Feminist Analyses: The Seventeenth and Eighteenth Centuries," in *Women and Reason*, ed. Elizabeth D. Harvey and Kathleen Okruhlik (Ann Arbor: University of Michigan Press, 1992), 20–21.

A Room of Her Own

1. Lynette McGrath, *Subjectivity and Women's Poetry in Early Modern England: Why on the Ridge Should She Desire to Go?* (New York: Routledge, 2017), 1–2.

2. Catherine Wilson, "Love of God and Love of Creatures: The Masham-Astell Debate," *History of Philosophy Quarterly* 21, no. 3 (2004): 289, https://www.jstor.org/stable/27744993.

3. Some early modern women had access to private libraries. See: Leah Knight, Micheline White, and Elizabeth Sauer, eds., *Women's Bookscapes in Early Modern Britain: Reading, Ownership, Circulation* (Ann Arbor: University of Michigan Press, 2018).

4. The historical research on Astell's life is slim. The authoritative biography is Ruth Perry, *The Celebrated Mary Astell: An Early English Feminist* (Chicago: University of Chicago Press, 1986). Most scholarship looks to this masterfully researched book for details of her life. This book also is the only published resource for reprints of Astell's poetry and personal letters. There are additional exceptional books whose authors did archival research that I am also indebted to: Sarah Louise Trethewey Apetrei, *Women, Feminism and Religion in Early Enlightenment England* (Cambridge: Cambridge University Press, 2010); Jacqueline Broad, *The Philosophy of Mary Astell: An Early Modern Theory of Virtue* (New York: Oxford University Press, 2015); Jacqueline Broad, *Women Philosophers of the Seventeenth Century* (Cambridge: Cambridge University Press, 2007); Patricia Springborg, *Mary Astell: Theorist of Freedom from Domination* (Cambridge: Cambridge University Press, 2005).

5. Perry, *The Celebrated Mary Astell*, 29.

6. Quoted in Christine Peters, "Single Women in Early Modern England: Attitudes and Expectations," *Continuity and Change* 12, no. 3 (1997): 325–45.

7. For more on the daily lives of girls in the seventeenth century, see: Perry, *The Celebrated Mary Astell*; Merry E. Wiesner-Hanks, *Women and Gender in Early Modern Europe* (Cambridge: Cambridge University Press, 2008); Sara Mendelson and Patricia Crawford, *Women in Early Modern England 1550–1720* (Oxford: Oxford University Press, 2000).

8. In 1723, Jonathan Swift wrote that "not one Gentleman's Daughter in a Thousand, should be brought to read, or understand her own Natural Tongue, or be Judge of the easiest Books that are written in it . . . They are not so much as taught to spell in their Childhood, nor can ever attain to it in their whole lives." Swift, "A Letter to a Very Young Lady on Her Marriage," in *The Works of Reverend Dr. Jonathan Swift Volume I* (Dublin: George Faulkner, 1768), 370.

9. G. W. Bernard, "The Dissolution of the Monasteries," *History* 96, no. 324 (2011): 390–409, https://doi.org/10.1111/j.1468-229X.2011.00526.x.

10. Perry, *The Celebrated Mary Astell*, 46.

11. Perry, *The Celebrated Mary Astell*, 48.

12. Perry, *The Celebrated Mary Astell*, 53.

13. Perry, *The Celebrated Mary Astell*, 49.

14. For studies on Cambridge Platonism, see: Ernst Cassirer, *The Platonic Renaissance in England*, trans. James P. Pettegrove (Edinburgh: Nelson, 1953); Stephen Darwall, *British Moralists and the Internal Ought* (Cambridge: Cambridge University Press, 1992); Sarah Hutton, "The Cambridge Platonists," in *Blackwell Companion to Early Modern Philosophy*, ed. S. Nadler (Oxford: Blackwell, 2002), 308–19; J. A. Passmore, *Ralph Cudworth: An Interpretation* (Bristol, UK: Thoemmes, 1990); C. A. Patrides, *The Cambridge Platonists* (Cambridge, MA: Harvard University Press, 1970); G. A. Rogers, J. M. Vienne, and Yves Charles Zarka, eds., *The Cambridge Platonists in Philosophical Context: Politics, Metaphysics and Religion* (Dordrecht, Netherlands: Kluwer, 1997).

15. Perry, *The Celebrated Mary Astell*, 57–59.

16. Astell, "The Invitation," reprinted in Perry, *The Celebrated Mary Astell*, 401–3.

17. Astell, "Affliction," reprinted in Perry, *The Celebrated Mary Astell*, 445.

18. Astell, "Solitude," reprinted in Perry, *The Celebrated Mary Astell*, 406.

19. Astell, "Heaven," reprinted in Perry, *The Celebrated Mary Astell*, 429.

20. Astell, "The Thanksgiving," reprinted in Perry, *The Celebrated Mary Astell*, 451.

21. Astell, "The Thanksgiving," 451.

22. Astell, "The Invitation," 401–3.

23. Astell, "The Thanksgiving," 451.

24. Astell, "Ambition," reprinted in Perry, *The Celebrated Mary Astell*, 405.

25. Astell, "Solitude," 406.

26. Astell, "Heaven," 430.

27. Apetrei, *Women, Feminism and Religion*, 83.

28. Astell, "Affliction," 445. "I can have liberty to Pray, / And to examine when I go astray."

29. Astell, "Affliction," 445.

30. Mary Astell, *A Serious Proposal to the Ladies*, ed. Patricia Springborg (Ontario, CA: Broadview Press, 2002), 80.

31. Astell, "Ambition," 405.

> *What's this that with such vigour fills my brest?*
> *Like the first mover finds no rest,*
> *And with it's force dos all things draw,*
> *Makes all submit to its imperial Law!*
> *Sure 'tis a spark 'bove what Prometheus stole,*
> *Kindled by a heav'nly coal,*
> *Their sophistry I can controul,*
> *Who falsely say that women have no Soul.*

32. Astell, "Ambition," 405.

33. Astell, "Heaven," 429.

34. Naomi Zack, *Bachelors of Science: Seventeenth-Century Identity, Then and Now* (Philadelphia: Temple University Press, 1996) 57–67.

35. Amy Froide, *Never Married: Singlewomen in Early Modern England* (Oxford: Oxford University Press, 2007), 17.

36. Astell, "Judgment," reprinted in Perry, *The Celebrated Mary Astell*, 417.

37. Froide, *Never Married*, 99.

38. Robert O. Bucholz and Joseph P. Ward, *London: A Social and Cultural History, 1550–1750* (Cambridge: Cambridge University Press, 2012), 157–58.

39. Janet Todd, *Aphra Behn: The Secret Life* (New Brunswick, NJ: Rutgers University Press, 1996), 1–8. Behn died in 1689, about a year after Astell arrived in London.

40. John E. Crofts, *Packhorse, Waggon and Post: Land Carriage and Communications Under the Tudors and Stuarts* (London: Routledge, 1967), 19, 38–40.

41. For more on highway robbery in early modern England, see: Gillian Spraggs, *Outlaws and Highwaymen: The Cult of the Robber in England from the Middle Ages to the Nineteenth Century* (London: Pimlico, 2001) and Peter Newark, *Crimson Book of Highwaymen* (Hopkins, MN: Olympic Marketing Corp, 1988).

42. Astell, "Death," reprinted in Perry, *The Celebrated Mary Astell*, 407.

43. Emily Cockayne, *Hubbub: Filth, Noise, and Stench in England, 1600–1770* (New Haven, CT: Yale University Press, 2008), 34, 54, and 63 (for smells and what to do about them); 56–57, 58, and 155 (for fleas); 60 (for pig hair brushes); 96 and 106 (for motion and noises of the carriage).

44. Astell, "Affliction," 445.

45. Perry, *The Celebrated Mary Astell*, 66.

46. Perry, *The Celebrated Mary Astell*, 66.

47. Perry, *The Celebrated Mary Astell*, 68.

48. Broad, *The Philosophy of Mary Astell*, 5.

49. Katherine R. Kellett, "Performance, Performativity, and Identity in Margaret Cavendish's 'The Convent of Pleasure,'" *Studies in English Literature, 1500–1900* 48, No. 2 (Spring 2008): 419–42, http://www.jstor.org/stable/40071341.

50. Astell, *A Serious Proposal*, 51–52.

51. Astell, *A Serious Proposal*, 77.

52. Astell, *A Serious Proposal*, 64.

53. Astell, *A Serious Proposal*, 83.

54. Astell, *A Serious Proposal*, 55.

55. Astell, *A Serious Proposal*, 94.

56. Astell, *A Serious Proposal*, 94.

57. Astell, *A Serious Proposal*, 59–60. "The Incapacity, if there be any, is acquired not natural" and "The Cause therefore of the defects we labour under, is, if not wholly, yet at least in the first place, to be ascribed to the mistakes of our Education," which "spreads its ill Influence through all our Lives."

58. Astell, *A Serious Proposal*, 139. She wrote, "As Prejudice fetters the Understanding so does Custom manacle the Will, which scarce knows how to divert from a Track which the generality around it take, and to which it has it self been habituated."

59. Astell, *A Serious Proposal*, 89.

60. Astell, *A Serious Proposal*, 68.

61. Astell, *A Serious Proposal*, 73.

62. Plato, *The Collected Dialogues of Plato*, trans. Lane Cooper (Princeton, NJ: Princeton University Press), 479.

63. Perry, *The Celebrated Mary Astell*, 232–81.

64. Astell, *A Serious Proposal*, 73.

65. Astell, *A Serious Proposal*, 73.

66. Astell, *A Serious Proposal*, 106–8.

67. Astell, *A Serious Proposal*, 112: "For when the passion of a Lover is evaporated into the Indifference of a Husband . . . unless he be a very good Man . . . a wise and good Woman is useful and valuable in all Ages and Conditions . . . [she] lives a cheerful and pleasant life . . . the most happy life on Earth."

68. Astell, *A Serious Proposal*, 74.

69. Astell, *A Serious Proposal*, 82–83. Astell doesn't acknowledge Malebranche's sexist statements. Perry says it's because she didn't read French (cf. Perry, *The Celebrated Mary Astell*, 78). But English translations of his work were available at the time. See Charles J. McCracken, *Malebranche and British Philosophy* (Oxford: Oxford University Press, 1983), 11.

70. Astell, *A Serious Proposal*, 77. Study was essential to her religious practice, because religion was nothing "without a good Understanding."

71. Astell, *A Serious Proposal*, 70–71. "A truly Christian Life requires a clear Understanding as well as regular Affections, that both together may move the Will to a direct choice of Good and a stedfast adherence to it," she wrote. "Reason and Truth are firm and immutable, she who bottoms on them is on sure ground."

72. Astell, *A Serious Proposal*, 74.

73. Lady Mary Wortley Montagu, *The Selected Letters of Lady Mary Wortley Montagu*, ed. Robert Halsband (London: Longmans, 1970), 3.

74. Astell to Norris, *Mary Astell and John Norris: Letters Concerning the Love of God*, ed. Derek E. Taylor and Melvyn New (Aldershot, UK: Routledge, 2005), letter 7, 129.

75. Astell to Norris, *Letters Concerning the Love of God*, letter 5, 101.

76. Perry, *The Celebrated Mary Astell*, 233–81.

77. Perry, *The Celebrated Mary Astell*, 244.

78. Astell, *A Serious Proposal*, 73–74. She also refers to her college as an "institution," *A Serious Proposal*, 100.

79. Perry, *The Celebrated Mary Astell*, 23.

80. Astell letters reprinted in Perry, *The Celebrated Mary Astell*, 355–99.

81. Perry, *The Celebrated Mary Astell*, 7.

82. See: Mary, Lady Chudleigh, *The Poems and Prose of Mary, Lady Chudleigh*, ed. Margaret J. M. Ezell (New York: Oxford University Press, 1993).

83. Perry, *The Celebrated Mary Astell*, 137.

84. Perry, *The Celebrated Mary Astell*, 138. For an appreciation of women's friendship in the seventeenth century, I'm indebted to Cornelia Wilde, *Friendship, Love, and Letters: Ideals and Practices of Seraphic Friendship in 17th-Century England* (Heidelberg: Universitätsverlag Winter, 2012).

85. Actual divorces were rare and required the involvement of Parliament.

86. For details on the duchess, see: Tovio David Rosvall, *The Mazarine Legacy: The Life of Hortense Mancini, Duchess Mazarin* (New York: Viking, 1969); and Susan Shifrin, *The Wandering Life I Led: Essays on Hortense Mancini, Duchess Mazarin and Early Modern Women's Border Crossings* (Newcstle upon Tyne: Cambridge Scholars Publishing, 2009). And from Astell sources: Broad, *Women Philosophers of the Seventeenth Century*, 127–28; Perry, *The Celebrated Mary Astell*, 151–56.

87. Mary Astell, *Political Writings*, ed. Patricia Springborg, (Cambridge: Cambridge University Press, 1996), 34.

88. Astell, *Political Writings*, 48: "She who Elects a Monarch for Life, who gives him an Authority she Cannot recall howcver hc misapply it, who puts her fortune and Person entirely in his Powers."

89. Astell, *Political Writings*, 11.

90. Astell, *A Serious Proposal*, 106.

91. Astell, *Political Writings*, 55.

92. Astell, *Moderation Truly Stated, or A review of a late pamphlet entitul'd Moderation a vertue: with a prefatory discourse to Dr. D'Aveanant concerning his late essays on peace and war* (London, 1704), xxxv–xxxvi.

93. Ruth Perry, "Mary Astell and the Feminist Critique of Possessive Individualism," *Eighteenth-Century Studies* 23 (1990): 455.

94. John Locke, *Two Treatises of Government*, ed. Peter Laslett (Cambridge: Cambridge University Press, 1988), 2 § 48.

95. Locke, *Two Treatises of Government*, 2 § 82.

96. Astell, *Political Writings*, 18.

97. Astell, *Political Writings*, 17.

98. John Milton, *Political Writings*, ed. Martin Dzelzainis (Cambridge: Cambridge University Press, 1991), 1.

99. John Milton, *The Prose Writings of John Milton with a Life of the Author by C. Symmons* (Oxford: Oxford University Press, 1806), 226.

100. Astell, *Political Writings*, 46–47.

101. Astell, *A Serious Proposal*, 235.

102. Line Cottegnies and Sandrine Parageau, introduction to *Women and Curiosity in Early Modern England and France*, ed. Cottegnies, Parageau, and John J. Thompson (Leiden, Netherlands: 2016), 6–9.

103. Bonnie Calhoun, "Shaping the Public Sphere: English Coffeehouses and French Salons and the Age of the Enlightenment," *Colgate Academic Review* 3, no. 7 (2008): 76.

104. Cottegnies and Parageau, *Women and Curiosity*, 8.

105. Londa Schiebinger, *The Mind Has No Sex?: Women in the Origins of Modern Science* (Cambridge, MA: Harvard University Press, 1991), 188.

106. Astell, *Political Writings*, 28.

107. She wasn't alone in this effort. Aphra Behn translated a work by French scientist Bernard Fontenelle, who wrote how the female intellect was in some ways superior to the male intellect: a woman could make "observations so learned that the greatest Philosophers in *Europe* could make no better." But Fontenelle also thought that women's curiosity was too uneven for the methodicalness of science, and their insights wouldn't culminate in a systematic understanding of the world. French philosopher François Poulain de la Barre was more generous. His work, translated into English in 1677 as *The Woman as Good as the Man*, proposed that women were as smart as men if not smarter, because their minds hadn't been corrupted by university teachings. It's possible Astell read his work and found it empowering. In one passage that might have been inspired

by Poulain, she expressed pride in her native wits: "I can't pretend a Multitude of Books, Variety of Languages, and the Advantages of Academical Education or any Helps but what my own Curiosity afford." Poulin's work was primarily theoretical and didn't have the religious dimension of Astell's. Possibly because it was written by a man, it also didn't have the same urgency with respect to women's causes.

108. Astell is inconsistent about whether women's intellectual sensibility is naturally superior to men's. See Astell, *Political Writings*, 31, 58; and Astell, *A Serious Proposal*, 202–3, in which she says, "Fathers find other Business, they will not be confin'd to such a laborious work, they have not such opportunities of observing a Childs Temper, nor are the greatest part of 'em like to do much good, since Precepts contradicted by Example seldom prove effectual."

109. Astell, *The Christian Religion, As Profess'd by a Daughter of the Church of England* (London, 1705), 103. Astell wrote, "A woman can *put on the whole armour of God* without degenerating into a masculine Temper."

110. Astell, *A Serious Proposal*, 99–100: It's "a love that thinks nothing within the bounds of Power" that connects us to a community in an unselfish manner, that has "no Interests here to serve, no contrivances for another [Person]."

111. Astell, *Political Writings*, 7–31. In a couple instances, Astell is more modest, saying she only wants women to learn a modest amount, or she would never expect women to take on roles outside of being a teacher or a mother. But as I've suggested before, these passages serve as as reassurances to her readers: she doesn't want to intimidate women (or men in power, for that matter) by the truly radical aspects of her philosophy.

112. Astell, *A Serious Proposal*, 203.

113. Luce Irigaray, *This Sex Which Is Not One*, trans. Catherine Porter (Ithaca, NY: Cornell University Press, 1985), 84.

114. Perry, *The Celebrated Mary Astell*, 239.

115. Perry, *The Celebrated Mary Astell*, 295–96.

116. Perry, *The Celebrated Mary Astell*, 100.

117. Virginia Woolf, *Three Guineas* (New York: Harcourt, Brace, 1938), 27, 33. Woolf says, "It must be an experimental college, an adventurous college. Let it be built on lines of its own. It must be built not of carved stone and stained glass, but of some cheap, easily combustible material which does not hoard dust and perpetrate traditions. Do not have chapels. Do not have museums and libraries with chained books and first editions under glass cases . . . It should explore the ways in which mind and body can be made to co-operate; discover what new combinations make good wholes in human life."

118. Virginia Woolf, *A Room of One's Own* (New York: Harcourt, Brace, 1929), 45.

119. Astell, *A Serious Proposal*, 108.

120. Astell, *A Serious Proposal*, 83.

121. Astell, *A Serious Proposal*, 120.

122. Patricia Hill Collins, *Intersectionality as Critical Social Theory* (Durham, NC: Duke University Press, 2019), 130.

123. Springborg, introduction to *A Serious Proposal*, 12; and Perry, *The Celebrated Mary Astell*, 129; Astell, *A Serious Proposal*, 202.

124. Astell, *A Serious Proposal*, 88–89.

125. "Inessential" is a direct reference to Elizabeth Spelman's incredible book *Inessential Woman: Problems of Exclusion in Feminist Thought* (Boston: Beacon Press, 1988).

126. Julia Kristeva, *Powers of Horror: An Essay on Abjection*, trans. Leon S. Roudiez (New York: Columbia University Press, 1982), 2.

The Women behind the Men

1. Plato, *Complete Works*, trans. D. S. Hutcheson (Indianapolis, IN: Hackett, 1997), 1714. In the "Halcyon" dialogue, there is mention that Socrates had two wives. (Scholars debate whether this dialogue was written by Plato or one of his contemporaries.)

2. Xenophon, *The Works of Xenophon*, trans. H. G. Dakyns (New York: MacMillan Company, 1897), 300.

3. Peter Abelard and Heloise, *The Letters and Other Writings*, trans. William Levitan (Indianapolis, IN: Hackett, 2007), 11.

4. Abelard and Heloise, *The Letters and Other Writings*, 11.

5. Abelard and Heloise, *The Letters and Other Writings*, 61.

6. See translator's footnote: Abelard and Heloise, *The Letters and Other Writings*, 55.

7. Quoted in Étienne Gilson, *Heloise and Abelard* (Ann Arbor: University of Michigan Press, 1960), 48.

8. Abelard and Heloise, *The Letters and Other Writings*, 55.

9. Abelard and Heloise, *The Letters and Other Writings*, 310.

10. Abelard and Heloise, *The Letters and Other Writings*, 110.

11. Abelard and Heloise, *The Letters and Other Writings*, 107 (for menstruation-friendly clothing); 109 (for less manual labor than men); 113 (for food and drink allowances).

12. In Abelard and Heloise, *The Letters and Other Writings*, 56, Heloise says Peter borrowed her ideas: "When it suited your own purposes in that letter to your friend, and did not think it beneath your dignity to set out at least some of the arguments I used when I tried to dissuade you from this marriage of ours." In the footnote, the translator writes that the concept of worth that Heloise presents in this letter makes its way into Abelard's later work in the *Ethics*. Waithe writes that "the quotes Heloise uses in *Epistola II* in her argument against marriage, all appear in Abelard's *Theologia Christiana*, Book II," which was likely written after their correspondence and which Heloise would not have seen as she was already living in the convent. See Mary Ellen Waithe, *Medieval, Renaissance, and Enlightenment Women Philosophers, A.D. 500–1600* (Dordrecht, Netherlands: Kluwer, 1989), 70.

13. Alice Chambers Bunten, *Life of Alice Barnham (1592–1650), Wife of Sir Francis Bacon* (London: Oliphants, 1928), http://sirbacon.org/ResearchMaterial/Barnham.htm.

14. Bunten, *Life of Alice Barnham*.

15. Naomi Zack, *Bachelors of Science: Seventeenth-Century Identity, Then and Now* (Philadelphia: Temple University Press, 1996), 57. Zack describes the "English *bachelor of science*" as "both an unmarried man and an individual whose life's work was centered on the New Science, and to a lesser degree, on the New Politics. These bachelors of science were inventing themselves as much as they were creating contexts for redefining women, the natural world, and those who came to be conceptualized as the inhabitants of the present Third World," 2. She notes that "Descartes, Hobbes, Boyle, Locke and Newton were lifelong bachelors," 57.

16. Stephen Gaukroger, *Descartes: An Intellectual Biography* (New York: Oxford University Press, 1995), xvi, 1–2; Susan Bordo, ed., introduction to *Feminist Interpretations of René Descartes* (University Park: Penn State University Press, 1999), 1–4.

17. Gaukroger, *Descartes*, 353.

18. Bordo, *Feminist Interpretations*, 5.

19. Matthew D. Mendham, "Rousseau's Discarded Children: The Panoply of Excuses and the Question of Hypocrisy," *History of European Ideas* 41, no. 1 (2015): 131–52, https://doi.org/10.1080/01916599.2014.965495; Mary-Ann Glendon, "Les Lettres Inedites de Marie-Thérèse Le Vasseur," *Columbia: A Journal of Literature and Art*, no. 18/19 (1993): 165–72.

20. Londa Schiebinger, *The Mind Has No Sex?: Women in the Origins of Modern Science* (Cambridge, MA: Harvard University Press, 1991), 220.

21. Quoted in Phyllis Stock, *Better Than Rubies: A History of Women's Education* (New York: Putnam, 1978), 107; see also: Susan Moller Okin, "Rousseau's Natural Woman," *Journal of Politics* 41, no. 2 (1979): 393–416, https://doi.org/10.2307/2129771.

22. Jean-Jacques Rousseau, *Emile*, trans. William H. Payne (London: Appleton Press, 1909), 263.

23. For an alternative reading of Rousseau that does away with the image of him as a solitary bachelor and acknowledges Levasseur as a "true companion," see "Thérèse Levasseur's Improvised Life with Rousseau," in *The Wives of Western Philosophy*, edited by Jennifer Forestal and Menaka Philips (New York: Routledge, 2021), 107–26; and also Glendon, "Les Lettres Inedites de Marie-Thérèse Le Vasseur."

24. Quoted in Rae Langton, "Duty and Desolation," *Philosophy* 67, no. 262 (1992): 482, http://www.jstor.org/stable/3751703.

25. Quoted in Langton, "Duty and Desolation," 483–484.

26. Andrea Nye, *Feminism and Modern Philosophy: An Introduction* (New York: Routledge, 2004), 14–15.

27. Immanuel Kant, *Observations on the Feeling of the Beautiful and Sublime and Other Writings*, ed. and trans. Patrick Frierson and Paul Guyer (Cambridge: Cambridge University Press, 2011), 39.

28. Quoted in Nye, *Feminism and Modern Philosophy*, 15.

29. For a discussion of Hippel and his relationship to Kant, see: Anthony J. La Vopa, "Thinking about Marriage: Kant's Liberalism and the Peculiar Morality of Conjugal Union," *Journal of Modern History* 77, no. 1 (2005): 7–8, https://doi.org/10.1086/429427.

30. Quoted in Langton, "Duty and Desolation," 493. For more on the subject, see: James Edwin Mahon, "Kant and Maria von Herbert: Reticence vs. Deception," *Philosophy* 81, no. 317 (2006): 417–44.

31. Quoted in Langton, "Duty and Desolation," 493.

32. Nye, *Feminism and Modern Philosophy*, 14.

33. Quoted in Langton, "Duty and Desolation," 499.

34. Quoted in Langton, "Duty and Desolation," 494.

35. Quoted in Langton, "Duty and Desolation," 500.

36. Quoted in Dale E. Miller, "Harriet Taylor Mill," *Stanford Encyclopedia of Philosophy*, Spring 2019, https://plato.stanford.edu/archives/spr2019/entries/harriet-mill/.

37. Helen McCabe, "'Political . . . Civil and Domestic Slavery': Harriet Taylor Mill and Anna Doyle Wheeler on Marriage, Servitude, and Socialism," *British Journal for the History of Philosophy* 29, no. 2 (2020): 3, https://doi.org/10.1080/09608788.2020.1750348. For an excellent overview, see: Helen McCabe, "Harriet Taylor Mill," in *The Philosopher Queens: The Lives and Legacies of Philosophy's Unsung Women*, ed. Rebecca Buxton and Lisa Whiting (London: Unbound, 2020).

38. Martha Nussbaum, "The Speech of Alcibiades," in *The Philosophy of (Erotic) Love*, ed. Robert C. Solomon and Kathleen M. Higgins (Lawrence: University Press of Kansas, 1991), 301.

39. Solomon and Higgins, eds., "Introduction to Plato," in *The Philosophy of (Erotic) Love*, 13.

"Fitts" and Starts

1. A list of indispensible resources on Masham: Richard Acworth, "Cursory Reflections upon an Article Entitled 'What Is It with Damaris, Lady Masham?'" *Locke Studies: An Annual Journal of Locke Research* 6 (2006): 189–97; Jacqueline Broad, *Women Philosophers of the Seventeenth Century* (Cambridge: Cambridge University Press, 2007); Jacqueline Broad, "A Woman's Influence? John Locke and Damaris Masham on Moral Accountability," *Journal of the History of Ideas* 67, no. 3 (2006): 489–510; James G. Buickerood, introduction to *The Philosophical Works of Damaris, Lady Masham* (Bristol, UK: Thoemmes Continuum Press, 2004); James G. Buickerood, "What Is It with Damaris, Lady Masham? The Historiography of One Early Modern Woman Philosopher," *Locke Studies: An Annual*

Journal of Locke Research 5 (2005): 179–214; Margaret Ezell, "'Household Affaires Are the Opium of the Soul': Damaris Masham and the Necessity of Women's Poetry," in *Write or Be Written: Early Modern Women Poets and Cultural Constraints*, ed. Barbara Smith and Ursula Appelt (Aldershot, UK: Ashgate Publishing, 2001), 49–65; Lois Frankel, "Damaris Cudworth Masham: A Seventeenth Century Feminist Philosopher," *Hypatia* 4 (1989): 80–90; Mark Goldie, *John Locke and the Mashams at Oates* (Cambridge: Cambridge University Press, 2004); Bridget Hill, "Masham, Damaris, Lady Masham (1658–1708)" in *Oxford Dictionary of National Biography*, ed. Lawrence Goldman (Oxford: Oxford University Press, 2006); Sarah Hutton, "Damaris Cudworth, Lady Masham: Between Platonism and Enlightenment," *British Journal for the History of Philosophy* 1, no. 1 (1993); Sarah Hutton, "Lady Damaris Masham," *Stanford Encyclopedia of Philosophy*, Winter 2020, https://plato.stanford.edu/archives/win2020/entries/lady-masham/; Marcy P. Lascano, "Damaris Masham and 'The Law of Reason or Nature,'" *Modern Schoolman* 88, no. 3/4 (July/October 2011): 245–65; Peter Laslett, "Masham of Otes: The Rise and Fall of an English Family," *History Today*, n.d.; Sheryl O'Donnell, "'My Idea in Your Mind': John Locke and Damaris Cudworth Masham," in *Mothering the Mind: Twelve Studies of Writers and Their Silent Partners*, ed. Ruth Perry and Martine Watson Brownley (New York: Holmes and Meier, 1984); Sue Weinberg, "Damaris Cudworth Masham: A Learned Lady of the Seventeenth Century," in *Norms and Values: Essays on the Work of Virginia Held* (Lanham, MD: Rowman and Littlefield, 1998).

2. On bachelors, see: Naomi Zack, *Bachelors of Science: Seventeenth-Century Identity, Then and Now* (Philadelphia: Temple University Press, 1996), 65. On Cambridge life, see: Elisabeth Leedham-Green, *A Concise History of the University of Cambridge* (Cambridge: Cambridge University Press, 1996).

3. Broad, *Women Philosophers*, 117. Broad says John Covel writes of a time when Anne Conway stayed with Cudworth in the Master's Lodge at Christ's Church, Cambridge.

4. For more on Ralph Cudworth's ideas, see: Gerald R. Cragg, ed., *The Cambridge Platonists* (New York: Oxford University Press, 1968); C. A. Patrides, *The Cambridge Platonists* (Cambridge: Cambridge University Press, 1970); J. A. Passmore, *Ralph Cudworth: An Interpretation* (Bristol, UK: Thoemmes, 1990).

5. Passmore, *Ralph Cudworth*, 80.

6. Quoted in Passmore, *Ralph Cudworth*, 80.

7. Masham to Locke, April 7, 1688, in John Locke, *The Correspondence of John Locke*, ed. E. S. De Beer, 8 vols. (Oxford: Clarendon Press, 1976–1989), vol. 3, no. 1040.

8. Marcy Lascano, "Heads Cast in Metaphysical Moulds," in *Early Modern Women on Metaphysics*, ed. Emily Thomas (Cambridge: Cambridge University Press, 2018), 9–28. Cudworth left his books to his older son, but it does seem that Masham had some of the manuscripts and books at Oates since her husband later sold some, and Francis Masham published some of Cudworth's manuscripts. Broad, "A Woman's Influence?"

9. Quoted in Broad, *Women Philosophers*, 116.

10. Anna Grigg wrote Locke in 1685 saying Masham was "a fair and intolerably Witty Lady" letter 820. Scholar James Buickerood agrees, and adds his own excellent description of her as "lively, very bright, intellectually disposed and accomplished, fun loving and capable of taking amusement in her youthful predilection to be vividly at odds with herself, others and the world at large." Buickerood, introduction, to *The Philosophical Works of Damaris, Lady Masham*, vii. But this part of his description I don't entirely agree with: "Not timorous or reticent." When Locke presses her on philosophical matters, and also on the question of her feelings for him, she holds back.

11. "I may have different sentiments from those I now have." Masham to Locke, January 6, 1682, *The Correspondence of John Locke*, vol. 2, no. 677.

12. For "Fitts," see Masham to Locke, February 27, 1682, *The Correspondence of John Locke*, vol. 2, no. 688. For early modern women's stress and performance anxiety, see: Ursula Appelt, *Write or Be Written*; Leslie Baker, "The Masculine Mind and the Woman's Body: Exploring the Strategies of Seventeenth-Century Female Philosophers Anne Conway and Damaris Masham to Reconcile Domesticity and Intellectualism" (master's thesis, Dalhousie University, 2008).

13. Masham to Locke, February 27, 1682, *The Correspondence of John Locke*, vol. 2, no. 688.

14. Masham to Locke, May 23, 1682, *The Correspondence of John Locke*, vol. 2, no. 710.

15. Masham to Locke, May 23, 1682, *The Correspondence of John Locke*, vol. 2, no. 710.

16. Masham to Locke, May 6, 1682, *The Correspondence of John Locke*, vol. 2, no. 704.

17. For more on the marital pressures on women, see: Amy M. Froide, *Never Married: Singlewomen in Early Modern England* (Oxford: Oxford University Press, 2005).

18. Zack, *Bachelors of Science*, 59.

19. Zack, *Bachelors of Science*, 60.

20. Masham to Locke, August 14, 1682, *The Correspondence of John Locke*, vol. 2, no. 726.

21. Masham to Locke, January 1683, *The Correspondence of John Locke*, vol. 2, nos. 751 and 752.

22. Masham to Locke, April 7, 1683, *The Correspondence of John Locke*, vol. 2, no. 763.

23. Masham to Locke, June 16, 1684, *The Correspondence of John Locke*, vol. 2, no. 779.

24. Masham to Locke, August 25, 1684, *The Correspondence of John Locke*, vol. 2, no. 784.

25. Masham to Locke, October 8, 1684, *The Correspondence of John Locke*, vol. 2, no. 787.

26. Masham to Locke, October 8, 1684, *The Correspondence of John Locke*, vol. 2, no. 787.

27. Masham to Locke, January 15, 1685, *The Correspondence of John Locke*, vol. 2, no. 805.

28. Masham to Locke, March 20, 1685, *The Correspondence of John Locke*, vol. 2, no. 815.

29. Masham to Locke, June 5, 1685, *The Correspondence of John Locke*, vol. 2, no. 823.

30. Masham to Locke, June 5, 1685, *The Correspondence of John Locke*, vol. 2, no. 823.

31. Masham to Locke, August 14, 1685, *The Correspondence of John Locke*, vol. 2, no. 827.

32. Masham to Locke, November 14, 1685, *The Correspondence of John Locke*, vol. 2, no. 837.

33. Masham to Locke, November 14, 1685, *The Correspondence of John Locke*, vol. 2, no. 837.

34. Masham to Locke, November 14, 1685, *The Correspondence of John Locke*, vol. 2, no. 837.

35. Masham to Locke, December 14, 1685, *The Correspondence of John Locke*, vol. 2, no. 839.

36. Masham to Locke, December 14, 1685, *The Correspondence of John Locke*, vol. 2, no. 839.

37. Masham to Locke, March 13, 1686, *The Correspondence of John Locke*, vol. 3, nos. 870 and 882.

38. Masham to Locke, October 9, 1686, *The Correspondence of John Locke*, vol. 3, no. 870: "Philander is a Name, that since I have seene you, has many times Reconcil'd me to the World when nothing else would . . . But Above All I have made use of it (though whether with so much Reason, or No, You and Heaven Can Onely Tell) when I Have beene Tempted to Beleeve that there was no such Thing Below (amongst your Sex at least) as an Undesigning and Honest Friendship; free from Unjust Ends; and Little Interests."

39. Masham to Locke, December 14, 1685, *The Correspondence of John Locke*, vol. 2, no. 839.

40. Masham to Locke, April 7, 1688, *The Correspondence of John Locke*, vol. 3, no. 1040: "I do not I confess think my self altogether Uncapable of Things of that Nature; And I am sure I have a Universal Love for All usefull Knowledge Beyond that Capacitie."

41. Masham to Locke, April 7, 1688, *The Correspondence of John Locke*, vol. 3, no. 1040: "I may much more Advantageously employ my Houres in Pursuing the End of these speculations then in indeavouring to Extricate those Difficulties that the Witts of Men have Intangled them with, Which being Needless to my self, can be no Part of my Obligations; who should not be likely to be in any Capacitie of Dispensing to Others: The Duty Certainly of those that Are."

42. Masham to Locke, April 7, 1688, *The Correspondence of John Locke*, vol. 3, no. 1040.

43. Masham to Locke, April 7, 1688, *The Correspondence of John Locke*, vol. 3, no. 1040.

44. Damaris Masham, *Occasional Thoughts in Reference to a Vertuous or Christian Life* (London, 1705), 199: "So that the best Fate which a Lady thus knowing, and singular, could expect, would be that hardly escaping Calumny, she should be in Town the Jest of the Would-be-Witts; the wonder of Fools, and a Scarecrow to keep from her House many honest People who are to be pitty'd for having no more Wit than they have, because it is not their own Fault that they have no more."

45. Masham, *Occasional Thoughts*, 175.

46. Masham to Locke, April 7, 1688, *The Correspondence of John Locke*, vol. 3, no. 1040. I'm not positing that Masham would pursue philosophy if there were no pleasure. As we learn in her first treatise, she insists that pleasure is our prime motivation; what I want to make sure is consistent and clear in this chapter, is that when she jumps into philosophy, it is because she is motivated by a pleasure that overcomes the suffering smart women face.

47. A reproduction of this drawing of Oates can be seen in Sheryl O'Donnell, "'My Idea in Your Mind': John Locke and Damaris Cudworth Masham," in *Mothering the Mind: Twelve Studies of Writers and Their Silent Partners*, ed. Ruth Perry and Martine Watson Brownley (New York: Holmes and Meier, 1984), 27.

48. Maurice Cranston, *John Locke: A Biography* (Oxford: Oxford University Press, 1985), 343.

49. Lynette McGrath, *Subjectivity and Women's Poetry in Early Modern England: Why on the Ridge Should She Desire to Go?* (New York: Routledge, 2018), 93.

50. "Damaris Cudworth Masham, Lady Masham (1659–1708)," Project Vox, accessed August 20, 2019, http://projectvox.org/masham-1659-1708/.

51. "Churchill, Awnsham, (1658–1728), of the Black Swan, Paternoster Row, London and Henbury, Dorset," *History of Parliament Online*, accessed August 20, 2019, http://www.historyofparliamentonline.org/volume/1690-1715/member/churchill -awnsham-1658-1728#footnote4_nb68f8k.

52. Damaris Masham, *A Discourse Concerning the Love of God* (London, 1696), 115–16.

53. "Churchill, Awnsham," *History of Parliament Online*.

54. Cranston, *John Locke*, 215.

55. Masham, *Discourse*, 27.

56. Masham, *Discourse*, 78.

57. Nicolas Malebranche, *The Search after Truth: With Elucidations of the Search after Truth* (Cambridge: Cambridge University Press, 1997), 116.

58. Malebranche, *The Search after Truth*, 116.

59. Since the Middle Ages, philosophers and laypeople alike believed that monstrous births were God's way of announcing sinners to the world. The word "monster" itself comes from the Latin *monere*, which means "to remind" or" to warn." People were obsessed with the stories of these births and loved to speculate about whom God was cautioning and why. By the early modern period, tales of monstrous births were regularly published in the newspapers and pamphlets, and their pictures were plastered on tavern walls. One account from England proclaimed that on April 17, 1613, a monster was born with "a strange and wonderful shape, with four legs, four arms, two bellies, proportionately joined to one back, one head, two faces, like double-faced Janus, the one fore, the other behind." Above the text was an etching of twins joined at the back, each trying to walk away from the other—a warning from God that the Catholics were tearing the country apart. Another pamphlet from 1609 reported "strange news out of Kent," and below the headline was a woodblock print of a baby standing in a meadow, waving its disklike palms and eighteen fingers as if to get the reader's attention. The infant had no head, and flush on its chest was a tiny face. Apparently, its mother had conceived it out of wedlock, and as divine punishment for not securing a husband as head of the family, her child was born without a head.

60. Charles McCracken, *Malebranche and British Philosophy* (Oxford: Oxford University Press, 1983), 11.

61. Masham, *Discourse*, 107.

62. Masham, *Discourse*, 108. Italics are Masham's.

63. Masham, *Discourse*, 32.

64. Masham, *Discourse*, 23.

65. Masham, *Discourse*, 36.

66. Masham, *Discourse*, 33. Italics are Masham's.

67. Masham, *Discourse*, 120–21.

68. Masham, *Discourse*, 126.

69. Masham, *Discourse*, 123.

70. Masham, *Discourse*, 62.

71. Masham, *Discourse*, 76–78. God's goodness and wisdom assure us that we are to seek our pleasures: "The love of Pleasure implanted in us . . . can never mislead us from the observance of the Law of reason." An obvious rebuttal is that some people seek self-destructive or harmful things. Masham responds to this by distinguishing between "present appetites" and delayed gratification: the pleasure we ought to follow is that which procures the greatest happiness, which is typically a future good.

72. Masham, *Discourse*, 67.

73. Masham, *Discourse*, 64.

74. Jean Le Clerc, "Discours sur l'amour divin, où l'on explique ce que c'est, & où 'lon fait voir les mauvaises consequences des explications trop subtises, que l'on en donne," in *Bibliothèque Choisie* (Amsterdam: Henri Schelte, 1705), vol. 7, 383.

75. Dr. Marcy Lascano, professor of philosophy at the University of Kansas, email correspondence with the author, May 31, 2020.

76. Broad, *Women Philosophers*, 130.

77. Masham, *Occasional Thoughts*, 8.

78. Masham, *Occasional Thoughts*, 70.

79. Masham, *Occasional Thoughts*, 202.

80. Masham, *Occasional Thoughts*, 22.

81. Masham, *Occasional Thoughts*, 24.

82. Masham, *Occasional Thoughts*, 204.

83. Masham, *Occasional Thoughts*, 39–40. Italics are Masham's.

84. Masham, *Discourse*, 65.

85. Masham, *Occasional Thoughts*, 33.

86. See: Locke, *Essays on the Law of Nature, the Latin Text*, ed. and trans. Wolfgang von Leyden (Oxford: Clarendon Press, 1954), 199. Locke says, "In fact, this [natural] law does not depend on an unstable and changeable will, but on the eternal order of things. For it seems to me that certain essential features of things are immutable, and that certain duties arise out of necessity and cannot be other than they are. And this is not because nature or God . . . could not have created man differently. Rather, the cause is that, since man has been made such as he is, equipped with reason and his other faculties and destined for this mode of life, there necessarily result from his inborn constitution some definite duties for him, which cannot be other than they are."

87. Masham, *Occasional Thoughts*, 63.

88. Ralph Cudworth, *A Treatise Concerning Eternal and Immutable Morality*, ed. Sarah Hutton (Cambridge: Cambridge University Press, 1996), 26.

89. Masham, *Occasional Thoughts*, 159.

90. Masham, *Occasional Thoughts*, 154–55.

91. Masham, *Occasional Thoughts*, 227–228.

92. Masham, *Occasional Thoughts*, 2; Regan Penaluna, "The Social and Political Thought of Damaris Cudworth Masham," in *Virtue, Liberty, and Toleration: Political Ideas of European Women, 1400–1800*, ed. Jacqueline Broad and Karen Green (Dordrecht, Netherlands: Springer, 2007), 111–22.

93. Masham, *Occasional Thoughts*, 190–191.

94. Mary Hays, *Female Biography* (London: Fry and Kammerer Printers, 1807), 499–500.

95. Susan Whyman, "The Correspondence of Esther Masham and John Locke: A Study in Epistolary Silences," *Huntington Library Quarterly* 66, no. 3/4 (2003): 288.

96. Hays, *Female Biography*, 499–500.

97. Masham, *Occasional Thoughts*, 200.

98. Victor Cousin, *Course of the History of Modern Philosophy*, trans. O. W. Wight (New York: D. Appleton, 1859), 178: "She [is] a person remarkable for her mind"; John Tulloch, *Rational Theology and Christian Philosophy in England in the Seventeenth Century: The Cambridge Platonists*, 1874, facsimile (Hildesheim, Germany: Georg Olms, 1966), 226: Masham "deserve[s] a niche in the history of English philosophy."

The Demons of Doubt

1. Damaris Masham, *Occasional Thoughts in Reference to a Vertuous or Christian Life* (London, 1705), 175: "And is not the incurring of general dislike, one of the strongest discouragements that we can have to any thing?"

2. Christia Mercer, "Descartes' Debt to Teresa of Ávila, or Why We Should Work on Women in the History of Philosophy," *Philosophical Studies* 174, no. 10 (2016): 2539–55, doi:10.1007/s11098-016-0737-9.

3. For more on Teresa of Ávila, see: Teresa of Ávila, *The Book of My Life*, trans. Mirabai Starr (Boulder, CO: Shambhala Publiations, 2008); Barbara Mujica, "Teresa de Ávila: Portrait of the Saint as a Young Woman," *Romance Quarterly* 63, no. 1 (January 2016): 30–39.

4. Adrian Piper, quoted in Lauren O'Neill-Butler, "Opinion | Adrian Piper Speaks! (for Herself)," *New York Times*, July 5, 2018, https://www.nytimes.com/2018/07/05/opinion/adrian-piper-speaks-for-herself.html.

5. Sandra Lee Bartky, *Femininity and Domination: Studies in the Phenomenology of Oppression* (New York: Routledge, 1990), 90.

6. Bartky, *Femininity and Domination*, 97.

7. Bartky, *Femininity and Domination*, 85.

8. Lili Loofbourow, "The Male Glance," *Virginia Quarterly Review* 94, no. 1 (2018): 36, https://www.vqronline.org/essays-articles/2018/03/male-glance.

9. See Mercer's comment about Anne Conway and her indebtedness to a medieval tradition of suffering in Mercer, "Descartes' Debt to Teresa of Ávila."

10. See Annette Baier's excellent discussion of theological and generative theories of love. Baier, "Unsafe Loves," in *The Philosophy of (Erotic) Love*, ed. Robert Solomon and Kathleen M. Higgins, 448.

Love and Loathing

1. Claudia L. Johnson, introduction to *The Cambridge Companion to Mary Wollstonecraft* (Cambridge: Cambridge University Press, 2002), 3.

2. Mary Wollstonecraft, *The Works of Mary Wollstonecraft*, eds. Janet Todd and Marilyn Butler, 8 vols. (New York: New York University Press, 1989), vol. 6, 243. The secondary literature on Wollstonecraft is wonderfully rich and vast. Here are some studies that helped me form a foundational understanding of her life and work: Charlotte Gordon, *Romantic Outlaws: The Extraordinary Lives of Mary Wollstonecraft and Mary Shelley* (New York: Random House, 2016); Lyndall Gordon, *Vindication: A Life of Mary Wollstonecraft* (New York: Harper Perennial, 2006); Barbara Taylor, *Mary Wollstonecraft and the Feminist Imagination* (Cambridge: Cambridge University Press, 2003); Janet Todd, *Mary Wollstonecraft: A Revolutionary Life* (New York: Columbia University Press, 2000).

3. Wollstonecraft to Gilbert Imlay, June 27 and 29, 1795, in *The Collected Letters of Mary Wollstonecraft*, ed. Janet Todd (New York: Columbia University Press, 2004), 306–7.

4. Wollstonecraft, *The Works*, vol. 6, 245.

5. Wollstonecraft, *The Works*, vol. 6, 248. Italics are Wollstonecraft's.

6. Wollstonecraft, *The Works*, vol. 6, 253.

7. Wollstonecraft, *The Works*, vol. 6, 253.

8. Wollstonecraft, *The Works*, vol. 6, 269.

9. For her rejection of Rousseau's primitive state, see: Wollstonecraft, *The Works*, vol. 6, 288 and 296; for her comments on evolution, 336; for her observation of the juvenile starfish, 281.

10. Gordon, *Vindication*, 235.

11. Gordon, *Vindication*, 250.

12. Wollstonecraft to Imlay, September 6, 1795, *Letters*, 320.

13. Wollstonecraft, *The Works*, vol. 5, 75 and 102.

14. Wollstonecraft, *The Works*, vol. 5, 140.

15. Wollstonecraft to Gilbert Imlay, November 27, 1795, *Letters*, 333.

16. That said, there are a fair number of scholarly books that take her seriously as a philosopher. See for example: Sandrine Berges and Alan M. S. J. Coffee, eds., *The Social and Political Philosophy of Mary Wollstonecraft* (Oxford: Oxford University Press, 2017); Rebecca Buxton and Lisa Whiting, *The Philosopher Queens: The Lives and Legacies of Philosophy's Unsung Women* (London: Unbound, 2020); Taylor, *Feminist Imagination*.

17. Wollstonecraft, *The Works*, vol. 5, 250.

18. I'm grateful to Barbara Taylor for this insight. See Taylor, *Feminist Imagination*, 56.

19. Monique Wittig, *The Straight Mind: And Other Essays* (Boston: Beacon Press, 1992), 20.

20. For more on the contemporary scholarship about the formation of our desires and its implications for feminism, see Amia Srinivasan, "Does Anyone Have the Right to Sex?" *London Review of Books*, March 22, 2018, https://www.lrb.co.uk/the-paper/v40/n06/amia-srinivasan/does-anyone-have-the-right-to-sex.

21. Marilyn Butler, introduction to *The Works of Mary Wollstonecraft*, ed. Janet Todd and Marilyn Butler, 8 vols. (New York: New York University Press, 1989), vol. 1, 7.

22. Butler, introduction to *The Works*, vol. 1, 11.

23. William Godwin, *Memoirs of Mary Wollstonecraft* (New York: Kessinger, 2008), 10.

24. Todd, *Mary Wollstonecraft*, 20.

25. Todd, *Mary Wollstonecraft*, 14; Wollstonecraft to Jane Arden, November 16, 1774, *Letters*, 16.

26. Wollstonecraft to Jane Arden, November 16, 1774, *Letters*, 16–17.

27. Todd, *Mary Wollstonecraft*, 22.

28. Godwin, *Memoirs*, 18–22.

29. Andrew Elfenbein, "Mary Wollstonecraft and the Sexuality of Genius," in *The Cambridge Companion to Mary Wollstonecraft*, ed. Claudia L. Johnson (Cambridge: Cambridge University Press, 2002), 228–45. For more on genius and sexuality in Romanticism, see Andrew Elfenbein, *Romantic Genius: The Prehistory of a Homosexual Role* (New York: Columbia University Press, 1999).

30. Todd, *Mary Wollstonecraft*, 23.

31. Wollstonecraft to Jane Arden, ca. late 1782, *Letters*, 38.

32. For more on the marriage plot in Wollstonecraft's age, see: Lisa O'Connell, *The Origins of the English Marriage Plot: Literature, Politics and Religion in the Eighteenth Century* (Cambridge: Cambridge University Press, 2019).

33. Wollstonecraft, *The Works*, vol. 1, 72.

34. Wollstonecraft, *The Works*, vol. 1, 73.

35. Todd, *Mary Wollstonecraft*, 40.

36. Gordon, *Vindication*, 41.

37. Gordon, *Vindication*, 32; Butler, introduction to *The Works*, vol. 1, 7.

38. Gordon, *Vindication*, 39.

39. Wollstonecraft to Everina, ca. late 1783, *Letters*, 40.

40. Wollstonecraft to Everina, ca. late 1783, *Letters*, 41.

41. Todd, *Mary Wollstonecraft*, 54.

42. Gordon, *Vindication*, 37.

43. Gordon, *Vindication*, 38.

44. Gordon, *Romantic Outlaws*, 66–67; Todd, *Mary Wollstonecraft*, 56.

45. Alan Richardson, "Mary Wollstonecraft on Education," in *The Cambridge Companion to Mary Wollstonecraft*, ed. Claudia L. Johnson (Cambridge: Cambridge University Press, 2002), 24–41, http://search.proquest.com/lion/docview/2137992285/citation/18CF6BB3FBE44807PQ/2.

46. Todd, *Mary Wollstonecraft*, 56.

47. Gordon, *Vindication*, 46.

48. Todd, *Mary Wollstonecraft*, 60; Gordon, *Romantic Outlaws*, 89.

49. Gordon, *Romantic Outlaws*, 90.

50. Londa Schiebinger, *The Mind Has No Sex?: Women in the Origins of Modern Science* (Cambridge, MA: Harvard University Press, 1991), 189; reproduction of the illustration on page 205.

51. Schiebinger, *The Mind Has No Sex?*, 203–5; 223–24.

52. Wollstonecraft, *The Works*, vol. 5, 103.

53. Simone de Beauvoir, *The Second Sex* (New York: Vintage Books, 1953), 301.

54. Wollstonecraft to her sister Eliza Bishop, ca. late November 1785, *Letters*, 63.

55. Todd, *Mary Wollstonecraft*, 58.

56. Gordon, *Romantic Outlaws*, 91.

57. Lowe, "Mary Wollstonecraft and the Kingsborough Scandal," *Eighteenth-Century Ireland / Iris an Dá Chultúr* 9 (1994): 44.

58. Quoted in Lowe, "Mary Wollstonecraft," 45.

59. Quoted in Lowe, "Mary Wollstonecraft," 45.

60. Butler, introduction to *The Works*, vol. 1, 8.

61. Wollstonecraft to Eliza Bishop, June 27, 1787, *Letters*, 129.

62. Ernest Lee Tuveson, *The Imagination as a Means of Grace* (Berkeley: University of California Press, 1960), 7.

63. Tuveson, *Imagination*, 19.

64. Taylor, *Feminist Imagination*, 60.

65. Taylor, *Feminist Imagination*, 63.

66. Quoted in Taylor, *Feminist Imagination*, 62.

67. Elfenbein, "Mary Wollstonecraft and the Sexuality of Genius," 234.

68. Wollstonecraft, *The Works*, vol. 5, 186.

69. Gordon, *Vindication*, 116.

70. Emma Garman, "A Liberated Woman: The Story of Margaret King," May 24, 2016, in Longreads, https://longreads.com/2016/05/24/a-liberated-woman-the-story-of-margaret-king/, accessed October 15, 2020.

71. Gordon, *Vindication*, 116, 120.

72. Wollstonecraft to Johnson, September 13, 1787, *Letters*, 134.

73. Taylor, *Feminist Imagination*, 146.

74. Wollstonecraft to Everina, November 7, 1787, *Letters*, 139.

75. Godwin, *Memoirs*, 44.

76. Butler, introduction to *The Works*, vol. 1, 9.

77. Butler, introduction to *The Works*, vol. 1, 9; Taylor, *Feminist Imagination*, 43.

78. Gordon, *Vindication*, 130–31; Taylor, *Feminist Imagination*, 191.

79. Taylor, *Feminist Imagination*, 32–33.

80. Gordon, *Vindication*, 131.

81. Taylor, *Feminist Imagination*, 25.

82. Quoted in Taylor, *Feminist Imagination*, 49. For more on the reception of Wollstonecraft's ideas, see: Regina M. Janes, "On the Reception of Mary Wollstonecraft's *A Vindication of the Rights of Woman*," *Journal of the History of Ideas* 39 (1978), 293–302.

83. Wollstonecraft, *The Works*, vol. 1, 89.

84. Wollstonecraft, *The Works*, vol. 1, 94.

85. Wollstonecraft, *The Works*, vol. 1, 103.

86. Wollstonecraft, *The Works*, vol. 1, 112.

87. Wollstonecraft, *The Works*, vol. 1, 121.

88. Wollstonecraft, *The Works*, vol. 1, 266.

89. Wollstonecraft, *The Works*, vol. 1, 186.

90. Wollstonecraft, *The Works*, vol. 1, 187.

91. Wollstonecraft, *The Works*, vol. 1, 266.

92. Wollstonecraft, *The Works*, vol. 1, 105.

93. Wollstonecraft, *The Works*, vol. 1, 131.

94. Wollstonecraft, *The Works*, vol. 1, 108.

95. Wollstonecraft, *The Works*, vol. 1, 216.

96. Wollstonecraft, *The Works*, vol. 1, 218–20.

97. Wollstonecraft to Everina, March 24, 1787, *Letters*, 113.

98. Godwin, *Memoirs*, 58.

99. Wollstonecraft to Henry Fuseli, ca. late 1792, *Letters*, 205.

100. Butler, introduction to *The Works*, vol. 1, 10.

101. Gordon, *Romantic Outlaws*, 229–30.

102. Gordon, *Romantic Outlaws*, 230.

103. Wollstonecraft, *The Works*, vol. 1, 143.

104. Taylor, *Feminist Imagination*, 125.

105. Godwin, *Memoirs*, 70.

106. Gordon, *Romantic Outlaws*, 232.

107. Gordon, *Romantic Outlaws*, 222–26.

108. Gordon, *Romantic Outlaws*, 237.

109. Gordon, *Romantic Outlaws*, 237.

110. Wollstonecraft to Imlay, December 29, 1793, *Letters*, 235.

111. Wollstonecraft to Imlay, December 29, 1793, *Letters*, 235.

112. Wollstonecraft to Imlay, January 1794, *Letters*, 239.

113. Wollstonecraft to Imlay, September 23, 1794, *Letters*, 265.

114. Wollstonecraft to Imlay, October 26, 1794, *Letters*, 270.

115. Butler, introduction to *The Works*, vol. 1, 11.

116. Wollstonecraft to Imlay, May 22, 1795, *Letters*, 293.

117. Godwin, *Memoirs*, 84.

118. Wollstonecraft to Imlay, October 10, 1795, *Letters*, 327.

119. Wollstonecraft to Imlay, March 1796, *Letters*, 338.

120. Godwin, *Memoirs*, 62–63.

121. Godwin, *Memoirs*, 84.

122. Wollstonecraft to Godwin, August 17, 1796, *Letters*, 348.

123. Godwin, *Memoirs*, 75.

124. Godwin to Wollstonecraft, August 22, 1796, *Godwin and Mary: Letters of William Godwin and Mary Wollstonecraft*, ed. Ralph M. Wardle (Lincoln: University of Kansas Press, 1977), 23.

125. Godwin, *Memoirs*, 105.

126. Godwin, *Memoirs*, 109.

127. Wollstonecraft to Godwin, March 11, 1797, *Letters*, 402.

128. Wollstonecraft to Godwin, June 6, 1797, *Letters*, 418.

129. Wollstonecraft to Godwin, July 4, 1797, *Letters*, 429.

130. Wollstonecraft to George Dyson, May 16, 1797, *Letters*, 412.

131. Wollstonecraft, *The Works*, vol. 1, 119.

132. Wollstonecraft to Dyson, May 16, 1797, *Letters*, 412.

133. Wollstonecraft to Godwin, September 4, 1796, *Letters*, 357.

134. Wollstonecraft to Godwin, September 4, 1796, *Letters*, 358.

135. Wollstonecraft to Godwin, September 15, 1796, *Letters*, 365.

136. Wollstonecraft to Godwin, August 1797, *Letters*, 436.

137. Wollstonecraft to Godwin, August 1797, *Letters*, 436.

138. Godwin, *Memoirs*, 114.

139. Taylor, *Feminist Imagination*, 246–47.

140. Taylor, *Feminist Imagination*, 28.

141. Garman, "A Liberated Woman."

142. Godwin, *Memoirs*, 73.

143. Virginia Woolf, *Virginia Woolf on Women and Writing: Her Essays, Assessments and Arguments*, ed. and introduced by Michèle Barrett (London: Women's Press Ltd., 1993), 98.

Heroes

1. Laura Mulvey, "Afterthoughts on 'Visual Pleasure and Narrative Cinema,'" in *Film Theory Reader: Debates and Arguments*, ed. Marc Furstenau (Abingdon, UK: Routledge, 2010), 222.

2. Mary Wollstonecraft, *The Complete Works of Mary Wollstonecraft*, ed. Janet Todd and Marilyn Butler, 8 vols. (New York: New York University Press, 1989), vol. 5, 189.

3. Wollstonecraft, *The Works*, vol. 1, 152–53.

Into the Hands of Virginia Woolf

1. Iris Murdoch, *Existentialists and Mystics: Writings on Philosophy and Literature* (New York: Penguin, 1999), 5–6.

2. For more on George Ballard, see: Ruth Perry, introduction to George Ballard, *Memoirs of Several Ladies of Great Britain: Who Have Been Celebrated for Their Writings or Skill in the Learned Languages, Arts, and Sciences* (Detroit: Wayne State University Press, 1985). Perry says Ballard was directly inspired by Elstob. More recently, scholar Laura Dawn Hollis argued that there wasn't sufficient evidence of this, and so the story as I tell it here reflects that uncertainty. See Hollis, "On the Margins of Scholarship: The Letters of Elizabeth Elstob to George Ballard, 1735–1753," *Lias* 42, no. 2: 167–268, https://doi .org/10.2143/LIAS.42.2.3141805.

3. Perry, introduction to Ballard, *Memoirs of Several Ladies*, 19.

4. Hollis, "On the Margins," 182.

5. Hollis, "On the Margins," 177.

6. Perry, introduction to Ballard, *Memoirs of Several Ladies*, 35.

7. Perry, introduction to Ballard, *Memoirs of Several Ladies*, 37.

8. See Melanie Bigold, "'Bookmaking Out of the Remains of the Dead': George Ballard's *Memoirs of Several Ladies* (1752)," *Eighteenth-Century Life* 39, no. 2 (2014): 28–46, https:// doi.org/10.1215/00982601-2645927.

9. Hollis, "On the Margins," 183.

10. Elizabeth Ogilvy Benger, "The Female Geniad," (London, 1791).

11. Woolf learned about Astell through the dissertation of Florence Smith, published in 1916. See "A Room of Her Own" for this discussion.

12. Joanna Russ, *How to Suppress Women's Writing* (Austin: University of Texas Press, 2016).

13. For a powerful study on how non-Kantian philosophies outside Europe were suppressed in the Western canon, see: Peter K. J. Park, *Africa, Asia, and the History of Philosophy: Racism in the Formation of the Philosophical Canon, 1780–1830* (Albany: State University of New York Press, 2013).

Bedtime Stories

1. Brian Black, *The Character of the Self in Ancient India: Priests, Kings, and Women in the Early Upaniṣads* (Albany: State University of New York Press, 2007), 148–55; David Buchta, "Gārgī Vācaknavī as an Honorary Male: An Eighteenth Century Reception of an Upanishadic Female Sage," *Journal of Hindu Studies* 3, no. 3 (2010): 354–70, https:// doi.org/10.1093/jhs/hiq028.

2. Quoted in Black, *The Character of the Self in Ancient India*, 150.

3. Scholars are unsure of Gārgī's status, too, and offer up the idea that she was more like "an honorary male." See Buchta, "Gārgī Vācaknavī as an Honorary Male."

4. All quotes from James L. Fitzgerald, "Nun Befuddles King, Shows *Karmayoga* Does Not Work: *Sulabhā's Refutation of King Janaka at MBh 12.308*," *Journal of Indian Philosophy* 30 (2002): 641–77, http://www.jstor.org/stable/23496945.

5. Ruth Vanita, "The Self Is Not Gendered: Sulabha's Debate with King Janaka," *NWSA Journal* 15, no. 2 (2003): 76–93, http://www.jstor.org/stable/4316972.

6. Fitzgerald, "Nun Befuddles King," 655.

7. Anonymous, *The Lives of the Ancient Philosophers, Containing an Account of their Several Sects, Doctrines, Actions, and Remarkable Sayings* (London, 1702), 536. For discussion of Cleobulina's feet-washing, see: Joan E. Taylor, *Jewish Women Philosophers of First-Century Alexandria* (Oxford: Oxford University Press, 2003), 220.

8. Ian Michael Plant, *Women Writers of Ancient Greece and Rome: An Anthology* (Norman, OK: University of Oklahoma Press, 2004), 29. Only a few fragments of Cleobulina's work exist today.

9. Except for a phrase here and there, the works of the many other Pythagorean women, whose lives taken together span a period of nine hundred years, are lost. The list includes Themistoclea, Theano, Damo, Myia, Melissa, Arignote, Timycha of Sparta, Aesara of Lucania, Perictione, Perictione II, and Theano II. For more, see: Mary Ellen Waithe, *Ancient Women Philosophers, 600 B.C.–500 A.D.* (Dordrecht , Netherlands: Kluwer, 1997), 12–27; Annette Huizenga, *Moral Education for Women in the Pastoral and Pythagorean Letters: Philosophers of the Household* (Leiden, Netherlands: Brill, 2013); Caterina Pellò, "Women in Early Pythagoreanism" (PhD diss., University of Cambridge, 2018), 114.

10. Pellò, "Women in Early Pythagoreanism," 10; Prudence Allen, *The Concept of Woman, Volume 1: The Aristotelian Revolution, 750 B.C.–A.D. 1250* (Grand Rapids, MI: Eerdmans, 1996), 143–59.

11. Plant, *Women Writers of Ancient Greece and Rome*, 41. A new class of prostitutes was invented in the sixth-century BCE in Greece: the hetaira (some sources also use hetaera). They were well educated and provided intellectual conversation and sex to one or two men (unlike the *pornê*, a separate class of prostitutes who provided sex to numerous anonymous partners). They were also allowed into intellectual spaces typically off-limits to all other women, including symposiums, where Greek men often discussed philosophical matters. See, Leslie Kurke, "Inventing the 'Hetaira': Sex, Politics, and Discursive Conflict in Archaic Greece," *Classical Antiquity* 16, no. 1, (1997): 106–50, doi: 10.2307/25011056.

12. Jane Donawerth, "Aspasia," in *Rhetorical Theory by Women Before 1900: An Anthology* (Lanham, MD: Rowman and Littlefield, 2002), 1.

13. Jakub Filonik, "Athenian Impiety Trials: A Reappraisal," *Dike—Rivista di Storia del Diritto Greco ed Ellenistico* 16 (2013): 28, https://doi.org/10.13130/1128-8221/4290.

14. Gabriele Cornelli, *Plato's Styles and Characters: Between Literature and Philosophy* (Berlin: De Gruyter, 2015), 308; Waithe, *Ancient Women Philosophers*, 83–106.

15. Marilyn Bailey Ogilvie, *Women in Science: Antiquity Through the Nineteenth Century: A Biographical Dictionary with Annotated Bibliography* (Boston: MIT Press, 1986), 31; Waithe, *Ancient Women Philosophers*, 197–98; Naomie Zack, *The Handy Philosophy Answer Book* (Canton, MO: Visible Ink Press, 2010), 47.

16. For more on Arete's father, Aristippus, see: "Aristippus," *Internet Encyclopedia of Philosophy*, accessed November 21, 2021, https://iep.utm.edu/aristip/.

17. Diogenes Laërtius, *Lives of Eminent Philosophers*, trans. R. D. Hicks (Cambridge, MA: Harvard University Press, 1925), bk. 3.

18. Laërtius, *The Lives of Philosophers*, bk. 6; R. Bracht Branham and Marie-Odile Goulet-Cazé, *The Cynics: The Cynic Movement in Antiquity and Its Legacy* (Berkeley: University of California Press, 2000), 373.

19. Quoted in Michèle Le Dœuff, *Hipparchia's Choice: An Essay Concerning Women, Philosophy, Etc.*, trans. Trista Selous (New York: Columbia University Press, 2007), 205; also see: Laërtius, "Hipparchia," *The Lives of Philosophers*, bk.6.

20. Heidi Marx, *Sosipatra of Pergamum: Philosopher and Oracle* (New York: Oxford University Press, 2021), 3, 73; Sarah Iles Johnston, "Sosipatra and the Theurgic Life: Eunapius Vitae Sophistorum 6.6.5–6.9.24," in *Reflections on Religious Individuality*, ed. Jörg Rüpke and Wolfgang Spickermann (Berlin: Walter De Gruyter, 2012), 99–118; Nicola Denzey Lewis, "Living Images of the Divine: Female Theurgists in Late Antiquity," in *Daughters of Hecate: Women and Magic in the Ancient World*, ed. Kimberly B. Stratton and Dayna S. Kalleres (New York: Oxford University Press, 2014), 274–97.

21. Marx, *Sosipatra*, 73.

22. For more on Hypatia, see: Edward J. Watts, *Hypatia: The Life and Legend of an Ancient Philosopher* (New York: Oxford University Press, 2017); Michael Deakin, *Hypatia of Alexandria: Mathematician and Martyr* (Amherst, NY: Prometheus Books, 2007); Soraya Field Fiorio, "The Killing of Hypatia," *Lapham's Quarterly*, January 16, 2019, https://www.laphamsquarterly.org/roundtable/killing-hypatia; Hardy Grant, "Who's Hypatia? Whose Hypatia Do You Mean?," *Math Horizons* 16, no. 4 (2009): 11–15, http://www.jstor.org/stable/25678812.

23. Deakin, *Hypatia of Alexandria*, 92–95, 104.

24. Hossein Kamaly, *A History of Islam in 21 Women*, Kindle ed. (New York: Simon and Schuster, 2020).

25. Dr. Leyla Amzi-Erdogdular, professor of history at Rutgers University, email correspondence with author, April 10, 2020.

26. Amzi-Erdogdular, email correspondence with author, April 10, 2020.

27. For the final quote, this translation is from Sufiwiki; another translation is found here: Margaret Smith, *Rabi'a The Mystic and Her Fellow-Saints in Islam* (Cambridge: Cambridge University Press, 2010), 10–13.

28. Kamaly, *A History of Islam in 21 Women*.

29. Sandra A. Wawrytko, "Women on Love: Idealization in the Philosophies of Diotima (*The Symposium*) and Murasaki Shikibu (*The Tale of Genji*)," *Philosophy East and West* 68, no. 4 (2018): 1314–44, https://doi.org/10.1353/pew.2018.0108; Kaori Shoji, "Setouchi Jakucho Takes Japan Back 1,000 Years," *New York Times*, January 23, 1999.

30. Gerda Lerner, *The Creation of Feminist Consciousness: From the Middle Ages to Eighteen-Seventy* (New York: Oxford University Press, 1994), 52–54. For a general overview of Hildegard, see: Barbara Newman, ed., *Voice of the Living Light: Hildegard of Bingen and Her World* (Berkeley: University of California Press, 1998).

31. Quoted in Allen, *The Concept of Woman*, vol. 1, 294.

32. For Hildegard on female orgasm, see Peter Dronke, *Women Writers of the Middle Ages: A Critical Study of Texts from Perpetua to Marguerite Porete* (Cambridge: Cambridge University Press, 1984), 175: "When a woman is making love with a man, a sense of heat in her brain, which brings with it sensual delight, communicates the taste of that delight during the act and summons forth the emission of the man's seed. And when the seed has fallen into its place, that vehement heat descending from her brain draws the seed to itself and holds it, and soon the woman's sexual organs contract, and all the parts that are ready to open up during the time of menstruation now close, in the same way as a strong man can hold something enclosed in his fist."

33. Allen, *The Concept of Woman*, vol. 1, 315.

34. For my understanding of the beguines, I'm grateful to Walter Simons, *Cities of Ladies: Beguine Communities in the Medieval Low Countries, 1200–1565* (Philadelphia: University of Pennsylvania Press, 2003).

35. This article proposes that the beguines' theology went further than the ideas of medieval philosopher Bernard of Chartres (who focused on self-annihilation but not deification), and preceded similar ideas found in Meister Eckhart: Juan Marin, "Annihilation and Deification in Beguine Theology and Marguerite Porete's Mirror of Simple Souls," *Harvard Theological Review* 103, no. 1, (2010): 89–109.

36. Simons, *Cities of Ladies*, 143.

37. Simons, *Cities of Ladies*, 131.

38. "Obituary: Marcella Pattyen," *Economist*, April 27, 2013, https://www.economist.com/obituary/2013/04/27/marcella-pattyn.

39. Jane Duran, "Julian of Norwich: Mysticism and Philosophy," *New Blackfriars* 90, no. 1029 (2009): 552–59, https://doi.org/10.1111/j.1741-2005.2009.01275.x; Julian quoted in Prudence Allen, *The Concept of Woman: vol. 2, The Early Humanist Reformation* (Grand Rapids, MI: Eerdmans, 2002), 416.

40. Claire Sahlin, *Birgitta of Sweden and the Voice of Prophecy* (Woodbridge, UK: Boydell and Brewer, 2001); Laura Saetveit Miles, "Looking in the Past for a Discourse of Motherhood: Birgitta of Sweden and Julia Kristeva," *Medieval Feminist Forum* 47, no. 1 (December 2011): 52–76; Unn Falkeid, "The Legacy of Birgitta of Sweden: Women, Politics, and Reform in Renaissance Italy," Department of Philosophy, Classics, History of Art and Ideas website at the University of Oslo, accessed November 22, 2021, https://www.hf.uio.no/ifikk/english/research/projects/the-legacy-of-birgitta-of-sweden/index.html.

41. Miles, "Looking in the Past for a Discourse of Motherhood," 56.

42. Barbara Obrist, "The Swedish Visionary: Saint Bridget," in *Medieval Women Writers*, ed. Katharina M. Wilson (Athens: University of Georgia Press, 1984), 236.

43. Earl Jeffrey Richards, introduction to Christine de Pizan, *The Book of the City of Ladies*, trans. Earl Jeffrey Richards (New York: Persea Books, 1982), xix–xx.

44. Christine de Pizan, *The Book of the City of Ladies*, trans. Earl Jeffrey Richards (New York: Persea Books, 1982), 3–5.

45. Cristina Malcolmson, "Christine de Pizan's City of Ladies in Early Modern England," in *Debating Gender in Early Modern England, 1500–1700*, ed. Cristina Malcolmson and Mohoko Suzuki (New York: Palgrave Macmillan, 2002), 15.

46. Sarah Lawson, introduction to Christine de Pizan, *The Treasure of the City of Ladies, or The Book of Three Virtues*, trans. with an introduction and notes by Sarah Lawson (London: Penguin Books, 2003), xiii–xxvii. Lawson says that although there are some modern editions of her works, Pizan is still generally unknown and not included in the pantheon of classic writers.

47. Sara Fredman, "Margery Kempe Had 14 Children and She Still Invented the Memoir," *Electric Literature*, February 27, 2020, https://electricliterature.com/margery-kempe -had-14-children-and-she-still-invented-the-memoir/; Lucy Johnston, "The Life of Margery Kempe," *Historic UK*, accessed November 22, 2021, https://www.historic-uk.com/ HistoryUK/HistoryofEngland/Mysticism-And-Madness-Of-Margery-Kempe/.

48. Therese Boos Dykeman, ed., *The Neglected Canon: Nine Women Philosophers* (Dordrecht, Netherlands: Kluwer, 1999), 81–82.

49. Quoted in "Marie Le Jars de Gournay (1565–1645)," *Internet Encyclopedia of Philosophy*, accessed November 17, 2020, https://iep.utm.edu/gournay/.

50. Anne R. Larsen, *Anna Maria van Schurman, "The Star of Utrecht": The Educational Vision and Reception of a Savante* (Abingdon, UK: Routledge, 2016), 34; Martine van Elk, *Early Modern Women's Writing: Domesticity, Privacy, and the Public Sphere in England and the Dutch Republic* (New York: Palgrave Macmillan, 2017), 170.

51. Elk, *Early Modern Women's Writing*, 185.

52. Elk, *Early Modern Women's Writing*, 184.

53. Jacqueline Broad, *Women Philosophers of the Seventeenth Century* (Cambridge: Cambridge University Press, 2007), 18–19. Carol Pal, *Republic of Women: Rethinking the Republic of Letters in the Seventeenth Century* (Cambridge: Cambridge University Press, 2012), 72–73.

54. Broad, *Women Philosophers*, 13–34.

55. Quoted in Broad, *Women Philosophers*, 21.

56. Quoted in Broad, *Women Philosophers*, 13.

57. See, René Descartes, *The Philosophical Writings of Descartes*, vol. 3, trans. John Cottingham, Robert Stoothoff, and Dugold Murdoch (Cambridge: Cambridge University Press, 1985).

58. Margaret Cavendish, *The Description of a New World, Called the Blazing World* (London: A. Maxwell, 1668), edition accessed online at Project Gutenberg, http://www.gutenberg .org/files/51783/51783-h/51783-h.htm; David Cunning, "Margaret Lucas Cavendish," *Stanford Encyclopedia of Philosophy*, Summer 2017, https://plato.stanford.edu/archives/ sum2017/entries/margaret-cavendish/.

59. Cavendish, *The Blazing World*, http://www.gutenberg.org/files/51783/51783-h/51783-h .htm.

60. Ellen Akins, "Review: 'Margaret the First,' by Danielle Dutton," *Minneapolis Star Tribune*, April 10, 2016.

61. Octavio Paz, *Sor Juana, or, The Traps of Faith*, trans. Margaret Sayers Peden (Cambridge, MA: Harvard University Press, 1988), 1–10; Lerner, *The Creation of Feminist Consciousness*, 4; María Elena de Valdés, *The Shattered Mirror: Representations of Women in Mexican Literature* (Austin: University of Texas Press, 2010), 73.

62. Dorothy Schons, "Some Obscure Points in the Life of Sor Juana," in *Feminist Perspectives on Sor Juana Inés de la Cruz* (Detroit: Wayne State Press, 1991), 53–54.

63. Philip J. Ivanhoe, professor of Confucian Studies and Eastern Philosophy at Sungkyunkwan University, and Hwayeong Wang, researcher of Confucian Studies and Eastern Philosophy at Sungkyunkwan University, email correspondence with author, April 5–10, 2020; Philip J. Ivanhoe and Hwayeong Wang, "Im Yunjidang," in *Women Philosophers from Non-Western Traditions: The First Four Thousand Years*, ed. Therese Boos Dykeman (Dordrecht, Netherlands: Springer, forthcoming).

64. Sungmoon Kim, "The Way to Become a Female Sage: Im Yunjidang's Confucian Feminism," *Journal of the History of Ideas* 75, no. 3 (2014): 395–416, https://doi.org/10.1353/ jhi.2014.0026.

65. Robert E. Buswell Jr., ed., *Religions of Korea in Practice* (Princeton, NJ: Princeton University Press, 2018); Youngmin Kim and Michael J. Pettid, *Women and Confucianism in Choson Korea: New Perspectives* (Albany: State University of New York Press, 2011).

66. Translation courtesy of Professor Philip Ivanhoe, professor of Confucian Studies and Eastern Philosophy at Sungkyunkwan University, email correspondence with the author, April 10, 2020.

67. Quoted in Londa Schiebinger, *The Mind Has No Sex?: Women in the Origins of Modern Science* (Cambridge, MA: Harvard University Press, 1991), 102.

68. Karen Detlefsen, "Émilie du Châtelet," *Stanford Encyclopedia of Philosophy*, Winter 2018, https://plato.stanford.edu/archives/win2018/entries/emilie-du-chatelet/.

69. Schiebinger, *The Mind Has No Sex?*, 64.

70. Carol Strauss Sotiropoulos, "Scandal Writ Large in the Wake of the French Revolution: The Case of Amalia Holst," *Women in German Yearbook: Feminist Studies in German Literature and Culture* 20 (2004): 98–121, https://doi.org/10.1353/wgy.2004.0006.

71. Scheibinger, *The Mind Has No Sex?*, 270.

72. Quoted in Sotiropoulos, "Scandal Writ Large," 109–10.

73. Jean Boyd and Beverly B. Mack, *Collected Works of Nana Asma'u: Daughter of Usman 'dan Fodiyo (1793–1864)* (East Lansing: Michigan State University Press, 1997), 4.

74. Boyd and Mack, *Works of Nana Asma'u*, 245.

75. Beverly Mack, professor emerita of African studies at the University of Kansas, email correspondence with the author, April 12, 2020.

76. Boyd and Mack, *Works of Nana Asma'u*, 13.

77. Margaret Fuller, *The Essential Margaret Fuller*, ed. Jeffrey Steele (New Brunswick, NJ: Rutgers University Press, 1992), 310.

78. Francine Prose, *The Lives of the Muses: Nine Women and the Artists They Inspired* (New York: HarperCollins, 2003), 141; Sandra A. Wawrytko, "Lou Salomé (1861–1937)" in *A History of Women Philosophers: Volume IV: Contemporary Women Philosophers*, ed. M. E. Waithe (Dordrecht, Netherlands: Kluwer, 1995), 69–102.

79. See Wawrytko "Lou Salomé (1861–1937)," 72–73.

80. Carol Diethe, *Nietzsche's Women: Beyond the Whip* (Berlin: Walter de Gruyter, 1996), 59–60.

81. Elizabeth G. Ametsbichler, afterword in Hedwig Dohm, *Become Who You Are, with an Additional Essay, "The Old Woman,"* trans. Elizabeth G. Ametsbichler (Albany: State University of New York Press, 2006), Kindle edition. Also see: Chris Weedon, "The Struggle for Women's Emancipation in the Work of Hedwig Dohm," *German Life and Letters* 47, no. 2 (April 1994): 182–92, https://doi.org/10.1111/j.1468-0483.1994.tb01529.x.

82. Ametsbichler, afterword in *Become Who You Are*.

83. Quoted in Diethe, *Nietzsche's Women*, 147.

84. For more on Gilman, see: Cynthia J. Davis, *Charlotte Perkins Gilman: A Biography* (Stanford: Stanford University Press, 2010); Charlotte Perkins Gilman, *The Living of Charlotte Perkins Gilman: An Autobiography* (New York: Appleton-Century, 1935).

85. Davis, *Gilman*, xvii.

86. Davis, *Gilman*, 190–91; Gilman describes gynæcocentrism in her novel *Herland* (New York: Pantheon, 1979).

87. Davis, *Gilman*, 210–12.

88. Gilman, *Autobiography*, 215, 333–35, 331.

89. Quoted in Patricia Hill Collins, *Black Feminist Thought* (New York: Routledge, 2000), 3.

90. See Nell Irvin Painter, "Sojourner Truth in Life and Memory: Writing the Biography of an American Exotic," *Gender and History* 2, no. 1 (1990): 3–16, https://doi.org/10.1111/j.1468-0424.1990.tb00073.x.

91. Anna Julia Cooper, *A Voice from the South: By a Black Woman of the South* (Chapel Hill: University of North Carolina at Chapel Hill Library, 2017), 71. For more on Cooper, see: Vivian M. May, *Anna Julia Cooper, Visionary Black Feminist: A Critical Introduction*

(Abingdon, UK: Routledge, 2007); Kathryn T. Gines, "Anna Julia Cooper," *Stanford Encyclopedia of Philosophy*, Summer 2015, https://plato.stanford.edu/entries/anna-julia-cooper/index.html#ref-2.

92. Cooper, *Voice from the South*, 68.

93. Cooper, *Voice from the South*, 13.

94. Cooper, *Voice from the South*, 68.

Monsters

1. "Catharine Cockburn (Trotter)," National Portrait Gallery, accessed November 22, 2021, https://www.npg.org.uk/collections/search/portrait/mw36258/Catharine-Cockburn-Trotter. Here are some excellent works of scholarship that helped me form my portrait of Cockburn: Melanie Bigold, *Women of Letters, Manuscript Circulation, and Print Afterlives in the Eighteenth Century: Elizabeth Rowe, Catharine Cockburn, and Elizabeth Carter* (Basingame, UK: Palgrave Macmillan, 2013); Jacqueline Broad, *Women Philosophers of the Seventeenth Century* (Cambridge: Cambridge University Press, 2007); Anne Kelley, *Catharine Trotter: An Early Modern Writer in the Vanguard of Feminism* (Burlington, VT: Ashgate, 2002); Patricia Sheridan, "Catharine Trotter Cockburn," *Stanford Encyclopedia of Philosophy*, Spring 2019, https://plato.stanford.edu/archives/spr2019/entries/cockburn/.

2. Catharine Trotter Cockburn, *The Works of Mrs. Catharine Cockburn: Theological, Moral, Dramatic, and Poetical*, 2 vols. (London, 1751), vol. 2, 190.

3. Cockburn, *Works*, vol. 2, 188 (Cockburn counts herself among the "*serieux*"); Bigold, *Women of Letters*, 94.

4. Cockburn, *Works*, vol. 2, 288.

5. Cockburn, *Works*, vol. 2, 288–89.

6. Kelley, *Catharine Trotter*, 3.

7. Thomas Birch, introduction to Cockburn, *The Works of Mrs. Catharine Cockburn: Theological, Moral, Dramatic, and Poetical*, 2 vols. (London, 1751), vol. 1, iv.

8. Birch, introduction to Cockburn, *Works*, vol. 1, iv.

9. Kelley, *Catharine Trotter*, 88; poem quotation from Cockburn, *Works*, vol. 2, 557–59.

10. Catharine Trotter (Cockburn), *Olinda's Adventures: or, The Amours of a Young Lady* (London: Augustan Reprint Society, 1969), 143. There are many variations on this title. Although I consulted this copy, I chose to refer to the shorter title *The Adventures of a Young Lady*. "About Threescore," she says of the age of the person she describes as "a Dutch Coll"; for more on *Olinda's Adventures*, see Melanie Bigold, "1693: *The Adventures of a Young Lady*," in *The Cambridge Guide to the Eighteenth-Century Novel, 1660–1820* (Cambridge: Cambridge University Press, forthcoming).

11. Trotter (Cockburn), *Olinda's Adventures*, 138.

12. Trotter (Cockburn), *Olinda's Adventures*, 137.

13. Broad, *Women Philosophers*, 143.

14. Holly Faith Nelson, "Piers [née Roydon], Sarah, Lady Piers," in *Oxford Dictionary of National Biography*, ed. H. C. G. Matthew and Brian Harrison (Oxford: Oxford University Press, 2004), https://doi.org/10.1093/ref:odnb/74078.

15. Shirley Strum Kenny, *British Theatre and the Other Arts, 1660–1800* (Cranbury, NJ: Associated University Presses, 1984), 31.

16. Quoted in Kelley, *Catharine Trotter*, 83–84.

17. The exact year is uncertain. Anne Kelley dates the performance to 1695/6, see: Kelley, *Catharine Trotter*, 16.

18. Kenny, *British Theatre*, 77–81.

19. Kenny, *British Theatre*, 31.

20. Leslie Stephen, "Colley Cibber," *Dictionary of National Biography* (London: Smith, Elder, and Company, 1899), 216.

21. Charles Gildon, "A Comparison Between the Two Stages, . . . 1702," *Review of English Studies* 1, no. 1 (January 1925): 96; see also Germaine Greer, *Kissing the Rod: An Anthology of 17th-Century Women's Verse* (New York: Farrar, Straus and Giroux, 1988), 408–9. Greer excerpts a letter from one of Cockburn's admirers, who described the noise from the pit of the third performance of *Agnes de Castro* as "Thunder-Claps of noisy Prattle during the whole Play."

22. Quoted in Kelley, *Catharine Trotter*, 248.

23. Kelley, *Catharine Trotter*, 90.

24. Aristotle, *The Complete Works of Aristotle*, ed. Jonathan Barnes (Princeton: Princeton University Press, 1984), vol. 2, 2318.

25. Cockburn, *Works*, vol. 2, 259; Pilar Cuder-Domínguez, *Stuart Women Playwrights, 1613–1713* (Abingdon, UK: Routledge, 2016), 104.

26. Cockburn, *Works*, vol. 2, 258.

27. Catharine Trotter (Cockburn), *The Revolution of Sweden*, electronic reproduction (Farmington Hills, MI: Cengage Gale, 2009), 17–18.

28. Trotter (Cockburn), prologue to *The Revolution of Sweden*.

29. Catharine Trotter (Cockburn), "Dedication to Lady Sarah Piers in *Love at a Loss* (1701)" quoted in Kelley, *Catharine Trotter*, 92.

30. Catharine Trotter (Cockburn), prologue to *Love at a Loss* (London, 1701). Eighteenth Century Collections online, Gale.

31. Paula R. Backscheider, "Stretching the Form: Catharine Trotter Cockburn and Other Failures," *Theatre Journal* 47, no. 4 (1995): 452, https://doi.org/10.2307/3208986.

32. Trotter (Cockburn), *Love at a Loss*, quoted in Kelley, *Catharine Trotter*, 92.

33. Cockburn, *Works*, vol. 2, 296.

34. Greer, *Kissing the Rod*, 408–9.

35. And although men attended theater in greater numbers than women and were traditionally the target audience, there was an increase in women audience members who were drawn to the productions of women playwrights. Women were also avid readers of plays. See Judith Milhous, *The Publication of Plays in London 1660–1800: Playwrights, Publishers and the Market* (London: British Library Publishing, 2015); Lucyle Hook, introduction to [anonymous], *The Female Wits* (Los Angeles, Augustan Reprint Society, 1967), Project Gutenberg edition, https://www.gutenberg.org/files/37546/37546-h/37546-h.htm; and Janet Todd, "Life after Sex: The Fictional Autobiography of Delariver Manley," *Women's Studies* 15, no. 1–3 (October 1, 1988): 43–55, https://doi.org/10.1080/00497878.1988.9978716.

36. Cockburn, *Works*, vol. 2, 320.

37. Laura Jean Bergthal, *Playwrights and Plagiarists in Early Modern England: Gender, Authorship, Literary Property* (Ithaca, NY: Cornell University Press, 1996), 162–203.

38. Quoted in Wendy Churchill, *Female Patients in Early Modern Britain: Gender, Diagnosis, and Treatment* (Abingdon, UK: Ashgate, 2012), 180, 210; Cockburn mentions colic in a letter to Thomas Burnet in *Works*, vol. 2, 160. (Due to a printing error, in some editions of the *Works*, vol. 2, the page sequence 177–92 is repeated but with new material. This letter from 1705 falls in the second sequence. See here for an example of the anomalous printing with the additional sequence: https://bit.ly/3oNzNX2. Melanie Bigold, senior lecturer in English at Cardiff University, email correspondence with the author, Monday, October 19, 2020).

39. Cockburn, *Works*, vol. 2, 165. I inferred this from a letter she wrote to her friend Burnet in 1704 in which she says she's not been in touch with her London friends.

40. Trotter (Cockburn) to Burnet, Salisbury, December 9, 1701, in Cockburn, *Works*, vol. 2, 156. This is the same Gilbert Burnet who may have dissuaded Queen Anne from funding Astell's college and who also proposed a site of women's learning in his own work. It seems his lack of support for Astell was political; she was aligned with the Tories whereas Burnet was aligned with the Whigs.

41. This poem captures the bias against women writers: "Yet *Hackney Writers*, when their Verse did fail / To get 'em Brandy, Bread and Cheese, and Ale, / Their Wants by Prostitution were supply'd." Quoted in Kelley, *Catharine Trotter*, 13.

42. Quoted in Kelley, *Catharine Trotter*, 15.

43. Trotter (Cockburn) to Burnet, Salisbury, December 9, 1701, in Cockburn, *Works*, vol. 2, 156.

44. Kelley, *Catharine Trotter*, 16.

45. Cockburn, *Works*, vol. 1, 87.

46. Cockburn, *Works*, vol. 1, 45, 51. She wrote that school learning "disuse[s] the mind to plain and solid truth" and that an "unbiased search of truth" required a person to "unlearn all their former knowledge" and "break through all the prejudices of men, and free them from a willing slavery."

47. Cockburn, *Works*, vol. 2, 155. "I found the adversary so weak, I could not doubt of vanquishing him with justice on my side."

48. Cockburn, *Works*, vol. 1, 48.

49. Cockburn, *Works*, vol. 2, 155.

50. Locke to Trotter (Cockburn) in John Locke, *The Correspondence of John Locke*, ed. E. S. De Beer, 8 vols. (Oxford: Clarendon Press, 1976–1989), vol. 7, letter no. 3234; Cockburn mentions the books but not the money, but Locke and other sources say she received both: Sheridan, "Catharine Trotter Cockburn."

51. Cockburn, *Works*, vol. 2, 189–90.

52. Trotter (Cockburn) to Burnet, London, August 8, 1704, Cockburn, *Works*, vol. 2, 175.

53. Trotter (Cockburn) to Burnet, London, August 8, 1704, Cockburn, *Works*, vol. 2, 175.

54. In this work, she argues that in matters of moral uncertainty the Bible—and not the pope—is the right guide to use. She rejects papal authority on the ground that no human is free of error, and so relying on one person's moral judgment leaves the church in a precarious position: it takes only one mistaken judgment by the pope to topple the validity of Christianity. A similar argument shows up in the work of a contemporary, Edward Stillingfleet, who also advocates democratizing the interpretation of Scripture, because a mistake of interpretation simply illustrates the weakness of human cognition and not the weakness of Christianity itself. See Cockburn, *Works*, vol. 1, 6.

55. Trotter (Cockburn) to Burnet, July 7, 1705, Cockburn, *Works*, vol. 2, 186. (This letter from 1705 appears only in some editions of the *Works*. See note 38, this chapter, above).

56. Cockburn, *Works*, vol. 2, 237.

57. Burnet to Trotter (Cockburn), Leipzig, July 5, 1704, in Cockburn, *Works*, 170.

58. Burnet to Trotter (Cockburn), Luxembourg, July 17, 1704, in Cockburn, *Works*, vol. 2, 171. Another one of Burnet's classic dude lines: "I have need of a kind virtuous friend, and as I can put trust and confidence in you, more then in any other of your sex, I know of in England of your age." I love the qualification after qualification in this one!

59. Cockburn, *Works*, vol. 2, 206.

60. Trotter (Cockburn) to Rev. Mr. Fenn. Ockham, July 18, 1707, in Cockburn, *Works*, vol. 2, 247. She says, "When that foolish unaccountable tenderness is joined with a well grounded esteem, it adds a great deal of agreeableness to the more solid advantages of a rational companion."

61. Trotter (Cockburn) to Patrick Cockburn August 4, 1707, in Cockburn, *Works*, vol. 2, 240.

62. Trotter (Cockburn) to Patrick Cockburn August 13, 1707, in Cockburn, *Works*, vol. 2, 242.

63. Cockburn, *Works*, vol. 1, xl.

64. The Oath of Abjuration required clergymen such as Patrick Cockburn to submit to the British monarch and agree to the repudiation of James Stuart as a claimant to the throne.

65. Kelley, *Catharine Trotter*, 23.

66. Catherine Gallagher, "Political Crimes and Fictional Alibis: The Case of Delarivier Manley," *Eighteenth-Century Studies* 23, no. 4 (1990): 502–21, https://doi.org/10.2307/2739182.

67. Quoted in Bigold, *Women of Letters*, 134–35.

68. Quoted in N. H. Keeble, ed. *The Cultural Identity of Seventeenth-Century Woman: A Reader* (New York: Routledge, 2002), 152.

69. Felicity A. Nussbuam, "'Savage' Mothers: Narratives of Maternity in the Mid-Eighteenth Century," *Cultural Critique*, no. 20 (1991): 126, https://doi.org/10.2307/1354225.

70. Marilyn Francus, *Monstrous Motherhood: Eighteenth-Century Culture and the Ideology of Domesticity* (Baltimore: Johns Hopkins University Press, 2012), 30–40.

71. Cockburn, *Works*, vol. 2, 575.

72. Bigold, *Women of Letters*, 133.

73. Cockburn, *Works*, vol. 2, 111.

74. Cockburn, *Works*, vol. 2, 111.

75. Cockburn, *Works*, vol. 2, 119.

76. Cockburn, *Works*, vol. 2, 119.

77. Cockburn, *Works*, vol. 1, 434; *Works*, vol. 2, 127 and 131.

78. Cockburn, *Works*, vol. 2, 54.

79. Cockburn, *Works*, vol. 1, 296. Here is evidence of her syncretism: she says that "moral virtue" and "moral sense" and "essential difference in relations to things" . . . "all three together make an immovable foundation for, and obligation to moral practice."

80. Cockburn, *Works*, vol. 2, 22, 81.

81. Cockburn, *Works*, vol. 2, 124.

82. Trotter (Cockburn), "Dedicatory Letter to Harriet Godolphin," in *The Revolution of Sweden*.

83. Cockburn, *Works*, vol. 2, 267–68.

84. Cockburn, *Works*, vol. 2, 307.

85. Cockburn to her niece, November 20, 1744, in *Works*, vol. 2, 322.

86. Cockburn to her niece, October 2, 1747, in *Works*, vol. 2, 333.

87. Greer, *Kissing the Rod*, 407.

88. Quoted in Bigold, *Women of Letters*, 92.

89. Bigold, *Women of Letters*, 95.

Muses

1. Amia Srinivasan, "Genealogy, Epistemology and Worldmaking," *Proceedings of the Aristotelian Society* 119, no. 2 (2019): 154, https://doi.org/10.1093/arisoc/aoz009.